Napoleon
To
Nasser

The Story of Modern Egypt

by

Raymond Flower

© 2001 by Raymond Flower. All rights reserved.

No part of this book may be reproduced, stored in a retrieval system, or transmitted by any means, electronic, mechanical, photocopying, recording, or otherwise, without written permission from the author.

ISBN: 0-7596-5392-5 (e-book)
ISBN: 0-7596-5393-3 (Paperback)
ISBN: 1-4033-5746-3 (Dustjacket)

This book is printed on acid free paper.

1stBooks — rev. 08/30/02

Important Dates

1798	Napoleon invades Egypt. Battle of the Pyramids (21 July) Nelson destroys French fleet at Aboukir (1 August)
1799	Napoleon returns to France. Hands over to Kleber
1800	Kléber is assassinated. Menou assumes command
1801	Abercromby's expedition.
1802	Treaty of Amiens. French and English evacuate Egypt.
1805	Mohammed Ali is elected Pasha of Cairo
1811	Massacre of the Mamelukes (1st of March), Toussoun leads an expedition force to Arabia
1820	Expedition to the Sudan
1824	Ibrahim lands in Morea
1827	Battle of Navarino
1831—41	Campaigns in Syria. Mohammed Ali created hereditary Pasha of Egypt (13 February 1841)
1848	Mohammed Ali's mind fails: Ibrahim and Abbas successively appointed as regents
1849	Death of Mohammed Ali. Abbas becomes Viceroy
1854	Said succeeds Abbas (July). Grants de Lesseps the concession to dig the Suez Canal (November)
1859	Work begins on the Suez Canal
1863	Ismail succeeds to the Vice-regal throne
1867	Ismail is created Khedive

1869	Opening of the Suez Canal (16 November)
1875	Disraeli buys Egypt's shares in the Suez Canal from Ismail
1878	Congress of Berlin
1879	Ismail is deposed by the Sultan. (June) Tewfik becomes Khedive
1881	Colonel Ahmed Arabi leads the Nationalist movement
1882	Great Britain intervenes and bombards Alexandria (July).
1882	Arabi is defeated at Tel el Kebir (13 September) and the British occupation of Egypt begins
1884	Cromer becomes the virtual ruler of Egypt
1885	Death of Gordon at Khartoum (26 January)
1892	Abbas Hilmy succeeds Tewfik as Khedive
1898	Battle of Omdurman (2 September)
1899	Anglo-Egyptian Condominium Agreement on the Sudan (19 January)
1907	Cromer resigns, is succeeded by Gorst
1910	Assassination of Boutros Ghali Pasha
1911	Gorst dies, is succeeded by Kitchener
1914	Great Britain declares a Protectorate over Egypt. The Khedive Abbas Hilmy is deposed
1918	Saad Zagloul Pasha demands the independence of Egypt
1919	Zagloul is deported. Revolutionary uprisings against the British
1922	Egypt's independence is declared, and Ahmed Fouad is proclaimed King (28 February)

1924	Wafd Party elected by a huge majority with Zagloul as prime minister. Murder of Sir Lee Stack (19 November)
1927	Death of Saad Zagloul Pasha
1936	Accession of King Farouk (25 April). Anglo-Egyptian Treaty signed (August)
1942	British tanks surround Abdin Palace and force King Farouk to appoint Nahas Pasha as Prime Minister (February). Captain Gamal Abdel Nasser starts plotting revolution. Rommel reaches El Alamein (July). The Battle of El Alamein (October)
1946	Anti-British disturbances in Cairo and Alexandria. British Army moves to the Canal Zone
1948	State of Israel proclaimed. The Palestine War
1951	Nahas Pasha abrogates the Anglo-Egyptian Treaty and proclaims Farouk 'King of Egypt and the Sudan'. Harassing tactics against the British Canal Zone base
1952	Burning of Cairo (26 January) The 'Free Officers' seize power (23 July) Farouk abdicates and leaves Egypt (26 July)
1953	Egypt is proclaimed a republic with Naguib as President and Nasser as Vice-President
1954	Conflict between Naguib and Nasser (February-March) Evacuation agreement made with Britain (July) Repression of Muslem Brotherhood after their abortive attempt to assassinate Nasser. Naguib is placed under house arrest (November)
1955	Bagdad Pact. Israeli raid at Gaza (February) Nasser at Bandung Conference (April) The 'Czech' Arms deal (September)

1956	Nasser is elected President (June) USA withdraws the offer to finance the High Dam (July) Nasser announces the nationalization of the Suez Canal Company (26 July). The Suez War: Israel attacks Egypt (29 October); Britain and France start 'preventive police action' (30 October). Landings at Port Said (5 November), cease-fire (6 November)
1958	Formation of United Arab Republic between Egypt and Syria
1961	Syria breaks away from the UAR. Nationalizations and confiscations in Egypt
1962	Nasser announces the 'National Charter'. *Coup d'etat* in the Yemen
1963	Egypt intervenes in the Yemen
1964	Khrushchev at Assouan
1967	Border incidents between Syria and Israel (April). The 'Six Day War'. Nasser resigns, but is re-instated by popular acclaim (June) Abdel Hakim Amer commits suicide (September)
1970	After consultations at Moscow, Nasser accepts the Rogers Plan for a settlement with Israel (July). Inter-Arab conference in Cairo: Nasser patches up the quarrel between Hussein and Arafat (27 September). Death of Nasser from a heart attack (28 September). Anwar el Sadat nominated President (1 October)

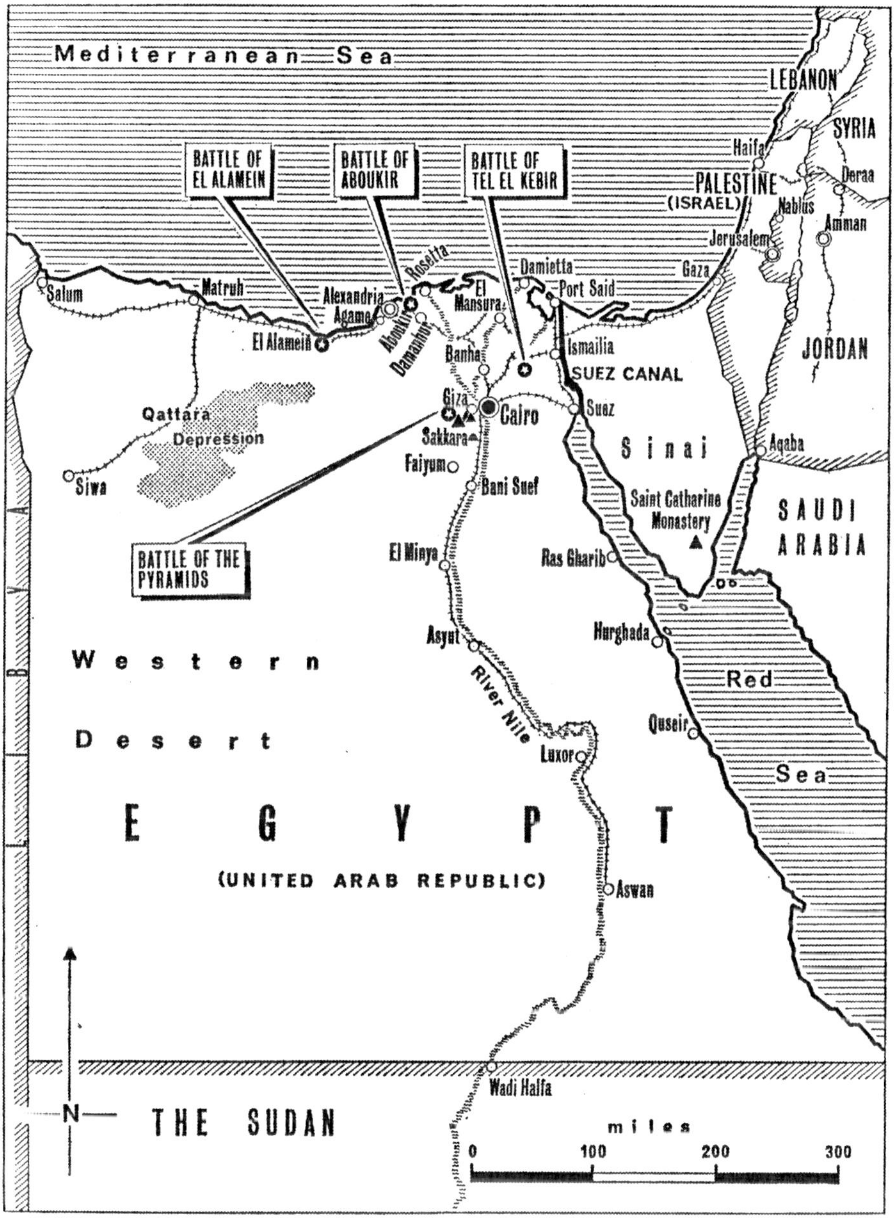
Mediterranean Sea
LEBANON
SYRIA
Haifa
Deraa
PALESTINE
(ISRAEL)
Nablus
Amman
Jerusalem
Gaza
JORDAN
BATTLE OF
EL ALAMEIN
BATTLE OF
ABOUKIR
BATTLE OF
TEL EL KEBIR
Rosetta
Damietta
Port Said
Salum
Matruh
Alexandria
Agami
El
Mansura
El Alamein
Abouki
Damanhur
Banha
Ismailia
SUEZ CANAL
Giza
Cairo
Suez
Qattara
Depression
Sakkara
Sinai
Aqaba
Faiyum
Siwa
Bani Suef
Saint Catharine
Monastery
SAUDI
ARABIA
BATTLE OF THE
PYRAMIDS
El Minya
Ras Gharib
Asyut
Hurghada
River Nile
Red
Western
Desert
Quseir
Luxor
Sea
EGYPT
(UNITED ARAB REPUBLIC)
Aswan
LIBYA
N
Wadi Halfa
THE SUDAN
miles
0
100
200
300

NAPOLEON TO NASSER
THE STORY OF MODERN EGYPT

Acclaimed by the Egyptian Ministry of Culture as 'The best book about modern Egypt to have been written by a Westerner,' RaymondFlower's highly topical account of the course of events from Napoleon's invasion of Egypt in 1798 until the death of Nasser in 1970 makes compulsive reading for all those who wish to understand the background of Egypt's recent history and contemporary renaissance.

'The author is a man who loves Egypt and its people. This love is the "leitmotif" of a graphic, evocative book with the tempo of the best kind of 55-minute TV documentary.'
Irish Press

'Very readable and, one would guess, very reliable. He knows, loves what he knows, but is not starry-eyed about it all.'
Methodist Recorder

'Raymond Flower's book on the last century and a half of Egyptian history is short, gay, and exhilarating... The author knows the country well, and likes its people, especially for their ready humour and natural gaiety. He has done them full justice in a book which has somehow avoided the rancour which creeps into everything connected with the Middle East..An excellent book.'
Terence Prittie in the *Jewish Chronicle*

'Amusingly written in a lively style and peppered with revealing anecdotes and asides. All this makes fascinating reading and provides...a solid introduction to modem Egypt.'
Magda Grey in *Tribune*

'An objective review based on facts rendered in a pleasant way that appeals to readers regardless of semantic levels.'
Dr Mustafa Munir, Director-General of Foreign Cultural Relations, Cairo in *Prism.*

Introduction to the New Edition

This book was absolutely up to date when it first appeared in 1972. Nasser had just died, thereby rounding off the era that had started with Napoleon. Since then, time and events have made the story more relevant than ever.

Anwar Sadat overturned the revolution that Nasser and he himself had carried out. The "revolution correction", he called it, reversing Nasser's policies which had stirred up nationalist sentiments in the Arab world and even further afield, but brought disaster to Egypt. Sadat got rid of the Russians and sought help from the West. He instituted an Open Door policy, and made peace with Israel. But his liberalising programmes made him the victim of the very forces that the revolution had unleashed.

With infinite patience Hosni Mubarak, who was standing beside Sadat when the assassins struck, worked to achieve stability. Mubarak has emerged as the great consolidator and pacifier. Under his guidance Egypt, though still struggling to contain extremist violence, has become a prosperous and relatively stable area in the turbulent Middle East.

The eventual outcome of the post-Nasser era remains to be seen. For six millennia, religion has been central to Egypt's history. The Nile Valley has always been ruled by "pharoah" figures, religious hierarchies, and a dominant upper class lording it over the fellaheen masses. Down the centuries, foreigners constituted this upper class—Hellenes, Romans, Mamelukes, Turks or Europeans.

By chasing out the Europeans, Nasser became the first fellah "pharoah", or "Rais" as he was popularly called. The configuration of the country seems to call for a dominant figure in command, whether appointed by force or by democratic process. Will this continue?

Undoubtedly, Egypt's seventh millennium will see many more spectacular changes.. Meanwhile, knowledge of the period covered by this book remains essential if you wish to understand the development of contemporary Egypt.

I hope you'll enjoy reading it.

Raymond Flower
2002

Prologue

Napoleon Versus England

On a freezing November night in 1797, as the sparse inhabitants of the valleys were huddled around their fire-places, a French military convoy hurried northwards across the Alps. Citizen General Bonaparte was returning from Italy.

Already, at twenty-eight, his career was astonishing. In barely five years he had risen from an unknown gunner captain to full command of the French forces in Italy—the leader of crack, devoted troops who had conquered the north of the peninsular, extinguished the Venetian Republic, and forced the Emperor to make peace. Living in semi-regal state and hailed by admirers as a modern Hannibal, he had brought the campaign to a triumphal conclusion a month previously with the Treaty of Campo Formio.

But in Paris—where the government was failing and a thousand conspiracies were afoot—he knew that he would have to tread warily. He had no illusions how little his prodigious success in Italy had endeared him to the corrupt and jealous Directory. And while his loyalty to the régime was still unquestioned (it was whispered by Paris wits that the price of his promotion had been marriage to the discarded mistress of one of the Directors—he could hardly afford to forget as he hastened towards the capital, that twice in the last five years he had been arrested and imprisoned, so that even at this stage a single false move could prove fatal.

The reason for his recall was no secret. By a decree dated 26 October, he had been appointed Commander of the Army of England—that is to say, of the invasion of Britain. The Treaty of Campo Formio had left the Republic with only her traditional enemy to contend with. But the longer Bonaparte reflected, the more certain he felt that an operation across the channel was not practical at the moment. The weakness of the French navy was the stumbling block, and he had no intention of being associated with failure.

From Mombello to Rastadt, and thence to Paris, he travelled at top speed. But his fame preceded him. At every village he had to stop and listen to speeches from the *maire,* and in every town to accept the hospitality of the municipality. Now and then he gave a hint of his thoughts to his travelling companions. 'What I have done up to now is nothing,' he muttered at one point to Miot de Melito, 'I am only at the beginning of the course I must run...Do you imagine that I triumph in Italy to underwrite that pack of lawyers who form the Directory—men like Carnot and Baras?' And later, at Rastadt; 'As for myself, dear Miot, let me tell you that I can no longer obey. I have tasted command, and I cannot give it up. I have made up my mind. If I cannot be master, I shall leave France.

His welcome in Paris pleased him hardly more than it pleased his detractors. Tricolours were everywhere and the cheering mobs seemed convinced that he had only to show his face in England to bring the British Empire to its knees. 'You expect me to be glad at such public demonstrations?' he was heard to exclaim, 'Why, there would be just as big a crowd to see me guillotined!' Grudgingly, the Directors followed the general mood and received him in state. Barras made a pompous speech, addressing him as the liberator of Italy and the pacificator of Europe. People stood on their tables a the Luxembourg to get a view of their hero. They saw a skinny, sallow figure dressed in a drab blue tunic and carrying a sword that trailed along the ground. Talleyrand, with whom he was on good terms, might enthuse over his '...charming personality...a pale complexion, a hint of fatigue' but word went around the salons that the young general looked like a puss-in-boots. His manner alternated between professional dryness and coarse familiarity. The best that could be said was that he had a rather pleasant smile.

As soon as possible, he escaped from all the fuss and flattery to his small house in the Rue Chantereine (re-named on his return, Rue de la Victoire) where, between the routine business of dealing with staff officers concerned with preparing stores and equipment for the invasion, he also conferred with less official characters such as retired fishermen and professional smugglers. Early in February he toured the north coast ports and, as his carriage slithered over the cobbled roads between Calais and Dunkirk, his suspicions were confirmed; an invasion of England under present circumstances would be a prescription for disaster. In due course, when the moment was right, he had every intention of engineering the downfall of the British Empire and the French government as well. But for the time being, 'the pear was not yet ripe'. On 5 March 1798 he proposed, instead, an expedition to Egypt. That same day, the Directors agreed.

Some twelve months previously, the French Consul in Cairo had sent in a lengthy memorandum suggesting that the time was appropriate for intervention in Egypt. This would be welcomed, he said, not only by the Egyptian people, who were victims of an oppressive and corrupt government, but also by Turkey, the suzerain power. It was no secret that the Porte was having trouble with the Mameluke Beys—who were maltreating the fifty or sixty French traders in the Delta. There was nothing new in the report; throughout the 1770s and 80s the French Foreign Ministry had been swamped with memoranda on the Eastern Question, and no one had taken much notice. But it so happened that this time the theme was repeated by an influential voice. Charles Maurice de Talleyrand, excommunicated Bishop of Autun, who was just back from the delights of colonial life in Philadelphia (where he had sensibly waited out the Reign of Terror) gave a public lecture at the Louvre 'On the advantages of new colonies for France, who lost important ones to England under the last kings'. If the idea had sparked a responsive chord with his audience in Paris, it had nearly fused the circuit with the young visionary holding court at Mombello.

Even as a subaltern, whiling away the dull and stuffy hours in a provincial barracks, Bonaparte had been fascinated by the East, filling his diaries with notes on such subjects as the history of Egypt and Carthage, the Tartars and the Turks, the measurements of the great pyramids, and even the dates and biographies of twenty-seven Caliphs—including details on the misconduct of their wives. *'Toute la Gloire vient de l'Orient, comme le soleil'* he had written. Now, suddenly, this Corsican with the blood of the Mediterranean in his veins, recalling the exploits of Alexander and Caesar and 'measuring his dreams with the callipers of reason' (as he told the Comtesse de Remussat) had seen how he could marry his vision of an Empire in the East with the pragmatic consideration of injuring England.

For as luck would have it, just two weeks after giving his lecture, Talleyrand became Foreign Minister. Immediately, Bonaparte was corresponding with his plans to gain control of the Mediterranean. 'The day is not far off,' he wrote to the new minister, 'when we shall appreciate the necessity, if we are going to destroy England, of seizing Egypt...with 25,000 men accompanied by eight or ten ships of the line, we could sail over and take it...the vast Ottoman Empire, which is dying day by day, obliges us to think...of the measures we must take to preserve our trade with the Levant.' Whether Talleyrand was ever wholly convinced or not (when the project later proved disastrous, both he and Napoleon gave full credit for the venture to the other) he was a diplomat not adverse to killing two birds with one stone. He could see that if the French did not occupy Egypt soon some other Power probably would; but perhaps most of all he preferred that so inconveniently popular a figure as Bonaparte should be safely employed on the Nile rather than loitering dangerously on the Seine.

Whatever Talleyrand's private motives may have been, the recommendations he made in favor of the expedition, which included a project for cutting a canal through the Suez isthmus and a plan to invade Syria after Egypt had been captured, were persuasive enough to win round the Directors. England's resources of supply were far afield, he pointed out to them, and a successful attack on her lines of communication would be a telling blow. Moreover, the possibility of a subsequent invasion of England before tackling India should be borne in mind. If the British fleet was kept busy around Alexandria a surprise assault across the Channel might perhaps be achieved. For rather dissimilar reasons, the Directory and Bonaparte thus saw eye to eye. Money to equip the expedition was obtained by a lightning raid on Switzerland, and in seventy-six days, working at maximum pressure and with remarkable secrecy, considering all the military, naval and civilian staff-work involved, the campaign was prepared.

Sitting in his wife's drawing room (Josephine herself was often out, usually in the bedrooms of either Barras or her dancing teacher, Monsieur Hyppolyte) Bonaparte mobilized his trusted staff along with the veteran troops who had served him so well in Italy, and with the help of Gaspard Monge, the scientist, and Bertholet, the chemist, persuaded an impressive number of specialists to join the expedition. To many intellectuals, the idea of retracing the tracks of the great armies of the ancient world acted like a magnet. Whereas England was piling up a far-flung empire, they sensed that the moment had come for revolutionary France to regenerate the Mediterranean, traditionally the hub of the world. Even Michelet, who was by no means an admirer of Bonaparte, noted that 'This was no ordinary conquest, spurred on by cupidity, but the fantastic, sublime hope of resurrection...' Before long, the nucleus of a whole university—astronomers, botanists, geometricians, mineralogists, archaeologists, orientalists, political economists, as well as musicians, painters and even poets—167 of them in all, mostly quite young, were heading for Toulon. Everything in the historic land of Egypt was to be meticulously studied. His soldiers might joke about this starry-eyed band and call them 'the donkeys', but to Bonaparte they were of the greatest importance. These were the men who would charter his reputation as a new Alexander.

Early in the morning of 19 May 1798, a coach drew up in front of the Hotel de l'Intendent at Toulon, and Bonaparte, with Josephine on his arm, came down the steps. Eye-witnesses agree that he showed no sign of emotion. Sitting back impassively in the carriage, he raised a finger now and then to return a salute. At the water's edge, Josephine gave him a farewell kiss. 'When will you be back?' she whispered in his ear. 'Maybe in six months,' he replied, shrugging his shoulders, 'Maybe in six years.' And, his foot already on the gang-plank, he added, almost to himself, 'Maybe, never...'

Meanwhile, on the other side of the Channel, the threat of a possible invasion from France was having very little effect on everyday life. If people in England were worried, it was about what was going on in the Navy. The disorders at Spithead were bad enough, but barely a month later there had been a full-scale mutiny in the Nore. No one suggested, of course, that a sailor's life was a 'cushy' one, but it still came as a shock to realize that the Fleet was manned largely by a process of kidnapping, the rations were low, medicines were pilfered by the ships' doctors, and neither pay nor pensions were adequate to support families the men seldom saw. Although the mutiny was suppressed with the utmost severity, it aroused public opinion sufficiently to pressure both Parliament and the Admiralty into a flurry of concessions, (and incidentally convinced quite a few foreign residents, who had experienced such things on the continent, that an English revolution was just around the corner).

In the midst of all this, the London newspapers gave warning that the French preparations in the channel ports were already far advanced. A secret agent had spotted General Bonaparte on the road between Furnes and Dunkirk, and another had reported a build-up of flat-bottomed boats at Brest. The invasion could not be far off. Then shortly afterwards, reports began coming in that France was planning some grand-scale operation, in the South. A British naval officer, whose swashbuckling exploits had landed him up as a prisoner of war in Paris, managed to get a message through that the Directory had their eye on Egypt and British trade in the Levant. When a few weeks later Sir Sidney Smith escaped from the Temple, Lord Granville had him to breakfast and took him on to the Palace. Sir Sidney told the King that Bonaparte's entourage included mathematicians, historians and geologists who would report on the antiquities and develop the resources of Egypt. It all sounded pretty far-fetched. Nevertheless, Pitt, the Prime Minister, decided that it was time 'to begin to think about the Mediterranean'. On 2 May the Admiralty instructed Lord St Vincent at Cadiz to send a detachment into the Mediterranean under Sir Horatio Nelson, who had recently arrived from England in command of HMS Vanguard. By the time the dispatch reached Lord St Vincent on 24 May, Nelson was already on his way to Toulon—and in trouble.

Only four days earlier, pacing up and down in his cabin, the Admiral had found himself 'exhilarated beyond description'. Although he had lost his right arm, he was back in command of a 'flying' squadron with secret orders to 'deal with the French'. After a brilliant sunset, the weather began to break, and by midnight Vanguard, while prepared for a gale, was in serious difficulties. Her main topmast went over the side, followed by the mizzen topmast. The storm lasted forty-eight hours, by which time Vanguard was almost a total wreck, and it was only by luck and good seamanship that she was towed safely into Oristano Bay in Sardinia, where by a superlative effort the damage was repaired in just four days.

But as it happened, these days had been critical. From a a merchant-man came the news that Bonaparte, with thirteen ships of the line and four hundred transports, had sailed from Toulon the day before the storm. The bird had flown. What is more, Nelson had not the faintest idea where the French had been heading. And to make matters worse, he was now becalmed.

The frustration he endured over the next two months can be read in his diary. 'The devil' he grumbled, 'has the devil's own luck.' Certainly, in this blindman's bluff round the Mediterranean, the elements were not on his side. With no frigates to bring him information, he twice again missed the French convoy by the narrowest of margins—indeed, during the night of 22 June, in foggy weather near Sicily, he passed so close to the slow-moving armada that Admiral de Breuys could hear the British signal guns. By then, having learnt that the French had captured Malta and had sailed east the previous week, Nelson was heading full speed for Alexandria, suddenly convinced that this was Bonaparte's goal. But arriving there on 28 June, he found that he had drawn a blank: the old eastern port was empty save for one Turkish ship of the line and four frigates, and the western or 'Franks' port held some fifty merchant sailing vessels of various nationalities. The French were aiming their mischief elsewhere. Or so it seemed. Yet the following day, look-outs in the Pharos of Alexandria had scarcely watched the sails of Nelson's squadron disappear over the north-eastern horizon in the direction of Asia-Minor than an immense French flotilla began to come into view from the north-west. While Nelson 'stretched the fleet over the coast of Asia' past Aleppo into the Gulf of Antayla and back via Crete to Syracuse, Napoleon reached the Delta as easily as either Alexander or Caesar had done in their day. Not until 23 July did Nelson realize that his original guess had been right—the mistake had been to arrive not too late but just a little too soon. By then Napoleon was preparing to enter Grand Cairo as a conqueror, and the history of modern Egypt had begun.

Chapter 1

The Volatile Mix

'The year 1213 of the Hegira (which began on 15 June 1798) marks the start of a period of great battles,' wrote Sheikh Abdel Rahman el-Djabarty in his journal. 'Of terrible events; of disastrous happenings; of appalling calamities and ever-increasing misfortunes; of successive trials and sufferings; persecutions; upheavals; of the overthrowing of the existing order, and continuous terrors; revolutions; administrative disorders; catastrophes and overall devastation; in a word, it was the beginning of a series of great misfortunes.'

The Sheikh's dismay was understandable—Napoleon was a disturbing influence. Yet it must be admitted that violence and sudden upheavals were nothing new to Egypt. Through the centuries life had gone on against a background of factions, vendettas and wars. For nearly 2,500 years the Valley of the Nile had been wholly under the heel of foreign conquerors. The last Egyptians to rule their own land, in fact, had been the Pharaohs. When the Saite Dynasty was finally swept away by Cambysus of Persia in 525 BC, Egypt had become progressively a stage for the elegance of Greece, the militancy of Rome, and the fanaticism of the early Christians. The only unchanging figure was the fellah, the Egyptian peasant who went on tilling his land, monotonously eking out a starvation existence—and exploited by whoever was in power.

The Fellah must be the oldest man in the world; he has seen everything. Through the Middle Ages he saw his country in the hands of independent Islamic rulers, for in 641 AD the Christians were replaced by the Arabs and the Caliphs of Damascus and Baghdad became the overlords of Egypt; and in the tenth century the country was once again conquered, this time by the Shia Fatimid rulers from Tunis.* The most celebrated successor to these North-African adventurers, who overran Syria and Sicily in their ceaseless struggle against the Crusaders, was the epic Salah el Din (known to the Crusaders, from whom he seized Jerusalem, as Saladin). Apart from building the citadel of Cairo—for the next six hundred years the nerve-center of Egypt—Saladin's influence was felt down the centuries in another way. Like the Caliphs of Baghdad, he ransacked the slave-markets of Asia Minor for young Christians to strengthen his Kurdish levies (the human raw material was not hard to find; at that time the markets of Constantinople were crowded with the children of refugees fleeing from the Tartars) and quickly shaped them into so efficient a fighting force that he was able to overrun Syria and finally drive the Crusaders out of the Holy Land. Before long the Mameluke system of military slavery, which existed only under the banner of Islam and has no exact parallel in history, developed into a complete social caste, with its special laws and traditions, that not only overthrew Saladin's own Ayyubid dynasty, but for six centuries ruled over Egypt with splendor and depravity.

The word mameluke has a curious mystique, although in Arabic it simply means 'chattel'—a possession, a slave; specifically, a white male slave purchased to be a recruit in the army. The basis of the mameluke system was its allegiance, not to the army itself, or indeed to the Crown, but to the individual master by whom the recruit had been purchased, and by whom he might in due course be given his franchise.

Once sold by his family—or as likely as not simply kidnapped from his village in the Caucasus by a dealer—the young boy would find himself with a shipload of others like himself heading for Cairo where, naked in the slave-market, he would wait to be bought by one of the Mameluke Beys. The break with his family and his home was complete; he had now lost his identity and even his religion and become a member of a military caste with strict rules and conventions. Yet although living in the cellars of the Bey's palace, he would find himself regarded as a sort of adopted child in his master's household regiment, loyal to his Bey and his fellow-slaves, and trained, as part of an élite fraternity, to despise fellahin and civilians alike, and even to look down on marriage and family life as fatal to his profession of a man at arms.

If luck was on his side in the slave-market, and he was bought by the Sultan himself or one of the more powerful Beys, the young mameluke would be sent to a military school where he would be taught to read and write, learn the Koran, and be drilled in the arts of warfare. Contact with the outside world was forbidden, and discipline was strict—enforced by a sort of prefectorial system, the older recruits, known as Aghas being in charge of the rest. While at school, the mameluke received no pay and had no rights; but once he had graduated he would be ceremoniously granted his freedom.

Viewed from this standpoint, slavery was simply a convention—a convenient means of recruiting apprentices of a warlike and aristocratic guild. After all, slavery was never regarded as a disgrace in the East; if anything it rated higher than hired service. The majority of the Mamelukes, of course, never had the opportunity of becoming free; many spent their whole lives as slaves; but every one of them—Sultan, Beys, and state dignitaries—went through the ranks in the same way, and moreover were proud of it. Twenty yeas after he had been bought as a child in Armenia for the equivalent of a hundred dollars, Barkuk became Sultan of Egypt. Twenty years after Barkuk bought him, El Muaiyyid became Sultan in his turn.* 'The young Circassian slave, once he set foot on the soil of Egypt, saw a career opening...and felt destined to be a lord," Arnold Toynbee remarks, adding tartly; 'but in a lordly station, he had the soul of a slave..."

Certainly it did not take long for the ambitious young mameluke to realize that the highest career opportunity was open to his talents. If through skill at riding, fencing, or throwing the javelin, or maybe by his good looks and fine bearing he could worm into the good graces of his Bey, he might be taken into his personal entourage and become 'keeper of the ink-pot' or 'bearer of the pipe', and in due course, if his luck held, be promoted to an 'Emir of Ten'—the lowest echelon of actual command, and with it the first heady initiation into Palace intrigue. Promotion meant wealth, and the possibility of rising in the hierarchy and forming a household of his own.

Ruling in the Citadel was the Sultan—the strongest of the Beys, who had successfully seized the crown.* He had his generals, the generals had their captains, the captains their lieutenants; and each of these subordinates had his squadron of troops at the disposal of his superior who had bought him and freed him, and to whom he owed allegiance. In such a set-up, strength, brute force and intrigue were the only security; the crown was constantly being menaced by the more powerful Beys and although son and even grandson might sometimes succeed the throne, a dynasty rarely continued beyond the second or third generation before being toppled by a fresh usurper. The figures speak for themselves; of the 250 Sultans who ruled Egypt during a single period of 300 years, only twenty-four died a natural death. In the frenzied splendor of the Citadel, the dagger and the poisoned cup were always ready, and not for nothing was medieval Cairo the authentic setting for the legends of the Thousand and One Nights.

With brutality, vengefulness and despotism the Sultans and their lieutenants ruled. Kait Bey—a supposedly enlightened sovereign whose fort overlooks Alexandria harbor on the traditional site of the Pharos—would personally flog the President of the Council of State and other high officials to exhort for more money for the Treasury. One of the Mameluke Sultans was said to have killed a horse with a single blow of his fist. But often the Sultan found it more enjoyable to kill men. He would order executions by the dozen, sometimes seizing the executioner's huge scimitar in his own hands to cut off a rebel's head. In a more merciful mood, he might just sever a hand or leg, or order the offender to be shod like a horse. In another mood, he would shower gifts on a friendly ruler or favorite who had caught his fancy. The state the Mamelukes kept was tremendous; hundreds of courtiers surrounded the Sultan, and each courtier had his own following. (Beyber's records show that 20,000 lbs. Of food were prepared daily at the Palace; and the daily cost of meat and vegetables in the time of El-Nasir averaged ten thousand dollars.) Their immense wealth, like that of Venice with whom they had commercial treaties, came from the Indian trade of the Levant. As masters of both Egypt and Syria, the Mamelukes levied customs dues on every bale of Oriental produce which arrived from the Persian Gulf and the Red Sea for transshipment to Venice. For six hundred years, while Europe was convulsed in turn by the Middle Ages, the Renaissance, the Reformation, the

Raymond Flower

Napoleon, hearing of Nelson's victory in 1798, swears by his sword to extirpate the English from the earth.

British Museum

Napoleon To Nasser

Typical Mamelukes. A contemporary portrayal by H. Alken. They were defeated by Napoleon in the Battle of the Pyramids, (1798) and destroyed by Mohammed Ali, 1811.

Mansell Collection

(Left)
Lejeune's painting of the Battle of Aboukir (1799) in which Napoleon drove the Turkish army into the sea.

Bulloz

Sir Sidney Smith repelling Napoleon's unsuccessful attack at Acre in 1799. Painting by Thomas Sutton; and (below) A British view of Napoleon's departure form Egypt, from Dr. Suntax's Napoleon 1814 Mansell Collection

Civil Wars, the struggle of nationalities and the balance of power, this military oligarchy did just what it liked in its corner of the Mediterranean.

'The Mamelukes' wrote Stanley Lane-Poole 'offer the most singular contrasts of any series of princes in the world. A band of lawless adventurers, slaves in origin, butchers by choice, turbulent, blood-thirsty and too often treacherous, these slave kings had a keen appreciation for the arts, which would have done credit to the most civilized ruler that ever sat on a constitutional throne...They show in their buildings, their decoration, their dress and their furniture a taste, a refinement which it would be hard to parallel in Western countries. It is one of the most singular facts in Eastern history that wherever these rude Tartars penetrated they inspired a fresh and vivid enthusiasm for art. It was tartar Ibn Toloun who built the first example of the true Saracenic mosque at Cairo; it was the line of Mameluke Sultans—all Turkish and Circassian slaves—who filled Cairo with the most beautiful and abundant monuments that any city can show.'

Yet with all this magnificence, they seldom seem to have time for a tender thought about hearth or home. In oriental fashion, they placed women well beneath man on the ladder of nature, tending to treat them as chattels in their homes—strictly for sensual convenience, nothing else. Their harems were filled with Egyptian, Nubian and Abbyssinian concubines but if they married at all—always to women of their own stock, that is to say Georgians or Circassians—they rarely had children from them. (Mameluke wives, often finding themselves to be in competition with the handsome young slaves, tended to abort themselves to retain their looks and their hold on their husbands.)* Life was so precarious in medieval Egypt, and the Mameluke armies were so constantly on the move, that the picture which emerges is essentially masculine and communal. Although they ruled over Egypt for so long, the Mamelukes were never a nation themselves; they remained perpetually a standing army of foreigners with no common ties or interests with the indigenous Egyptians—who were really the slaves. 'A pack of foreign wolves ruling over millions of sheep with perfect impunity,' as Lane-Pole put it.

The discovery of the Atlantic route round the Cape in 1498 by Vasco da Gama was a blow to their power, which disintegrated when seventeen years later a Mameluke army was chased out of Syria by the Ottoman Sultan—and then decisively beaten near Cairo. From that time onwards, until 1914, Egypt officially formed part of the Turkish Empire.

But throughout their dominions—every bit as extensive as the Eastern Roman Empire once had been—the Turks took hardly more interest in each individual province than a banker might take in a factory whose shares he had bought but which he never had time to visit. The regular encashment of Tribute money was the Porte's only real concern. So although the administration of Egypt was left nominally in the hands of a Pasha sent from Constantinople, and everything was done in the name of the Sultan, the Mameluke Beys (outwardly, of course, professing the utmost profound veneration for His Imperial Majesty) continued to live in luxurious splendor off the backs of the rest of the population, and to intrigue amongst themselves in a chronic struggle for supremacy. As the power of the Porte itself began to crack, the position of the Pasha became increasingly awkward; for the isolated representative of a formidable but sluggish Power to be left to simmer in the cauldron of citadel intrigue was bound to be explosive.

In 1769 when Clive and Warren Hastings were colonizing Hindustan, and Turkey was embroiled in a war with Russia, the Beys took their chance. They slaughtered the Turkish garrison in Cairo and sent the Pasha packing. For a brief instant of history, nudged on by Venice and Russia, the Mamelukes relived an echo of their former glory; sweeping across Syria and Arabia their leader Ali Bey reached Mecca and was hailed as Caliph—but not for long. A judicious bribe, and Constantinople learnt with relief that a dagger in the back had put an end to such inconvenient ambitions. For Egypt, it was something of a tragedy; Ali Bey had the makings of an enlightened ruler who did much to stamp out corruption and make life for the fellahin easier. His place was taken by two of the younger Beys, Ibrahim and Mourad, who divided the power between themselves under the theoretic authority of the Pasha and nearly ruined the country. Their greed for money was never-ending, and on top of their ruthless requisitioning came a succession of bad Niles and decimating epidemics.

When Bonaparte reached Egypt, he found the husks of civilization, and a country in weary bondage. But he found also that the Egyptians, throughout these calamitous centuries, had learnt to develop a fatalistic attitude towards life, and to come to terms with their gaudy overlords. Like many oppressed people, they had become curiously conservative, living in a state of negative contentment which they were unwilling to hazard. The arrival of the French promised to bring fresh horrors to their essentially placid lives, and in assuming that they would welcome him gratefully as a liberator, Bonaparte made the first—but not the last—of his major blunders in Egypt.

Raymond Flower

Notes:

In 969 El-Moizz, the fourth Caliph of the heretical Fatimid Dynasty (who since 909 had held the whole Barbary Coast from Fez to the Egyptian border) sent an army of 100,000 men under the command of his Sicilian slave Gohar against Egypt. Gohar defeated the Ikshid governors at Gizeh—where Napoleon was to triumph over the Mamelukes eight centuries later—and immediately began to lay out a palace-city for the Caliph, choosing a site on high ground just to the north of Fustat, then the capital of Egypt. The Arab historian Makrisi relates that Gohar himself marked out an area of ground measuring 1200 by 1600 yards with poles, between which bells were hung on cords; it was intended that the haruspices and astrologers should ring them when the signs showed that the propitious moment had arrived to turn the first sod. But as it happened, a kite-hawk perched on one of the ropes and set off the signal, to the consternation of the astrologers...(these kite-hawks are ubiquitous in Cairo, even today, and will suddenly swoop down and snatch the food off your plate if you are eating out of doors). However, since the signal had been given, the digging began, and as the planet Mars—El Kahir, the planet of war and discord, was in the ascendancy, the new city was given the name of El Kahira, instead of Mansuriya as originally intended. Hence Cairo, the millenary of which was celebrated in 1969.

Agha means literally 'big brother'. Even after the military school, close links remained between the Agha and his 'ini' who sometimes even adopted the Agha's name.

The Sultan Qalun was known as 'El-Alfi' because he cost 1000 dinars. Beybars, on the other hand, was sold for only 40 dinars because he had a cast in one eye. Yet Maliktimar fetched 5000 dinars on account of his astonishing physical beauty.

Perhaps the nearest comparison to a mameluke, Emir or Bey, was a medieval Baron in Europe.

Homosexuality was very current among the Mamelukes and to some extent the whole system was based on this, as Napoleon noted.

Chapter 2

Battle of the Pyramids

In the coffeehouses of the Khan-el-Khalil and the Franks quarter, behind the mushrabiya of harems, in the council chamber of the Citadel where galloping messengers from Alexandria had just gasped it out, everyone in Cairo suddenly heard the news. Two days previously, the word raced around, ten warships had anchored off Alexandria, followed shortly by another fifteen. A party of officers, landing in a rowing boat, had told the Governor, Sayed Mohamed Korein, that they were Englishmen on the track of a vast French armada which had left on an unknown destination. These Englishmen believed that the French intended to make a surprise attack on Egypt, which the inhabitants would be unable to repulse. They proposed, therefore, to anchor off Alexandria and await the French fleet, and in the meantime wished to buy provisions and fresh water.

The Governor had given them short shrift. He did not see how an invasion of Egypt by the French could concern the English—more likely, he thought, it was the English who wished to subjugate Egypt. 'This country belongs to the Sultan,' he told them sternly. 'If you wish to fight the French, you can do so outside Egyptian waters. The whole of the Mediterranean is open to you.'

In the excitement the incident caused in Cairo, it was felt that the Governor had acted with dignity. Three days later, news came that the English ships had sailed away. But hardly had the hubbub died down when the clatter of hooves was heard again through Bab-en-Nasr, and this time the inhabitants of the capital were shocked to learn, as they lingered over their coffee and shishas, that a vast armada 'which covered the sea without end' was outside Alexandria.

During the afternoon of 1 July, the messengers reported, some French officers had come ashore and spoken with their consul; and in the evening the whole fleet had moved towards the Bay of Agami, a few miles to the west. At dawn the following morning, the French were spread outside the walls of Alexandria 'like locusts'.

Not until later could the Egyptians console themselves with the knowledge that the landing had not gone at all as Bonaparte had planned. The Bay of Agami—now a fashionable resort—abounds in submerged reefs and submerged rocks, and as often happens in the summer, there was a heavy swell and huge breakers pounded the shore. But Bonaparte, realizing how crucial it was to be out of the way before Nelson returned and the Egyptians were alerted, had given orders to disembark whatever the risk. Many of the landing craft became waterlogged; others were driven back; some sank. During the night, little more than a brigade was able to get safely ashore. Nearly everyone was seasick; about thirty were drowned. Bonaparte himself scrambled weakly on to the beach soon after midnight, and exhausted, crumpled on to the shore.

For the time being, the suks of Grand Cairo buzzed with details of how Sayed Korein, calling on all good Muslims to repel and destroy the invader, had rejected all offers of negotiation and attacked with weapons (alas! Quite inadequate!) at his disposal. The Kachef of Behera, hastily summoned, had brought in his Bedouins. But to no avail. The Bedouins fled, the French quickly scaled the crumbling defenses of the town, and the unfortunate Sayed Korein was forced to surrender.

Nor in the consternation which greeted the news was it noticed that among the French casualties had been two of their principal generals. That Klèber should have been hit on the head and Menou knocked cold by a falling stone as he climbed the wall would have been splendid material for the humorists. But this was no time for joking; in a sudden panic, many of the inhabitants of Cairo packed their belongings and fled out into the desert. Fanatics shouted that the Christians should be massacred. A vast crowd made its way to Ibrahim Bey's palace on the Nile where military and religious leaders were meeting to discuss the emergency. Through the night, the deliberations went on; Ibrahim was in favor of negotiating with the French, Mourad would hear nothing of it. Proudly recalling the past victories of the Moslems over the Crusaders, he was spoiling for a fight. 'Let the heretics come,' he ended the meeting by yelling, 'I will trample them under my horse's hooves!'

In his ignorance of anything that went on outside Egypt, Mourad was so contemptuous of all foreigners that he genuinely believed he would 'slice up the French like water-melons' The French would never risk a battle on land, he reasoned, and would only fight in boats, on the Nile. To foil them, he ordered a massive iron chain, three hundred feet long, to be stretched across the river, and alongside it, a boat armed with cannons. This would be more than a match for any European *Frangis*, he declared.

After ceremonial prayers, Mourad Bey set out at the head of his forces to challenge the invaders.

Those who remained behind were far from sharing his confidence. Nerves were so jittery that the authorities ordered all the coffeehouses to remain open throughout the night, and there the inhabitants shook their heads over the French General's proclamation which had been smuggled in by refugees from Alexandria.

'People of Egypt!' they read, 'You will be told that I come to destroy your religion—do not believe it. Be assured that I come to restore your rights, to punish the usurpers, and that I respect, more than Mamelukes, God, his Prophet, and the Koran...the French also are true Moslems. The proof is that they have been to Rome the Great and destroyed the throne of the Pope, who always incited the Christians to make war on the Moslems...happy, thrice happy are those

Egyptians who side with us...but woe, woe to those who side with the Mamelukes...there shall be no salvation for them, and their memory shall be wiped out.'

For the man in the street, the situation was as bewildering as their first encounter with the French at Shubrakheit, on the Nile near Damanhour, undoubtedly was for the Mamelukes. To be confronted by serried squares of steel bayonets which erupted a murderous hail of lead from every side must have been unnerving to the Mameluke cavalry as if they had been confronted with an army of supermen from outer space. The Mamelukes still lived in the atmosphere of the Middle Ages. War, as they conceived it, was a matter of ferocious charges and individual combat—and who could match them with horse and sword? But this cold, precise and annihilating discipline of the French was something new in their experience. To add to their confusion, Mourad's own gunboat caught fire; the powder store went up with a terrifying explosion, and all the occupants were blown into the Nile. Dazed and helpless, Mourad took to his heels and went back to Cairo. One of his Beys, still true to the traditions of chivalry, rode back and challenged the French leader to single combat—but the troops of the Republic, thirsty and exhausted, were in no mood for such pleasantries. With a swift volley they reduced the gorgeously damascened figure into a heap of bloodstained loot.

In Cairo, consternation now gave way to panic. All available hands were press-ganged into service, and frenzied efforts were made to dig trenches and set up barricades at the approaches to the city. Dervishes whirled through the tortuous streets accompanied by the weird music of reed pipes and drums, which however unwelcome to European ears, has a strange fascination for the Arab, and, like *Marseillaise*, fills its hearers with a fierce longing for action and excitement. When Sayed Omar, chief of the Cherifs, emerged from the Citadel with the great banner of Islam, he was joined by thousands in a ragged and endless procession through the city, encouraged by Sheikhs reciting passages from the sacred Book of Bokhari. Prices rose astronomically. No one had any weapons worth speaking of; such as there were fetched huge premiums, and most people had to equip themselves with sticks and stones. No longer swept, the streets choked high with filth; outrages of all sorts began to occur, and inevitably the blood-curdling cry of 'Death to the Christians!' began to be heard. Churches were violated, foreigners' homes looted, and but for Ibrahim Bey's personal intervention, the whole European quarter would have been destroyed. On his orders, the Christians were escorted to the safety of the Citadel, and even his own Palace where his wife, with notable courtesy, looked after them until the dangers were over.

Hour by hour the bazaars buzzed with fresh rumors, and speculation about the plans of the French increased. No one knew from which direction they would come. Some said the French army was following the west bank of the Nile, others were sure it was the east bank—or possibly both. It never crossed the minds of the Mameluke chiefs to send out patrols, or even advance parties to slow up the invaders; and Abdel Rahman el-Djabarty, who chronicled these events, made a sad little entry in his Journal that, despite the sobering experiences at Shubrakheit, both Mourad and Ibrahim still regarded the enemy with such contempt that the measures they ordered for the city's defense were quite inadequate.

The French, meanwhile, were not without troubles of their own. Years later, at St Helena, Napoleon still had vivid memories of that scorching march across the plains of Behera. 'Melancholy and sadness prevailed in the army,' is how he chose to describe the sufferings of his men during the prodigious hardships of the approach to Cairo; 'As the Hebrews wandering in the wilderness, complained and angrily asked Moses for the onions and fleshpots of Egypt, the French soldiers constantly regretted the luxuries of Italy.' They would not have been human if they hadn't. In the burning heat of a July dust storm, with the temperature around 115°F, they found themselves trudging endlessly along the endless beds of canals, nearly boiled alive with their heavy uniforms and equipment, their throats parched by the heat and the dust and the equipment— and without a drop of water to drink. At each successive village the wells had been sabotaged, and their rations, consisting exclusively of dry biscuits, only served to make them thirstier. Such water as they saw was usually a mirage; but less substantial were the Bedouins who harassed them from a distance all the way to Cairo, capturing and mutilating any stragglers. Even so, many fell behind, shattered by heat prostration and thirst. 'Behind us,' recalled a young Lieutenant, Nicholas Desvernois, we left a trail of corpses.' Had it not been for the crops of watermelons in the fields, they would have lost a good many more.

Then suddenly, at the end of a fortnight, the Pyramids came into view—and with them reports that the Mamelukes were massed by the Nile. Unwisely, the Beys had split up their forces: while Ibrahim remained on the East Coast fronting Cairo to head off the French should they come that way, Mourad with the bulk of the army had crossed over to the West Bank—confident his cavalry could make mincemeat of the invaders. Had he forced the French to attack across the river, it might have been quite another story.

As it was, Bonaparte lost no time in seizing his opportunity. 'We saw that their cannons were not upon the field carriages,' runs his own account of the Battle of the Pyramids. 'As soon as I had satisfied myself that the artillery was not movable...that neither it nor the infantry would quit the entrenched camp, or that if the latter should come forth it would be without artillery... we resolved to prolong our right wing, and to follow with the movement of that wing with our whole army passing out of the range of the guns.'

When Mourad saw what was happening—that the French were attempting to outflank him and separate his cavalry from his infantry—he gave the order to attack. In an incomparable setting, 'the last great cavalry charge of the Middle

Ages,' as historians have called it, must have been a breathtaking sight. To one side, behind the Nile and the cultivated fields beyond, gleamed the medieval silhouette of Grand Cairo, topped by the Citadel; to the other, a few miles away, loomed the classic apricot-tinted shapes of the Pyramids. From what is today the riverside corniche between Embaba and the Pyramids road, a glittering line of six thousand horsemen, each with his personal retainers following behind, suddenly spurted forwards with incredible speed. Writing later, Lieutenant Vertrey, who was in the leading French division, retained a confused but vivid impression through clouds of dust of the thunderous crump of galloping of hooves, of pennants flying over the horses' heads, and of richly dressed riders with their huge green turbans crouching low in the saddle, scimitars in hand. The French had barely time to take action stations before the crunch came: 'In an instant we had formed our square, ten men deep, to take the shock...our soldiers fired with such coolness that not a single bullet was wasted.' With parade ground discipline, the French infantry fired, re-loaded and fired again. The effect was murderous; the first wave of Mamelukes fell almost to a man. Those who wheeled round the squares were caught in a crossfire which came from all directions. 'The blazing wads of our muskets penetrated at the same time as our bullets through their rich uniforms, which were embroidered with gold and silver and floated as lightly as gauze,' Vertrey recalls. 'The carnage was atrocious,' adds Millet, a private, 'The corpses of men and horses presented a terrible spectacle, so bloody was the massacre.' With suicidal courage, the Mamelukes—outnumbered by at least three to one—continued to pit individual feats of bravery against the business-like discipline of four French Divisions for more than an hour until Mourad, realizing that the game was up, fled in the direction of the Pyramids.

'From this moment,' declares Vivant Denon, the artist (who was sketching it all furiously from the cover of a palm tree) 'it was no longer a battle; it was a massacre.' Moments later, the French were on top of the entrenchments at Embaba, savagely hacking down everything in sight. A sandstorm began to blow up, making the river very choppy, and through the dust and din Abdel Rahman el-Djabarty, watching from the far bank, was appalled to see Embaba go up in flames and thousands of figures—cavalry, infantry and camp followers—throw themselves into the Nile in a desperate stampede for safety. Many of the Mamelukes galloped full tilt into the water and were swept to the bottom by the weight of their armor. 'The Eastern army, says Djabarty, 'began to scream at the top of their voices...but the more sagacious among them ordered them to be quiet, saying that the Prophet and his disciples fought with sabre and sword, not with screams and barks like dogs; but nobody listened to them.' By this time, the onlookers—Ibrahim Bey among the first—were taking to their heels, escaping with what possessions they could carry into the desert. Before making off, the Beys set fire to hundreds of Nile boats; and as Bonaparte moved into Mourad's country house at Giza with his staff, the domes and minarets of Cairo were lit up by a fearsome *son et lumière* which even silhouetted the far-off Pyramids as the mob took over, stealing and burning whatever they could find. 'From the tops of those Pyramids, forty centuries look down on you!' Bonaparte had declaimed to the soldiers around him as the battle was about to begin; in the flickering glow the scene was now of one of the richest loots ever encountered—jeweled weapons, damascened armor, priceless carpets, silks and silverware along with the gold which the Mamelukes habitually carried in their baggage in case they had to flee suddenly. Booty was fished literally from the bottom of the Nile. 'Never' says Djabarty, 'had Egypt seen so many horrors. Never have we seen such things in the history of nations; to hear is not to see.'

On 23 July 1798, the first French contingents moved cautiously into the city. The population, which only a few hours previously had 'sobbed, struck their own faces, and screamed, "Woe to us! Now we are the slaves of the French!" watched curiously as the 'poilus' of the day, quite unarmed, strolled through the streets joking with the passers-by who, gulping back their astonishment, lost no time in selling them whatever they needed at grossly inflated prices. Soon the bazaars were trading gleefully and the coffeehouses had re-opened. At four o'clock in the afternoon of 26 July, to a fanfare of trumpets and drums, the hero of revolutionary France made his entry into Grand Cairo and was installed in the most sumptuous of the Mameluke palaces (that of Elfy Bey at Ezbekieh, which later became the site of Shepheard's Hotel). For Napoleon Bonaparte, the dream of an Empire of the East was taking shape; for Egypt itself, thrust so abruptly into the world of the emergent nineteenth century, a new, European dominated chapter was beginning, which would reach its apogee 154 years later to the day, indeed, almost to the hour—with its own revolution, and its own hero.

In ten prestigious volumes—the most valuable achievement of the whole expedition—the French savants compiled a formidably detailed picture of Egypt at this period. Bonaparte also jotted down his impressions and it is intriguing to see eighteenth century Cairo through the sharp eyes of the twenty-nine year old conqueror. He began, as a good soldier should, by looking at the basic problems of water and defenses: 'Cairo is situated half a league from the Nile; old Cairo and Boulac are its ports. A canal which croses the city is usually dry, but fills during the inundation, at the moment when the dyke is cut, an operation which is never performed until the Nile is at a certain height, when it becomes the occasion of a public festival. The canal then distributes its waters amongst numerous channels; and the square of El-Bekir (Ezbekieh) as well as most of the squares and gardens of Cairo, is under water. All these places are traversed in boats, during the flood. Cairo is commanded by a citadel placed on a hill, which overlooks the whole city. It is separated from the Mokattem hills by a valley. An aqueduct, which is a remarkable work, supplies the citadel with water. For this purpose there is at Old Cairo, an enormous and very high octagonal tower, enclosing a reservoir, to which the waters of the Nile are raised by a hydraulic machine and from which they enter the aqueduct. The citadel also draws water from Joseph's well, but it is not so good as that of the Nile. This fortress was not in a state of defense, but neglected and falling to ruin...Cairo is surrounded with high walls, built by the Arabs, and surmounted by enormous towers; these walls were in a bad state, and falling through age; the Mamelukes never repaired anything. The City is large; half of its walls abut on the desert, so that dry sands are met with on going out by the Suez gate, or those which are towards Arabia.'

Having disposed of such basic logistics, he was able to take a more general look at the city, just as any tourist might have done: 'The population of Cairo is considerable, being estimated at 210,000 inhabitants. The houses are built very high and the streets made narrow, in order to obtain shelter from the sun. From the same motive the bazaars, or public markets, are covered with cloth or matting. The Beys have very fine palaces of an Oriental architecture, resembling that of India rather than ours. The Sheikhs also have very handsome houses. The okel are great square buildings with very large inner courts, containing whole corporations of merchants. Thus there is the okel of Seur rice, the okel of the merchants of Suez, and of Syria. On the outside, and next the street, they each have a little shop of ten or twelve feet square, in which is the merchant with samples of his goods. Cairo contains a multitude of the finest mosques in the world; the minarets are rich and numerous. The mosques in general serve for the accommodation of pilgrims, who sleep in them; some of them occasionally contain as many as 3,000 pilgr ims; amongst them is Jemilazer (The Mosque University of Al Azhar), which is said to be the largest mosque in the East. These mosques are usually courts, the circuit of which is surrounded by enormous columns supporting terraces; in the interior is found a number of basins and reservoirs of water, for drinking or washing. In one quarter, that of the Franks, are a few European families, a certain number of houses may be seen here, such as a merchant of 30,000 or 40,000 livres a year might have in Europe; they are furnished in the European style with chairs and beds. There are churches for the Copts, and some convents for the Syrian Catholics...There is a vast number of coffee-houses, in which people take coffee, sherbet, or opium, and converse on public affairs...'

Meandering next into a dissertation on slavery, he noted that Mourad and Ali had been sold to some of the Beys at a tender age by merchants who had purchased them in Circassia...it is the same with the pashas, viziers, and sultans,' he added, with unconscious irony: 'it was ... a long time before the Egyptians could understand that all the French were not my slaves...'

There were other things, too, that they found hard to understand; for the Egyptians, many aspects of the French occupation seemed not far from the incomprehensible. Amid a deluge of proclamations—remarkable for their free use of the Almighty—citizens who had lived all their lives in the shadow of the Citadel and were therefore well inured to the idiosyncrasies of despotic decree learned with surprise that the benefits of the Rights of Man, as interpreted by a true son of the Revolution, were about to be heaped on them. The sight of Bonaparte, dressed as a Grand Sheikh and participating in religious festivals, they were prepared to cheer; but the behavior of his troops—though normal enough for an army of occupation—was bound to offend their Moslem susceptibilities. They saw the French drinking, swearing, and making love in public. They noted with growing aversion their uninhibited ways not only with European women but also with the harem—whom they encouraged to appear in public unveiled. They were irritated that Copts, Syrians and Jews should begin to give themselves airs, and outraged when the military commandant had certain mosques and cemeteries destroyed in his drive to clean up the city. To many it seemed as though everything had been shattered save man's faith in Islam and in Allah, who had punished them for their sins by giving victory to the infidel.

In these first heady days Bonaparte, well-meaning maybe, but ignorant in the ways of the East, may have felt quite confident that his policy of peaceful coexistence was beginning to work. It was true that, as he wrote to Menou, he found it necessary to have five or six people beheaded every day in the streets of Cairo. But on the other hand the Divan of Sheikhs he had handpicked to govern under his jurisdiction were proving pleasantly cooperative. His flirtation with Islam, which he pushed to the extent of holding Moslem prayers and appearing, somewhat incongruously, in flowing Egyptian robes, was politically astute—and also a seductive form of self-indulgence. And no prospect could be more intoxicating than the virtual regeneration of Egypt that was being planned by the newly formed Institut du Cairo.

If a shadow existed, it was Josephine's behavior. Her indiscretions were no longer a secret, even in Cairo. And Nelson, of course. But of Nelson's activities, he had no news at all.

Chapter 3

The End of a Dream

Nelson, likewise, was in the dark. With not a hint of the momentous happenings in Egypt, he was still cruising aimlessly around the Mediterranean, and even his closest officers could hardly realize how bitterly despondent the fruitless search had made him. To his medical adviser he complained of heart trouble—which that gentleman diagnosed as nervous indigestion. The lack of news of the enemy, the admiral insisted, had broken his heart. 'More people perhaps die of broken hearts than we think', he added with unnaval emotion.

Then, suddenly, the news came. On 28 July 1798 it was learnt, from a captured French wine-brig, that Bonaparte's target had been Egypt—just as he had originally suspected. The same evening, there was confirmation from Turkish sources. The heart symptoms vanished; his return journey to Alexandria took less than four days. Soon after noon on 1 August, Nelson's fleet sighted Pharos and Pompeii's Pillar—from which a tricolor was flying, although there were no French ships in the harbor. An hour later, forgetting in his excitement to salute the quarter deck, a midshipman rushed up with the news: 'Enemy sail in sight!'

Before disappearing inland, Bonaparte had ordered Admiral de Breuys, if he could not remain at Alexandria itself, either to sail for French-occupied Corfu, or to find a suitable anchorage along the coast. Since he had insufficient provisions for the voyage to Corfu, and most of the Expeditions stores were still on board, de Breuys chose Aboukir Bay. Sheltered there in the western curve behind a low spit of land linked to a small fortified island with dangerous reefs although anchored nearly two miles out from the shore because the water was so shallow—de Breuys felt confident that, with his ships in line and nearly five hundred guns covering the seaward approach, there was little danger of his fleet being taken by surprise. It was pure bad luck that on the first day of August a good many of the crews were ashore filling water casks and digging wells (with other detachments protecting them against the Bedouins), and also that the admiral opposing him was in a mood bordering on recklessness.

Indeed Nelson, who had repeatedly said 'I will bring the French fleet into action the moment I can lay hands on them', was in no mood to let the enemy take up battle stations during the cover of darkness. However dangerous an immediate attack might be, delay was worse. With that touch of genius which marked him as England's greatest sailor, he noted instantly that 'where there is room for a French 74 to swing, there is room for an English 74 to anchor', and set course to attack the enemy's van and center from both sides; a brilliant and daring decision which carried the day. As the fiery sun sank below the horizon ten British 74s turned sharp to the wind, abreast of the reefs, rounding all the dangers in one prodigious sweep, and minutes later were raking the French with fire from the landward side as well as the seaward side—moreover so obliquely that, whereas Nelson's ships could fire on two French ships at once, de Breuys could not direct both his broadside batteries against them. To add to the Frenchmen's distress, since no one had ever expected to be attacked from that side, the starboard guns were loose, and piled up with every sort of bric-a-brac, in itself a source of deadly splinters.

Throughout the night, continuous flashes of broadsides pierced the soft, smoke-hung darkness, but watchers on the shore could spot only the glimmer of the lanterns which Nelson had ordered on British masts to distinguish them from the enemy. Even so, both sides fired sometimes on their own ships, and the reminiscences of those who took part in that harrowing night give a picture of isolated drama in a barely controlled confusion. Quite early on, de Breuys was killed; a canon ball scythed him in half on the bridge of his flagship, l'Orient. Soon afterwards, Nelson was hit—but not seriously wounded. A little before ten o'clock, l'Orient caught fire. The flames, fed by paint and oil buckets on deck, spread rapidly along her newly painted sides, and within half an hour the ship had to be abandoned. (Her last chaotic moments were immortalized, somewhat inaccurately, by Mrs. Hemens in the poem about the boy who stood on the burning deck.) Then, suddenly, she blew up with a blinding detonation which shook a twenty-mile radius from Alexandria to Rosetta, and a hail of red-hot wreckage, mingled with corpses, came flaming down. In the stunned silence that followed, there was complete darkness for fully ten minutes before the firing resumed.

Dawn came up on the surprising scene of a totally dismembered French fleet. Out of the thirteen sail-of-the-line, nine had been taken and two burnt; of the four frigates, one had been burnt and sunk. Only one 74 and two frigates escaped to fight another day.

L'Orient took with her to the depths of Aboukir Bay the body of Admiral de Breuys, the treasure of St John of Jerusalem which had been confiscated from the Maltese, and over half a million pounds in gold and diamonds which had been stolen from the Swiss republic to finance the expedition to Egypt. So now Bonaparte was not only cut off from home, but he was penniless too.

Nelson's dispatches, announcing the victory at Aboukir, took two months and a day to reach London—and such was the First Lord's emotion on reading them that he is reported to have collapsed on the floor of his office.

Bonaparte heard the news on 8 August as he was returning to Cairo after some mopping-up operations in the eastern delta. Norry, the architect, who happened to be riding alongside him, remembers that Bonaparte dismounted slowly and walked a few steps away. 'So the navy has gone...' he was heard to mutter, '...is this the end?' Then, turning back, he went on in a matter-of-fact tone of voice: 'Well, this upset will urge us on to greater things. Egypt used to be the center of civilization. We shall have to recreate the Egyptian Empire...'

For this, the first requirement was a cleaned-up and contented Cairo. But although the Arab proverb says, 'kiss the hand you cannot sever', and for centuries the Egyptians had been doing just that, they seemed to be progressively less inclined to get on kissing terms with the French. Basically, the trouble was the age-old incompatibility of East and West—which Bonaparte's spring-cleaning tactics, however well meaning, could only serve to aggravate. Even as Bonaparte tightened his grip on the capital and developed his ideas of what an orderly and popular government should be, it became obvious that theories on the 'rights of man' and other revolutionary French catchwords could have little impact on the inward-looking Egyptians. For one thing, they could not grasp what he was aiming at; for another, they had no desire for any such changes. However fetid and stomach-turning the atmosphere in the narrow alleys of Cairo with its compounded aroma of spices, urine and rotting humanity might be, this was how they had always known it; however harshly the Mamelukes may have used them, this was what they understood.

Essentially, with their deep-rooted faith in Islam and their consequent loyalty to the Sultan—to them the greatest and most powerful ruler in the world—the men and women of Egypt never pinned their troubles to anything more remote than the bullying of the local officials. There was not a fellah in the land who did not believe that if he could only meet the Sultan in person, his wrongs would be immediately and miraculously righted. Moreover, the Egyptian's whole attitude towards government was misunderstood by the French.

Although the indigenous administration was bad, and the benefits it gave pretty meager, ordinary Egyptians were conscious of being dependent on the 'hakooma', a necessary and morphous evil which offered them a sort of paternal protection, and which was traditionally entitled to tax them—to their last penny, if it could, to a good deal less if they were clever, and after all, with the help of a bribe, this could usually be arranged. Under the Mamelukes, they were often harshly taxed, and suffered acts of wanton cruelty, but by and large they were free from any discipline. They could work if they chose, or they could sit in the sunshine and do nothing. In their daily life no one bothered them.

Now, suddenly, Bonaparte began eroding these liberties, and the blessings of modern civilization seemed nothing if not an avalanche of bothersome regulations. The man in the street found he must pay a fee for such things as births, marriages and deaths; that he needed a permit to go on any sort of journey; that he was responsible for the actions of anyone he invited to his house; that he would be summonsed if he failed to surrender his mule to the French, or to keep the road outside his house watered by day and lit by night. The indignity of being required to wear a tricolor cockade in his turban as a sign of submission was something he could bear (after all, it cost nothing) but harder to stomach was the systematic robbery by which the French administrators sought to re-place the treasure which had sunk with their flagship. Owners of landed property, for example, were ordered to produce their title-deeds, and when, as frequently happened, these failed to pass scrutiny, the land was sold off and credited to the French republic.

To make matters worse, these regulations were enforced with Mameluke rigor—and more than Mameluke thoroughness—by the Copts and the Jews who, under one pretext or another, could now force their way into Moslem houses and even violate the harem. With smoldering rage the Egyptians came to realize that the French were worse than the Beys; instead of liberty they had brought bureaucracy. Government by the Mamelukes had been maddening, for sure, but at least it was predictable; government by the French was not only maddening but unpredictable too.

On 10 October Sheikh Abdel Rahman el-Djabarty spent an agreeable morning in the library of the newly established Institut du Caire. It was not his first visit and he was charmed, as always, by the cordial way he was received by the French professors—a welcome, he noted with approval, extended to all Egyptians who showed an interest in the arts. On this occasion he admired some books on ancient history illustrating the lives of the apostles and the miracles they had performed. He was particularly taken by a large volume dealing with the story of the Prophet, depicted with a sword in his right hand and a book in his left, and surrounded by his followers. Up on the first floor, he saw an intriguing piece of machinery: a telescope which could be taken to pieces and packed into a small box. A chemist entertained him with a curious experiment. He poured a liquid into a test-tube, and then added another liquid. A colored smoke formed and when this disappeared the liquids had turned into a solid yellow substance which, when touched, felt like stone. The chemist repeated the performance with different liquids and produced next a blue stone, and finally a red one. He then took a white powder and struck it with a hammer, causing an explosion like a gun going off. Everyone jumped like rabbits, and the chemists roared with laughter.

Leaving the building, Sheikh el-Djabarty saw that the alleys were plastered with proclamations. The French were always up to something new, he reflected as he read them. Not content with seizing houses whose title deeds were unsatisfactory, they were now proposing to levy a tax on all remaining freehold property. As he passed through the teeming streets, he noticed an ominous tension in the air. The crowds were rallying together; it looked as if trouble was brewing. As darkness fell, weapons which had been hidden were brought out, and suddenly a huge mob, with Sayed Badry at their head, rushed screaming along the streets. Revolt had broken out.

Napoleon To Nasser

Mohammed Ali with British naval officers at Alexandria in May 1839. Painting by David Roberts. Mansell Collection.

Disraeli purchasing the Khedive's shares in the Suez Canal as seen by Punch. Mansell Collection

A British view of de Lesseps in 1883. Mansell Collection

23

Raymond Flower

The opening of the Suez Canal. Blessing the Canal at Port Said in the presence of the Imperial and Royal Visitors, December 1869.
Mansell Colleciton

The Khedive Ismail, Sovereign ruler of Egypt. He was deposed by the Sultan in 1879.

Mansell Collection

Ahmed Arabi Paha, portrayed when in prison in Cairo in 1882 after his defeat by the British.

Mansell Collection

Lord Cromer became virtual ruler of Egypt in 1884 and was succeeded by Sir Eldon Gorst in 1907

National Portrait Gallery

Earl Kitchener of Khartoum (top right). As Sirdar of the Egyptian army he drove the Mahdists out of the Sudan and crushed them at Omdurman in 1898.
Mansell Collection

Wilfrid Scawen Blunt 1840-1922 (right) championed Egyptian and Arab nationalist interests during the heyday fo English jingoism.

In some ways it was a glimpse into the crystal ball—a microcosm of all the anti-colonialist rebellions which would explode during the next century and a half not only in Egypt but in many lands where the hand of Europe lay too heavily. The screaming mob, armed with stones, spears and razor-sharp knives storming through the streets; the French area commander and his guard savaged—followed by indiscriminate looting and frenzied erection of barricades when the troops were ordered in. Fighting went on all day until Bonaparte, losing patience at last, ordered the city to be shelled from batteries mounted at the Citadel, and finally directed their fire on the great mosque of Al Azhar itself. Sheltering behind a parapet, el-Djabarty watched incredulously as the city crumbled under a tornado of shells. 'When the people saw the shells fall,' he noted unhappily, 'a thing they had never experienced before, they called on the Almighty to save them from such misfortunes.' More realistically, a delegation of Sheikhs hastened to Bonaparte to ask for terms. 'You began the revolt' he answered them shortly, 'I shall finish it.' Not until the Sheikhs begged for mercy did he order the firing to cease.

Shortly afterwards, French troops took up positions all over the city and cavalry clattered into the sacred precincts of Al Azhar—where they too ran amok. Horses were tethered to the Kiblah, furniture hurled around and the Koran kicked about the floor. El-Djabarty, aghast, saw soldiers spit on the carpets, urinate on the walls, and litter the mosque with broken wine bottles. So much for rebellion. Heavy fines were imposed all round, and ten Sheikhs believed to have been implicated were stripped naked and shot in the Citadel. 'Sedition is dead', Bonaparte cautioned the others, 'beware, lest you involve yourselves in fresh misfortunes.' But from now on he flirted no more with Islam, and the citizens of Cairo no longer referred to him admiringly as Sultan el Kebir Bonaparte. Indeed, as the dust settled in the souks, passers-by halted at street corners to hear the latest news from the Porte. Copies of an Imperial Firman were passed around, in which the French were branded as infidels, liars, and monsters of every description.

Soon afterwards, it became known that Turkey had declared war on France.

Perspiring all too freely in the elaborate gold lace of his uniform, which reached almost up to his ears *(liberté, égalité* and *fraternité* had in no way diminished his taste for *costumes de fantaisie)* the devoted and ever competent little Berthier listened skeptically to his Chief's plans for a campaign in Syria. Bonaparte was not the man to let the Turks steal a march on him; however unpropitious it might be to leave Cairo in its actual hair-trigger state—to say nothing of the growing unrest in the provinces—he could hardly ignore the hostile army which was being assembled at Rhodes, nor the occupation of El Arish (a coastal village inside Egyptian territory) by the Turkish governor of

Acre. If the Turks were spoiling for a fight, he told Berthier, they should have one; he would capture Acre, raise the whole Christian population of Syria and Armenia against the Porte, and 'turn the Turkish Empire upside down'. These elliptical instructions were swiftly translated into lucid military orders, and on 11 February 1799 a force of some 13,000 set out across the Sinai desert to the tune of a hastily composed jingle, *Partant pour la Syrie*.

Two men stood in Bonaparte's way: Ahmed el Djezzar, the Turkish Governor of Acre, and Sir Sidney Smith, Commodore of the British squadron in the eastern Mediterranean. Of Djezzar ('the butcher') who had started life in the Cairo abattoirs, it was said that by applying his trade to politics he had become the greediest, the cruelest, and probably the most redoubtable figure south of Constantinople. Of Sir Sidney—who, after enlisting in the navy at the age of twelve, had been promoted captain at nineteen and knighted (for free-lancing with the Swedes) at twenty-six—his personal file at the Admiralty recorded, with barely disguised approval: 'a recklessness in running into danger, and great resources of mind in getting out of it with credit.' Freshly escaped from the notorious Temple in Paris—where he had been imprisoned after his activities at Toulon—Sir Sidney had a personal score to settle with the French.

This unlikely combination, and 'that miserable hole' grumbled Bonaparte at St Helena, 'made me miss my destiny.'

Built on a tongue of land jutting out into the sea, and protected on the landward side by massive ramparts, Acre had figured prominently in the destinies of such figures as Nesho the Egyptian, Solon the Greek, and Richard Coeur-de-Lion. At the news that Bonaparte was marching north, Sir Sidney guessed that this would be his target; and before the French arrived, he had already captured seven of their gunboats transporting stores, munitions, and more important still, the siege artillery. So that when Bonaparte reached Acre, he found his own guns pointing at him from the ramparts he had intended them to breach. An immediate first attack was easily repulsed. A second, more costly in casualties and even less successful than the first, resigned Bonaparte to the slow and tedious machinery of a siege. Despite the French sapping and mining, the little garrison of British marines and Turkish irregulars made ceaseless sorties; an eye-witness inside the walls describes the 'frenzied keening of the Moslem women, gyrating madly and throwing dust in the air' to excite their men to ever-greater feats of bravery in the nightly raids which Sidney Smith took a huge delight in leading, while Ahmed Djezzar sat at his palace gateway doling out a silver dollar for the head of each Frenchman laid at his feet.

To Bonaparte, who always depended on mobility for his success, such a stalemate was intolerable. It was as though he had stubbed his foot against a rock, kicked it away—and barked his shin. Night after night he paced fretfully up and down the small hill overlooking Acre which is still known as Coeur-de-Lion.

'The fate of the East,' he said, pointing angrily, 'depends on that petty town. Behold the key to Constantinople...and of India!'

It was a key he was fated never to possess. However much he might soothe his frustration with grandiose visions—'I will overturn the Turkish Empire and found, in the East, a new and grand Empire which will fix my name for posterity...perhaps I shall return to Paris by Andrianople, or by Vienna, having annihilated the House of Austria'—it was plain that his adventure in the East had turned sour on him. Furthermore, after two months of digging and mining, of sorties and artillery duels, the French were faced with a hazard as decimating as ever the enemy could be. Over 1,000 men, according to the records, had died of plague (as against 1,200 killed by the enemy) and 2,300 more were ill and wounded.

The showdown came when, on the fifty-first day of the siege, a large fleet of Turkish reinforcements appeared on the horizon. That night, consolidating the grenadiers of every regiment into a dense mass of *sturm-truppen*, Bonaparte launched a last devastating onslaught. But even this ten hour holocaust was in vain, although at one point the tricolor was hoisted briefly on one of the towers. Once the reinforcements began to land, it was obvious that the assault had failed—so completely, indeed, that he had no choice but to pull together what was left of his shattered forces and move off the plain back to Egypt.

Both protagonists now made use of their pens, each characteristically. 'General' wrote the sailor, elegantly twisting the knife in the wound, 'circumstances remind me to wish that you would reflect on the instability of human affairs. In fact, would you have thought that a poor prisoner in a cell of the Temple prison...would have compelled you in the midst of the sands of Syria, to raise the siege of a miserable, almost defenseless hamlet. Such events, you must admit, exceed all human calculations. Believe me, General...Asia is not a theatre for your glory. This letter is a little revenge that I give myself.'

Bonaparte, who, it is said, never forgave him for this, was only too acutely aware of the instability of human affairs, and the techniques for manipulating men. The report which he sent back to Cairo was as distorted as any of our twentieth century communiqués: 'In three days time, we shall start back *en route* for Cairo...' he told the Egyptians, '...I shall bring many prisoners and captured flags with me. I have overthrown the palace of Djezzar and the walls of Acre; I have bombarded the town until not a stone remained standing. The inhabitants fled by sea. Djezzar is mortally wounded...'

Leaving a trail of sick and disabled in their wake back across the desert, the French retreat to Egypt was a disastrous affair—but not so their entry into Cairo. This was as triumphant as any demagogue could wish; with flags flying and drums banging it took five hours for the haggard remnants to pass through the palm-strewn streets, but the Egyptians were not seriously fooled, and were mainly intrigued to see how pale and weary the soldiers seemed after their experiences up in Syria.

The following month gave Bonaparte a genuine excuse for a victorious parade.

The Turkish army—which Hassan Moustapha Bey had been assembling at Rhodes—finally put in an appearance at Aboukir Bay, captured the fort, which was manned by a single French platoon, and then squatted indecisively on the narrow strip of land which forms the western tongue of the bay. Far from indecisive was the attack which Bonaparte, still smarting from the memory of Acre, launched furiously against their entrenched positions, and this time succeeded in carrying the day.

'The blue column as it advanced to the assault was repulsed twice', states Sir Sidney Smith, who, once again, was in the thick of it all, 'but the barbarous custom of the Turks, of cutting off the heads of their fallen enemies, to effect which they ran forward irregularly, produced a burst of indignation amongst the French infantry, which rallied them; the suddenness of their return to the attack discomforted the unconnected defenders of these imperfect lines; the sea was soon covered with hundreds of fugitives swimming off to us.' One of these was a young Albanian officer named Mohammed Ali who was later to become ruler of Egypt.

Once again Bonaparte rode triumphantly through Cairo, this time with the captured Moustapha Bey convincingly at his side. But already his thoughts were far from Cairo. For during the formalities after the battle, Sir Sidney, with studied and perhaps malicious courtesy, had handed Bonaparte a bundle of two-months-old newspapers. From these he had learnt that the *Gotterdammerung* he had always expected had caught up with the incompetent regime in Paris. His conquests in Italy had been reversed; the French armies were retreating all across the map; France itself was in the throes of civil discord—and *La Patrie* was in quite serious danger of invasion.

In Egypt the outlook was gloomy—and in any case, what was glory on the Nile compared to the power, the imperial gilt, the azure and the flaming crimson, which even now he could scent in Paris? Little matter if it meant deserting his army in the face of all discipline. During a single night after reading the newspapers, his decision was taken. Pretending to be off on a routine visit to the provinces he slipped quietly out of Cairo and, accompanied only by a few handpicked aides, set sail for France.

The secret of his departure was so well kept that even Kleber, appointed his successor, learnt the news by letter too late to ask for explanations. Characteristically, Bonaparte had written: 'When I reach Paris I shall chase out this gang of lawyers who mock us...and I will consolidate this magnificent colony.' But in fact no one knew better than Napoleon that the expedition had been a fiasco.

Soon the drawing rooms of Paris would be full of stirring sketches depicting the triumphs of the Army of the Nile. Court painters would produce large, smooth canvasses showing the Conqueror of Egypt on horseback under translucent skies contemplating the Sphinx, or urging his gallant countrymen to trample down writhing, ebony-skinned enemies. But the letters home from these same warriors, intercepted at sea by the British fleet, showed quite a different side to the story: 'This infernal Egypt is nothing but a waste of sand. Since we have been here we have done nothing but suffer', wrote a despairing officer. *'Nom de Dieu,* bring us our baggage and our brandy', wailed another, 'the whole army has dysentery from drinking the local water. *'Nom de Dieu,* wine, brandy and rum! 'I fear we have been horribly deceived by this much-vaunted expedition', lamented a colonel; 'the most uncultivated district in France is a thousand times more beautiful than this promised land...picture a collection of dirty, ill-built pigeon lofts, and you have some idea of Alexandria...as for Cairo, the wealthiest, the largest and most magnificent city in the world —it is the vilest and most miserable kennel on the face of the earth.'

Without any doubt the expedition would have to be written off as a failure. For the Egyptians, it would be just another passing phase, which in a few years would be forgotten. Yet its effects were enduring; it thrust Egypt into the Europe of the nineteenth century; it spelt the beginning of the end of the Mamelukes; and—thanks to the labors of the Institut du Caire and their magnificent *Description de l'Egypte*—it was the outset of many projects and much of the French cultural influence which remain to this day. Students plotting the rise of imperialism will note that here was the first full-blooded attempt on the part of a European country to colonize in this area; admirers of Napoleon will recognize that the adventure in Egypt was a curtain raiser for the flamboyant career that followed.

But the requiem for Napoleon in Egypt was expressed succinctly, if not too elegantly, by Kleber, as he stood reading the letter from the man who had been his chief. *'Ce petit salaud'*, he exploded furiously, *'a foutu le camp avec ses culottes pleines de merde*!

On 7 March 1801, just eighteen months later, a pink-faced young Englishman leant on the side of a sailing vessel in Aboukir Bay, and, 'his imagination wound up to the most horrible anxiety', watched the vanguard of Sir Ralph Abercromby's expeditionary force make an assault landing against the French positions on the mainland.

'We saw our troops crowded in flat boats, sitting without their muskets loaded, and unable to return any of the heavy fire they were suffering from' wrote Morgan Morgan Clifford of the 12th Light Dragoons in his journal; 'many boats we saw sunk or torn to pieces by shells, and the men struggling in the water...' Once they approached the edge of the surf, the enemy—hitherto concealed—came storming down the beach. 'We heard the three cheers of the English soldiers, we saw the boats reach the shore, and the troops jump on land. The enemy rushed on them, whilst a body of their cavalry charged furiously the Guards, who were on the left of the line, and all was smoke and confusion...'

After a quarter of an hour, the scene brightened: the English appeared on the high ground behind, chasing a retreating enemy, and 'all now was joy'. By ten o'clock that evening, the whole of the expeditionary force had been landed, and, the beachhead consolidated, Abercromby pushed on towards Alexandria. Near the present Sporting Club two murderous clashes took place—(I never saw a field so strewed with dead' reported a British commander) which Morgan Clifford predicted would 'decide the fate of Egypt'. What no crystal ball could tell him was that this first appearance of the Union Jack on Egyptian soil would open a century and a half of Anglo-Egyptian relations—until that well-loved, and too often best-hated symbol was finally—and irrevocably—struck at Port Said two days before Christmas, 155 years later.

Ironically enough, if the British were in Egypt at all, it was due to a muddle at Whitehall. Soon after Bonaparte had deserted his army in Cairo to become First Consul in Paris, Sir Sidney Smith, from his grandstand view of the situation aboard Le Tigre, had written to his Sea-Lord that he 'had positive grounds for saying that Kleber is Bonaparte's most determined and dreaded enemy', and that in his opinion the very last thing Napoleon desired was to see Kleber and his army back in France. If the French could be eased out of Egypt, not only would the Turkish army be saved from probable extermination (no one knew better than he what a rabble they were) but another cat would be let loose among the pigeons in France.

General Kleber, a haughty Alsatian of the *Ancienne Ecole*, who had come to terms with a revolutionary government he despised, counterpointed this theme. With none of the grandiose visions of his predecessor, he had always been lukewarm about the expedition to Egypt, and as the difficulties of occupation increased, his pessimism grew. Soon his only thought was how to extricate the French from Egypt without disaster.

It was not too difficult, under the circumstances, to negotiate an agreement between the Turks and the French by which the French army was to be given a safe and honorable opportunity to withdraw from Egypt within three months. At the beginning of 1800, Sir Sidney, who had contrived with the pen what even his inspired swashbuckling had failed with the sword, could gleefully report to London that the French were evacuating Egypt.

Their Lordships' reply came as an unpleasant shock. While the French were busy preparing to hand over Cairo to the Turks, a frigate was bound for the Mediterranean with implicit instructions from Whitehall that the French were on no account to be permitted to leave Egypt 'upon any other terms than those of giving up their arms and surrendering as prisoners of war.'

The inhabitants of Cairo, who had watched with ill-concealed delight the departure of the French, were mystified by the sudden feverish resumption of military activity in the capital. A red-faced Kleber made known to his troops the British conditions. 'Comrades,' he roared from a tricolor-draped dais, 'a French soldier has only one reply to such insolent communications. Victory!' Before his temper had cooled, the French had annihilated the Grand Vizier's army at Matariah, and were once again firmly the masters of Egypt.

When, three months later, the news of this debacle reached their Lordships in London, they could not help feeling, petulantly, that Sir Sidney Smith was responsible for such an unsatisfactory state of affairs. 'Why,' said Mr. Fox fretfully, 'Egypt should be of such importance to the French, was a thing he had never been able to discover'. Nevertheless, it was felt that 'something ought to be done.' A number of memoranda were drafted for the edification of ministers concerned, and in due course it was decided to send an expeditionary force under Sir Ralph Abercromby to deal with the French.

Meanwhile, Cairo had flared up in another revolt. Some 6,000 Turks, escaping from Matariah, infiltrated into the capital to give the exasperated citizens the impetus for a general uprising against the occupation forces. Yet even as the French were re-establishing control, after a month of skirmishing—during which the suburb of Boulac was razed to the ground—an event occurred which nearly provoked them to destroy the whole city of Cairo.

On a drowsy June afternoon, as he was strolling unguarded in the garden of Elfi's palace, Kleber was assassinated. A young Moslem Arab from Aleppo—hired for the job, it transpired by some Turkish officers in Palestine—stole up to the General as if seeking alms, and knifed him four times. Kleber died on the spot, and as the news spread, the French troops ran amok ('We cut down with our sabers all the men and children we came across' as a sergeant gleefully wrote home.) Djabarty, terrified like everyone else of the repercussions which might follow, was amazed that Soliman, who confessed to the murder, was given an official trial instead of being put to death immediately. But the outcome was the same: Soliman was executed (along with a few sheikhs for good measure) with every refinement of torture the military tribunal could devise. He had struck his blow for freedom, so he thought—but, ironically, his action only served to prolong the occupation. For Kleber, whose sole desire was to get the army back to France, was succeeded by Menou, a stout little man who looked more like a pastry-cook than a general, and whose passion to remain in Egypt was so great that he officially embraced Islam and changed his name to Abdullah Menou, as well as marrying an Egyptian girl.

Fifteen months of skirmishing, punctuated by some bloodthirsty battles, particularly around Alexandria, only served to emphasize the stalemate. By 1802 there was little steam left on either side, and even Menou was prepared to welcome the Treaty of Amiens under which Egypt was evacuated by both British and French substantially along the lines that Sir Sidney Smith had arranged two years before. The bald fact was that after Bonaparte had quit, the Egyptian campaign had degenerated into little more than a sideshow. The *petit salaud* had given star quality to the expedition, if nothing else. And unconsciously he had paved the way for his successor, Mohammed Ali, whose story is Egypt's for the next half century.

Chapter 4

The Founder of a Dynasty

As the Turkish expeditionary force was being chased into the sea at Aboukir by the French in 1799, Sir Sidney Smith—who himself had a narrow escape—hauled a drowning soldier into his gig. He gave artificial respiration to the young Albanian with the bushy beard and piercing gray eyes, and sent him off to the safety of his flagship, remarking that in another five minutes the little blighter would have been dead.

Thus entered the Egyptian scene the man who was to succeed where Napoleon had failed. For by a series of sharp and decisive actions this Albanian irregular was to make himself the master of the country and the creator, to all intents and purposes, of nineteenth-century Egypt. Whereas Augustus boasted that he had found Rome built of brick and left it built of marble, Mohammed Ali could say that he found Egypt a chaos and left it a country. A dictator in the old Oriental style, his influence went far beyond the borders of the Delta. He captured the holy places of Arabia, tyrannized the Sudan, caused havoc in Greece, and stretched his dominion to the frontier of Turkey itself; so that in his heyday he was king in all but name of an empire comparable in extent to the Ptolomaic. A full century before Lenin and Mao, Mohammed Ali turned the whole of Egypt into a single state farm, with himself as the greatest landowner and sole tradesman. For five decades he colored the course of events in the Near East, creating what came to be known as the 'Egyptian Question' to the dismay of the chanceries of Europe.

Yet in a strange way the destiny which enabled this bully-boy from Macedonia to found a dynasty which endured until 1952 also ordained that, for all his autocracy and diplomatic skill, he would never take the final step to full independence, remaining to the end the vassal of his Turkish suzerain. Putting the cart before the horse, Mohammed Ali made Egypt an Empire before it was actually a nation.

As he used to tell visitors, he was born the same year as Napoleon (1769) and in the same place as Alexander—the little port of Cavalla in Macedonia. Little is known of his origins, but it seems that, orphaned quite early, he was brought up by the mayor of the town, who married him at eighteen to a fairly well-off relative After he had done nicely as a tax collector, and even better as a tobacco dealer, he appears to have tired of Cavalla and enlisted as an officer in the Albanian contingent sent by Turkey to join with the British in driving the French out of Egypt. When both English and French evacuated Egypt in 1802 after the

Peace of Amiens, Mohammed Ali remained in the service of the Pasha nominated by Turkey to govern the country.

No sooner had the British and French disappeared than anarchy erupted as the various political factions began a frantic struggle for power. Insofar as they could take sides at a distance, France favored the Albanians and Britain the Mamelukes, who, since the battle of the Pyramids, had lost any real military strength, although they still had a hold on the land; it was characteristic of Whitehall to plump for this picturesque but moribund aristocracy. Elfi Bey, whose magnificence had much impressed London (where a company was even floated to finance his fortunes in Egypt) was the British candidate for Pasha.

To Mohammed Ali, now second in command of the Albanian contingent, it seemed clear that these factions were fighting for little more than the power to indulge in licensed robbery. Recognizing the strategic and commercial position of Egypt at one of the vital cross-roads of the world, with only the sea and the desert as frontiers, and alive to the fertility of the land and the docility of its people, he was fascinated by the immense scope for power that Egypt offered. Before long he was scheming to grasp the chance of his life.

No record tells by whose knife the deed was done, but at dawn one morning the head of Tahrir, his friend and commander, was dropped through a Cairo window, and Mohammed Ali, as next in rank, took command of the Albanian troops. 'With these crude soldiers, who soon became his personal bodyguard, he supported both Turks and Mamelukes in the Civil War, while pretending to be nothing more than a police chief keeping order in the capital, and a good friend of the Egyptians', explains Alan Moorehead in *The Blue Nile*. 'No student of the lives of racketeers and party bosses can fail to recognize here the sly and ruthless maneuverings of a cunning man. He lurks on the sidelines with the cold, unblinking eye of the lizard, and at the right moment strikes...' At first he supported the Mamelukes against the Turks. Next, when the Mamelukes were settled back in power, he coerced their leader, Bardissy, into raising such stiff taxes to pay his Albanians that Cairo burst once more into revolt. He then appeased the riot by ostentatiously forcing Bardissy to remit the taxes—after which he chased the Mamelukes bodily out of Cairo and confiscated their property.

All this was artfully done in the name of the Sultan. Mohammed Ali was punctilious throughout to pay lip service to the Turkish governor, Kourschid, who was nominally in Power. But at the same time, while patrolling the streets, he passed himself off as a demagogue and quietly built up a following of his own among the Sheikhs and the semi-religious, semi-merchant middle class of the 'suks', the real Egyptians whose nationalistic feelings were stirring, and who later would bring Arabi, Zagloul and Nasser to power. Their support was necessary for the final trial of strength, which could not be long delayed. In the provinces brigands and marauders were plundering the fellahin; whole villages were abandoned; and in Cairo itself janisseries, Mamelukes, bashi-bazouks and military riff-raff of all descriptions pillaged the shops and violated harems. It was too much for even the long-suffering Egyptians.

The crunch came one morning in May 1805 when, exasperated beyond endurance, the people of Cairo, led by their Sheikhs and the heads of the various guilds, gathered in an immense crowd in front of the Beit el Kadi (the law courts) and lodged a noisy complaint against the governor. Throughout the day the 'suks' were seething as the demonstration grew. When no answer came from the governor, the crowd moved to Mohammed Ali's house and clamored for him to be nominated as Pasha.

In what was probably the first real demonstration of Egyptian national consciousness, Sheikh el Sharkawy, the Rector of Al Azhar, and Sayed Omar Makram, the head of the religious communities, ceremoniously deposed the Turkish governor and 'in the name of the people' invested Mohammed Ali with the fur mantle and robe of Pasha 'in virtue of his rectitude and benevolence and in accordance with the terms stipulated by the people', an act which prompted Drovetti, the French Consul, to send an acid report to Paris about 'These people who have never heard the fable about the frogs who asked for a king.'

To the Turkish governor it was an unheard-of affront. Outraged that the fellahin should defy the might of the Sublime Porte, he turned the guns of the citadel on the crowds below. But Mohammed Ali was not to be caught so easily; dragging his own guns up on to the Mokattem hills, he besieged the unfortunate Pasha in the Citadel itself. In due course the Porte, with its usual pragmatic disdain, confirmed the appointment of Mohammed Ali to succeed him, accepting that the soft natured, so long despised, illiterate fellahin had at last, after centuries of subjugation, made a positive move to assert their rights. Although still a vassal of Constantinople, Mohammed Ali was the ruler of their choice.

But in the Ottoman Empire it was one thing for an obscure young tobacco trader to gain power, and another thing to keep it. A few months later a Turkish flotilla appeared at Alexandria with an imperial decree transferring Mohammed Ali to Salonica, and an ugly situation was only averted when the Turkish admiral accepted a bribe of 4,000 purses (the personal fortune of a Coptic money-lender hastily expropriated by Mohammed Ali) to persuade the Sultan, whose concern with Egypt was purely mercenary, that more money could be expected through Mohammed than through the Mamelukes. In November 1806, Mohammed Ali was once again confirmed as Pasha.

Four months later, he was faced with a more serious challenge.

After an unsuccessful attempt to persuade the Sultan to join in with Russia against France—which culminated in an abortive *coup de main* in the Dardanelles—the British, once again at loggerheads with Turkey, decided it would be advantageous to lay hands on Egypt. If Elfi and his Mamelukes were reinstated, it was argued, Britain would not only have mastery of the shores of

Egypt, but solid commercial benefits into the bargain. General Frazer was therefore dispatched with what was termed in official language a 'reconnoitering' expedition to see what he could do. He was perfectly well aware that he could hardly expect to conquer the country with his small force of 7,000 men when Napoleon had failed with over 50,000, but he was relying on the active co-operation of the Mamelukes to open the way for him.

Mohammed Ali, who was grappling with the Mamelukes in Upper Egypt at the time, made no secret of his dismay (horses were even saddled for flight, if need be, eastwards to Palestine and Syria) but he still had a trick or two up his sleeve. Elfi and Bardissy died suddenly and simultaneously of 'indigestion' after drinking their coffee, and a deputation of Sheikhs and Ulemas from Cairo helped Mohammed Ali to patch up relations with the remaining Mamelukes. 'The French have no religion' intoned the Ulemas from the mosques, 'whereas the English are devout Christians who hate other religions. It is not right that you should side with the Infidel against the Moslems.' One may smile at the argument, but nevertheless it prevailed, and the British were left to fight their battles alone.

Like Bonaparte, they landed at Agami, and after Alexandria had been occupied without any resistance, a detachment was sent to take Rosetta. A contemporary Egyptian account relates that 'They entered early in the morning without a shot being fired, sauntering around the narrow streets as if they were on leave.'

But about the time when the sun was at its hottest, and the troops in their stifling red uniforms were lolling against latticed walls to protect themselves from the noonday heat, a signal was given by the Egyptian commander and from every window, housetop and street corner came a murderous hail of shot. The luckless detachment, set upon suddenly by turbaned figures brandishing scimitars, was taken completely by surprise, and the commanding officer. General Wauchope, and several hundred men were killed before a retreat, in considerable disorder, could be made to Alexandria.

The news of this defeat of the infidel electrified Cairo. It gave Mohammed Ali the shot in the arm that he needed; even the most hesitant Mamelukes now joined him and—spurred on by the haranguing of Omar Makram and the Ulemas—everyone who could manage to arm himself followed the army to Rosetta. Here General Stewart with the 31st, the 35th and the 78th of Foot had taken up a position at El Hammad and were besieging the town. The General had been unable to procure horses in Alexandria, and his sensations, as he watched Mohammed's high-blooded Arabs pour past, can hardly have been pleasant. The Egyptians attacked with the full weight of their cavalry, and in a three hour battle inflicted one of the most humiliating defeats ever experienced by a British force in the East.

Napoleon To Nasser

    Britain's sea-power prevented reports of the reverse from reaching Europe, but public opinion in England, which had already stomached much unpleasant news from the Continent as Napoleon proceeded on his remorseless way, was deeply shocked to learn that five hundred British soldiers had been marched as prisoners into the Cairo slave market between the heads of as many of their dead comrades set up on poles. Short of a full-scale invasion, all General Frazer could do was ask for terms—which Mohammed, who had expected a violent reaction from England, was only too glad to give. In September the 'reconnoitering' expedition reembarked, and the only trace left of its presence is the tombstone of a soldier of the 78th in the courtyard of the Greek Patriarchate in Alexandria. But for Mohammed Ali, who had fought alongside Abercromby six years before, this victory over the British was of incalculable value. Overnight, the Pasha had ceased to be an adventurer, a leader of the bashi-bazouks. He had become a power to be reckoned with. He was no longer a foreign Albanian, but a full-scale Egyptian hero the defender of Moslem Egypt against the Infidel. On the other hand the Mameluke Beys, by conspiring with the British against the Pasha, had now burnt their boats. For a while, Mohammed Ali quietly left them alone. But already he was planning a *coup de grace* to liquidate them once and for all. The day of reckoning for the Mamelukes was to come.

    With a vengeance it came, too. 'For every drop of blood that Mohammed Ali spilt that day', commented Dr Bowring (a British MP on a mission to Egypt) in his account of what happened on the afternoon of Friday 1 March 1811, 'he saved more than one innocent person.' Rarely, he reported to his employers in London, had the people of Cairo been treated to such a dazzling spectacle. Clustering in the great square below the Citadel and overflowing into the bazaars, sightseers jostled each other along the route the procession would take. The occasion was the investiture of Mohammed's son Toussoun—a lad in his teens—with a Pelisse of Honor as he left for Arabia at the head of an expedition to capture the holy cities of Mecca and Medina. All the Mameluke Beys and their followers had been invited. By midday, some five hundred with their splendidly mounted retinues had ridden up the steep approach and through the forbidding gates of the Citadel, festooned with banners and religious motives. Only the aged Ibrahim Bey, like the fox in the fable, had been too wary to leave his stronghold at Beni Suef and had sent an apocryphal reply listing those whose footsteps had led to the lion's cave. For the others, it was a welcome opportunity of returning to the delights of Cairo. They pointed out that for some time now the Pasha had shown a more conciliatory spirit towards the Mamelukes who, since 1807, had withdrawn into the provinces of Upper Egypt, and were busy adding to their acres rather than fomenting trouble politically. Besides which, the laws of hospitality protected them. If the Pasha had anything in mind, it was most likely to offer them an olive branch.

Raymond Flower

Their welcome at the Citadel was reassuring. Ceremoniously, Mohammed Ali received his guests in the great presence-chamber, greeting each Bey in turn. Coffee and delicacies were served; narguilas passed round, and the customary rituals performed. Yet as the Pasha retired along with the Sheikhs, Cadis, and other civilians to make way for the military procession, some people noticed that his normally florid face was whiter than usual.

In due course the procession formed up, with the Mameluke Beys in the central place of honor, and the glittering cavalcade moved slowly down the steep curving passage to the gates of the city. A Kurdish detachment was in the van, with some Janisseries behind; next the Albanians, and following them, the Mamelukes on horseback, their superbly jeweled robes and armour sparkling in the sunshine. Bringing up the rear were the Turkish contingents, and although everyone could see that Albanian soldiers were stationed at vantage points all along the route, it was not until the heavy gates of El Azab were suddenly closed that the Mamelukes scented a trap. At that moment the Albanians opened fire, and as the troops in front and behind attacked, the Mamelukes found themselves caught in a murderous fusillade from all sides. Against guns, their swords were useless, and the narrow lane became a pandemonium of plunging horses and men struggling for their lives. The action only lasted fifteen minutes—but in those fifteen minutes the military caste which had held the country in its grip for so many centuries was ruthlessly exterminated.

When the dust settled, leaving behind them a scene like a butcher's shambles, the Pasha's soldiers spread grimly through the city, killing and pillaging. In the panic-stricken suks the word went round that all the Mamelukes had perished. Only a single Bey named Emin, it was whispered, had managed to dodge the massacre, climb the ramparts on horseback, and leaping fifty feet into space on to the rocks below, had escaped into the desert—creating thus the last epic legend of the Mamelukes.*

The Pasha's Genoese doctor related afterwards to his family that Mohammed Ali had been pacing up and down a small room, when he brought him the news. 'A great day for your Highness' he murmured obsequiously. The Pasha made no reply. 'Water, water!' was all that he said.

A young Italian, Giovanni Finati, of the village of Zeilo near Ferrara, was in the Albanian contingent at the Citadel and has left his own on-the-spot account of the now legendary massacre. 'Before dawn the drums were beating throughout the city to call the troops together as for some great parade,' he writes. 'Few of us had received any intimation of this beforehand, so that all hurried from their quarters to know what it meant, and were marched off to the Citadel as they arrived and stationed there.

'No specific instructions were given, but each man was strictly charged after his arms had been examined, on no account to quit the post assigned to him, and to wait there for further orders.

'The hour of audience was at hand, and a procession of about 500 Mameluke officers of higher or lower degrees presented themselves at the gate of the Citadel and went in. They made rather a splendid show, and were led by three of their generals, among whom Saim Bey (sic) was conspicuous; when entered they proceeded directly onwards towards the palace, which occupies the highest ground, and as soon as their arrival there was announced to Mohammed Ali and Hassoun Pasha, who were sitting in conference together within, an immediate order was given for the introduction of the three chiefs who were received with great affability, both Pashas entering into a good deal of conversation with them, and many compliments and civilities passed.

'After a time, according to Eastern custom, coffee was brought, and last of all the pipes, but at the moment when these were presented, as if from etiquette, or to leave his guests more at their ease, Mohammed Ali rose and withdrew, and, sending privately for the captain of his guard, gave orders that the Citadel should be closed, adding that as soon as Saim Bey and his associates should come out for the purpose of mounting, they should be fired on till they dropped, and that at the same signal the troops, posted throughout the fortress, should take aim at every Mameluke within their reach; while a corresponding order was sent down at the same time to those in the town, and to such even as were encamped without, round the foot of the fortress, to pursue the work of extermination on all stragglers that they should find, so that not one of the proscribed body might escape...For myself,' adds Giovanni with a touch of self-righteousness, 'I have reason to be thankful that though I was one of the soldiers stationed at the Citadel that morning, I shed none of the blood of those unhappy men, having had the great good fortune to be posted at an avenue where none of them attempted to pass, or came near to me, so that my pistols and muskets were never fired...the work of rapine lasted six days, and although present at many of these scenes with a comrade of mine, I bore little part in them, and shall hardly be accused of having laid hands on a very large share of the plunder when I mention that, with the exception of a saddle, richly mounted in silver gilt, and a slave girl that belonged to one of them, I took no advantage of the permission given to make prize of whatever we found in the houses.'

Certainly the whole order of Mamelukes had now ceased to exist. Those remnants which had lingered in Upper Egypt with Ibrahim fled south into the Sudan; the women married Mohammed Ali's officers, and youngsters who had been spared were drafted into his new military and naval establishments. The massacre of the Mamelukes,' wrote the British Consul, 'was an atrocious crime, but it was a necessary prelude to all subsequent reforms.' Exactly who would benefit from these reforms was quite another matter.

For with the French and the British out of the way, and internal opposition crushed, the ferocious little Albanian was now effectively dictator of Egypt. The simple fact, of course, was that the people had only changed masters. One robber

Pasha had replaced a hundred robber Beys. Like the Mamelukes, Mohammed Ali looked on the Egyptians themselves as a race of serfs—useful to further his personal ambitions, but whose well being was of no consequence. As Moursi Saad el Dine has put it: 'Egypt became a paradise for the Turks and the Albanians and all the other hirelings...In fact, at that time, the native people of Egypt were simply termed fellahin or peasants.'

The difference was that Mohammed Ali exploited them with far more intelligence and success than his predecessors; in the process he brought the country out of the Middle Ages, and gave it a stability of sorts.

With true dictator's instinct, his first care was to make sure that he had an invincible army to maintain his position, and a well-filled treasury to exploit it. To take care of the latter he argued, like Joseph in Genesis, that 'the land is the Pharaoh's', and, basing himself on the ancient Islamic system which drew a hazy distinction between private and public property, he issued a decree expropriating all landowners—including the religious foundations and wakfs—and concentrating the whole agricultural resources of the country in his own hands. By acquiring the crops at source, it was not difficult to sell them at whatever profit he felt inclined.

From monopolizing the agricultural products, it was then a comparatively short step to make himself the sole proprietor of manufactured goods, and the sole importer and exporter. Soon all the produce and property of the country was under his direct control. For import and export operations he formed partnerships with the trading Consuls of the Foreign Powers—which had the advantage of putting the local diplomats in his pocket. Essentially a man of action rather than a theoretician (although he picked up some political philosophy in a lengthy correspondence with Jeremy Bentham); the economic concept which caught his imagination, encouraged by his foreign advisors who could smell a rake-off, was that with raw materials near at hand and cheap labor, it was only a question of importing machinery and technical aid from Europe to industrialize the country and lay the foundations of an industrial revolution parallel to those of Britain and France. That in the prevailing conditions of Egypt a century and a half ago this was merely wishful thinking took some time to become clear, and meanwhile the Pasha launched himself into manufacture as blithely as any of today's emergent states—but without foreign aid to buttress his projects.

In 1818 two factories opened in Cairo to make coarse woolen cloth for the army. A year later, when a French mechanic brought the matter to his notice, no time was wasted in erecting factories for the ginning, spinning and weaving of cotton: soon twenty-nine were in operation. Within ten years factories had sprouted throughout the country producing such varied commodities as sugar, arms, gunpowder, ropes and tarbouches. Iron foundries, steel and copper works and machine shops were backed up by a complex of spinners, weavers, smiths, engravers, joiners and forgers—all with the Pasha as managing proprietor, whose management techniques were often surprising. For instance, when the notoriously twisty Mahmoudiah canal linking Alexandria to the Nile was under construction, Mohammed Ali asked a French engineer what he thought of the plans.

'Your Highness must pardon my suggestion that your canal will be very crooked,' replied the expert.

'Do your rivers in France run in a straight line?' enquired the Pasha blandly.

'Of course not.'

'Who made them? Was it not Allah?'

'Assuredly, your Highness.'

'Well then,' said Mohammed Ali triumphantly. 'Do you think that you or I know better than Allah how water ought to run? I imitated him with my canal. Otherwise it would soon have been only a dry ditch, not a canal.'

The problem about such centralized control—which initially received a good press in Europe as the work of an enterprising potentate—was to find suitable men to keep the wheels turning. It was not surprising under the circumstances that in practice his schemes fell desperately short of the excellence they may have had in theory. From the outset, the model factories were run at a loss, and with no accountants to underscore the economic facts of life, the Pasha was soon involved in a race without end to meet not only the deficits of his internal policy but also the expenses of the extensive wars he was constantly fighting. Soon taxation became as crushing as under the Mamelukes, and local officials returned to their savage methods to screw the last piaster out of the wretched fellahin.

'Boundless ambition was the motivating force behind Mohammed Ali', says William Lane, a nephew of Gainsborough the painter, who, dressed in Arab clothes with a turbaned fez on his head, managed to look so much like an Arab that his neighbors genuinely believed he was from Saudi Arabia. Living in a house near the Khan el Khalil, Lane frequently had his Moslem friends in for tobacco and coffee, and from characters such as Sheikh Ahmed—a Saaderyeh dervish with a penchant for chewing live snakes and glass chandeliers—as well as from day to day experiences in the suks, he gathered together the material to write his delightful and now classic account of conditions in Cairo in the early nineteenth century. Even so he confessed it difficult to form a definitive opinion about the Pasha, chiefly because of the extraordinary secrecy which hedged all goings-on at the Citadel, and political affairs in particular. While Lane could see that the man in the street was being progressively impoverished, it was also a fact that 'anarchy had given way to tranquillity, and undisguised fanaticism to at least an affected toleration'. The Pasha's power was nerve-rackingly absolute: a simple horizontal motion of the hand and any of his subjects would be executed on the spot without further ado. But, thought Lane, he was not so much inclined to be cruel as autocratic, and even this had its lighter moments. When, for instance, an old man managed to run up to him and, grasping his sleeve, complained that he had been reduced to destitution by having his sons conscripted into the army, the Pasha did not brush him aside. He ordered that the richest man in the village should give him a cow.

Punishments, moreover, were designed to fit the crime. A butcher who sold meat underweight had the missing ounces carved off his back. An official, who had maltreated a baker, was baked in his victim's oven. Oriental justice, as recorded by Lane, had the violent but naive charm of a kindergarten game.

A peasant, he relates, was called upon by the local Nazir to pay 135 piasters in taxes. The man's only asset was a cow, so it was put up for sale. But as no one in the village had sufficient money to buy it, the Nazir ordered the butcher to slaughter the beast, and sixty fellahin were compelled to buy a piece at a piaster a time, the butcher receiving the cow's head for his trouble. The peasant managed to lodge a complaint, as a result of which the Nazir, the butcher and the sixty peasants were summoned, together with their Sheikh, to appear before a judge.

'Was the value of this man's cow sixty piasters?' asked the judge.

'Oh our Master' said the peasants, 'her value was indeed more!'

The Nazir, declared the Sheikh, oppressed everyone under his authority. Was the cow not worth at least 120 piasters? Yet he had sold for sixty. This was unfair to the owner.

The Judge thereupon ordered the Nazir to be stripped and bound. Then he turned to the butcher.

'Butcher,' he said, 'do you not fear God? You have killed the cow unjustly.'

The butcher protested that he was bound to obey the Nazir's orders. Had he not, he would have been beaten and his house would have been destroyed.

'If I order you to do a thing, will you do it?' asked the Judge.

'I will do it,' answered the trembling butcher.

'Slaughter the Nazir', said the Judge.

The butcher slit his throat.

'Now cut him up into sixty pieces.'

The sixty peasants who had bought the meat of the cow were then called forward, and each was made to pay two piasters for a piece of the Nazir's flesh; the butcher was given the head, and the 120 piasters were handed to the owner of the cow.

Note:

Most serious historians tend to dismiss the story of Emin Bey's dramatic leap as simply being a myth. But Giovanni Fineti, who was present at the massacre said: 'Another chief, Amin Bey, who was the brother of Elfi, urged the noble animal which he rode to an act of greater desperation, for he spurred him until he made him climb upon the rampart, and preferring rather to be dashed to pieces than be slaughtered in cold blood, drove him to leap down the precipice a height that has been estimated at from 30-40 feet or even more; yet fortune so favored him that though the horse was killed in the fall, the rider escaped. An Albanian camp was below and an officer's tent very near the spot on which he alighted; instead of shunning it he went in and throwing himself on the rites of hospitality, implored that no advantage might be taken of him; which was not only granted but the officer offered him protection, even at his own peril, and kept him concealed so long as the popular fury and excesses of the soldiery continued.' Fineti even declares that he saw Amin Bey some years later in Syria.

Chapter 5

Not a Nation but an Empire

Crack! A bullet whistled past the ear of the French officer training cadets in the scorching desert at Assouan. It was not the first time a cadet had shot at Colonel Séve. Grasping his riding whip, he lined up the company and, accusing them of stupidity, negligence and—worse still—bad marksmanship, unceremoniously flogged each cadet in turn. Then, throwing away his whip, he stood erect and ordered them to load their muskets and fire at him if they would. Ashamed, the youths dropped their arms, and ran weeping to his feet.

By such apocalyptic methods the veteran officer, who had fought at Waterloo and later became the celebrated Soliman Pasha (after whom Cairo's fashionable street was until recently named) won the respect of the unruly elements he had been given to train into a disciplined corps of officers, and built up the basis for a new 'model' army.

As a soldier himself, Mohammed Ali's first love was for the army; indeed, since the basis of his whole foreign policy was to bribe or bully the Sultan into giving him hereditary authority over Egypt (and to gain independence by playing off the various powers against the Porte) to have a strong standing army was obviously of supreme importance to him. But an initial attempt to drill his own Albanians—who had helped him to power—into disciplined troops triggered off a mutiny which nearly sent him to the same fate as the Mamelukes (as it was, he only escaped by cutting the dykes and flooding Cairo) and a subsequent experiment using slaves from the Sudan was equally disappointing. Of 20,000 Sudanese who were herded into barracks in Egypt, it is said that all but 3,000 died of grief, like caged animals: army life was too much for them.* It was only then, as a last resort, that Mohammed Ali turned to the native Egyptian.

If Egypt had remained under foreign domination for so many centuries, it was largely because the fellah had never fought, and, in many people's view, never would. Certainly, of all the misfortunes that the Egyptians suffered under Mohammed Ali, conscription was what they hated most. Rather than let their children be taken off to the army, they mutilated them. 'Peasant women would destroy one of their sons' eyes with rat poison' describes an Egyptian writer of the period. 'As Copts...were exempt, young Moslems would have a cross tattooed on their wrists. Other fellahs had their teeth pulled out, knowing that a soldier needed all his teeth for opening cartridges.'

Nevertheless the poorer villagers (who could not bribe the Sheikh-el-balad) were marched into barracks in chain-gangs, and although a great many of them died, by 1820 Mohammed Ali had raised a well-trained national army with which for some twenty years he substantially altered the balance of power in the Eastern Mediterranean and challenged the Porte itself. To the extent that with the help of those fellah regiments he raised Egypt from a despised province of a decadent empire into a military power, Mohammed Ali can be said to have brought about the re-birth of the indigenous Egyptian and paved the way for the first leaders of Egyptian nationalism, Arabi and Ali Fahmy.

He fought four campaigns: in Arabia, in the Sudan, in Greece and in Syria. The first of these campaigns was mainly to ingratiate himself with the Sultan. The Wahabis, an ultra-puritanical Moslem sect, had recently gained control of the Holy Cities of Mecca and Medina, but since neither the Pashas of Damascus nor Baghdad were inclined to do anything about it, Mohammed Ali seized on the opportunity to put the Sultan in his debt and establish himself clearly as the new leader of the Arab world. He sent his son Toussoun to Arabia at the head of an expeditionary force. Hardly had Toussoun landed at Yanbu, on the west of Arabia, than he immediately went into action against the Wahabis in the hilly Jedeed Bogaz area, a few miles inland. The seventeen-year-old commander was popular among the troops, but had next to no experience of warfare. Once again Giovanni Finati has left a participant's account of the affair.

'Toussoun himself came forward to encourage and animate his men, calling to many of them individually by their names and adjuring them in their religion and their country', recalls the young mercenary from Ferrara. But from their vantage point on top of the hills 'the Wahabis could pour their bullets down on us almost with impunity, and this occasioned a most dreadful slaughter.'

By midday the sun, reverberating fiercely off the arid landscape, grew so intolerably hot that fighting became impossible, and by a sort of mutual consent there was a truce for several hours—the soldiers slumped down in the shade of such palm trees as they could find and munched dates. But in due course the cravings of thirst grew intolerable 'so that the signal given for action at four o'clock in the afternoon was received with a desperation that was like joy...the ferocity and carnage that followed was indescribable and continued until long after sunset when all at once some panic or disaster turned the fortune of battle and we were put completely to the route.' There was a flight and a pursuit, but 'in such disorder and confusion that the miserable remnant which reached our camp with Toussoun found it quite untenable against an enemy master of the field.' They stayed just long enough to set fire to the camp equipment and tents—abandoning even the paymaster's chest in their haste—and fled back to the ships.

Giovanni and another lad, almost at the end of their tether with fatigue and thirst, managed to scramble to the top of some dunes and, burying themselves in the sand, had a grandstand view of the scene. Some time after midnight they crawled down on all fours and picked their way cautiously through the ruins of the camp, carefully keeping out of the way of those who were stripping the bodies for loot. The Gods were obviously on their side: first they lighted on some provisions, and then, after feeding and drinking, they stumbled on 400 golden crowns scattered about the ground. (The next we hear of Giovanni, he had left the army and had set up as a Tourist Guide in Cairo.)

Later, after being massively reinforced from Korseir, Toussoun was able to advance on Medina and Mecca—where the first man to reach the Prophet's tomb was, oddly enough, a Scotsman named Keith who had Islamised and was subsequently appointed Governor of the Holy City. But in the vast deserts of Arabia the Wahabites were more than a match for Toussoun, and victory came only when Mohammed Ali and his eldest son Ibrahim had personally taken charge. In September 1818, after seven dreary years of fighting, Ibrahim finally crushed the Wahabis at Deraya, and their leader Abdulla Ibn Saud was sent to Constantinople to pay the traditional penalty for rebellion.

Even so Wahabism—which compels the most rigid observance of every rite and ceremony prescribed by ancient tradition, and forbids the use of tobacco, scents and other luxuries—did not die out. Today, a descendant of Ibn Saud challenges the claims of Arab nationalism which lap at the shores of Saudi Arabia. The Arabian campaign, however, left Mohammed Ali ruinously short of money and men, and it was largely to remedy these deficiencies that he began looking south towards the Sudan. Two motives prompted him into the wilderness south of Assouan: gold and slaves. A full-grown Sudanese was worth 40 Egyptian pounds on the Cairo market, and Burkhardt, the Swiss explorer, had whetted the Pasha's appetite with tales of potential wealth in the mountains of Ethiopia. In June 1820 the die was cast, and a straggling procession of boats made its way from Boulac up the Nile. The expedition comprised 3,400 infantry, 1,500 cavalry, some artillery, and a contingent of Ababdeh Arabs. In charge was Ismail, Mohammed Ali's younger son.

A monotonous brutality, alternating with sickening cruelties marked the two years' campaign. Very little opposition was met until the great bend of the Nile at Kosti: here Ismail easily routed the tribe of Shagiyehs and occupied Berber. Shortly afterwards, Shendy surrendered, and Ismail's little army pushed laboriously on to Cape Khartoum—the junction of the White and Blue Niles, so called because it resembled an elephant's trunk. (Here, three years later, the city of Khartoum was founded.) At this point, his brother-in-law Ahmed Defterdar went west in search of negro slaves, but Ismail was drawn always further southwards by the lure of gold. 'This thirst for gold', wrote a Frenchman travelling in his suite, 'was the principal motive which drew this prince ever onward.' So far, from the strictly military point of view, it had been easy as stealing sweets from children: the local tribes had been too stunned to put up much resistance. But now it was the climate rather than the inhabitants which slowed and finally halted Ismail's advance. Two thousand miles deep into the virtually uncharted bowels of Africa, he found himself bogged down by the rains, with malaria and dysentery sweeping through the ranks: only the arrival of his brother Ibrahim saved him from disaster. Even so, he had to turn back without gold, and with only a trickle of slaves to send back to Cairo.

Apart from terrorizing the Sudan, he had accomplished nothing, and moreover the hatred he and his Turks had aroused all along the river was now intense. At Shendy, on the way back, it boiled over. Probably it was frustration, the exhaustion of a fruitless campaign, which prompted him to turn on the proud Malik Nemr of Shendy—whom he had already humiliated eighteen months before—and accuse him of secreting the gold in Dongola. 'Fill my boat with gold within five days or I drive a stake through your heart', he shrilled arrogantly in his high-pitched voice (an eyewitness account says he even struck the ruler across the face with his stick). That night, as a banquet was being held in Ismail's lushly decorated tent, some of Nemr's men crept up and set it on fire: Ismail and his suite were burned alive inside.

Mohammed Ali's reprisals for the death of his son were immediate and appalling: the Defterdar Ahmed raged up and down the Nile, burning every town and village to the ground and leaving a trail of spine-chilling atrocities in his wake. By 1823 some 50,000 Sudanese had been massacred; virtually the whole valley of the river from Assouan south laid waste, and the frontiers of Egypt had shifted over 2,000 miles of scorched earth as far as the borders of Ethiopia.

The little Albanian 'condottiere' was now in his fifties. William Turner of the Foreign Office, who passed through Cairo while serving on the staff of the British Ambassador in Constantinople, left this description of him: 'At eight o'clock I rode with Mr. Aziz to visit the Pasha in a small palace just outside a gate of the city on the road to Boulac...we found the Pasha in a small room, in one corner of which he was seated; he beckoned me to sit which I did without taking off my hat. He was dressed in a dark crimson pelisse, with a striped silk vest, and a projecting white turban, wearing a saber, and a knife in his bosom, set with diamonds most profusely. He was a thin man with a dark and designing countenance, and a penetrating eye. There was something savage in his look, and even his smile reminded one of Richard III's power to "smile and smile and murder while he smiled".'

It was the smile of the murderer who was now respectable; the village bully who had become a powerful tyrant—and whose ambitions, moreover, were already focussed on the distant horizons of his native land. The heroic struggle of the Greeks for independence, which fired the imagination of Lord Byron and liberal-minded people throughout Europe, excited Mohammed Ali too—but for quite a different reason. Like Napoleon, he saw the chance to use Egypt as a springboard towards the Ottoman Empire itself. Two ways led to Constantinople: by sea through the Aegean, and by land across Macedonia. Both on sea and on land, the Egyptian forces were stronger than the unreliable army and navy of the Turks.

In 1822 as a first step, he captured Crete, sending a bagful of human ears to the Sultan as proof; his reward was to be named the titular Pasha of the island. Two years later, the Sultan led right into his hand; things were getting desperate for the Turks in Greece. If he could make good the title by force of arms, promised the Porte, he would be appointed as Pasha of all Morea. The expedition which Ibrahim took across the Mediterranean (60 warships and 16,000 troops in 100 transports) astonished everyone in Europe. It was incredible that Mohammed Ali could have built up such a powerful army and navy in Egypt in so few years out of nothing. Colonel Séve had served his master well.

Ibrahim's invasion broke the backbone of the Greek revolt. Athens fell; then, after a long siege, Missolonghi. But his success—or rather the appalling cruelty which accompanied it—was his undoing. To exterminate whole towns and send the inhabitants of others into slavery was all very well in the seclusion of Arabia, or central Africa, but not in Hellas itself, under the gaze of a continent whose education had left it a soft spot for Greece. Public opinion in Europe was violently outraged by Ibrahim's behavior. A convention was called in London (1826) and Britain, France and Russia (who were beginning to fear that the affair might spark off a full-scale European war) sent their joint fleets to keep an eye on things. It was probably sheer bad luck that the afternoon in 1827 that they entered Navarino harbor where the Turko-Egyptian fleet was anchored, a bored and trigger-happy Turk chose to use the crew of a British boat for target practice. Like a match to petrol, a battle flared up; by evening the whole of the combined fleets of Egypt and Turkey had been destroyed. Even before Admiral Codrington appeared off Alexandria with an ultimatum, and the French landed an expedition in Morea, Mohammed Ali realized that the game was up. He had lost his fleet, and Ibrahim brought back to Egypt less than half the army he had set out with; moreover the rewards promised by the Sultan were withheld on the grounds that the Egyptians had failed to deliver the goods.

Cicero it was who labeled his contemporaries as 'heavy men', and Mohammed Ali, to Turkish eyes at least, had become just this—the useful local party boss had developed into a potentially dangerous bore. His beady eyes were never still. From his newly built palace at Ras el Tin, overlooking Alexandria harbor, they scanned the Mediterranean, unblinkingly aware that the efforts that he had made on behalf of his master in Arabia and Greece had done him no good. Loyalty to the Sultan had manifestly exhausted its usefulness. The discovery of a plot by the Sultan to have him assassinated brought matters to a head.

In 1831 he struck, sending Ibrahim off again, this time across Sinai into Palestine where, joined by a fleet at Jaffa, the Egyptians took Acre by storm: an important success (remembering Napoleon's fiasco at the same spot) which gave the expedition an impetus that swept it from victory to victory across Syria and Anatolia and made nonsense of the panicky Imperial Firman of 2 May 1832, declaring Mohammed Ali an outlaw and deposing him from the Pashalik of

Egypt. By the end of the year Ibrahim had crushed a huge Turkish army inside the boundaries of Asia Minor and had occupied Konia, the ancient capital of the Ottoman Sultans. Only 100 miles away was Constantinople itself.

'Ibrahim had achieved the impossible' noted D. A. Cameron in his study of Mohammed Ali. 'This had been done by Egyptian fellahin in the depth of winter among a dominant race which ruled them as slaves...the Egyptians had defeated the Turk in three pitched battles against odds, had outfought him, out-marched him, out-maneuvered him, and taken him captive. Yet, such is the paradox inherent in the land of Egypt, that all this time a Turkish bashi-bazouk would be going from village to village, flogging the fellahin, and sending them in gangs, like flocks of sheep, to learn how to conquer his countrymen. With the help of a few score Turkish boys and pashas, and a few hundred sergeants, Mohammed Ali had raised the money and the men for the Egyptian victory over the Ottoman Empire.'

Palmerston and Wellington were adamant to stop Mohammed Ali reaching Constantinople and regenerating the Porte (central to British policy was the maintenance of the Ottoman Empire against Russian ambitions). As war minister and general, they had overthrown Napoleon, and would not stand for any other military adventurer—particularly one who had built up so unsavory a reputation in Greece. Pressure was brought on Mohammed Ali to recall his army; in return, the Firman declaring him an outlaw was annulled, and a new Firman (6 May 1833) gave him the Pashalik of Syria.

He now had control over territory extending from equatorial Africa to the Taurus mountains. But by the very feat, extraordinary in itself, of exploding the province of Egypt into an extensive empire before it was even an independent nation, he had overplayed his hand, and stretched the resources of the country beyond all sustainable limits. Nineteenth century Syria, which included Palestine, the Lebanon, Damascus, Tripoli, Aleppo and Adana, was five times as large as the Nile Delta, and its variegated races were unwilling, like the docile fellahin, to submit to any sort of tyranny from outside, and particularly the rough, heavy-handed methods of Ibrahim. Moreover, it was becoming clearer every day that Mohammed Ali was moving towards an outright declaration of independence. From the Sultan's point of view, the position was as intolerable as Ian Smith's revolt in Rhodesia seemed a century and a half later. Indeed, in the House of Commons, Palmerston compared the position of Mohammed Ali to that of a Lord Lieutenant of Ireland trying to make himself a separate hereditary sovereign over Ireland and Scotland.

Mohammed Ali saw things in quite a different light. To the British Consul-General he complained that he could never allow everything that he had created—the arsenals, the fleet, the factories with their new machinery, the workmen trained in Europe, the schools and the mines, the roads and the canals, his whole personal empire, in fact—to revert to the Porte and be lost, while the very livelihood of his family went in jeopardy. His anxiety was that of any self-made man.

But Palmerston, back in England, did not care about Mohammed Ali's worries. His only concern was to keep the Turkish Empire from breaking up and the Russians from Constantinople.

'The Cabinet agreed that it would not do to let Mohammed Ali declare his independence, and separate Egypt and Syria from the Turkish Empire' he stated. 'That would result in a conflict between him and the Sultan, the Turks would be defeated, the Russians would fly to their aid, and a Russian garrison occupy Constantinople and the Dardanelles, which, once in their possession, they would never quit.'

The French, on the other hand, had a foot in both camps. While openly assuring the Sultan of their support, they were privately encouraging Mohammed Ali in the hope of increasing their influence in Egypt.

Matters came to a head in 1838 when a commercial treaty was signed between Britain and Turkey which opened up the Turkish Empire to British trade, and consequently threatened to wreck Mohammed Ali's private system of state trading. The viceroy demanded commercial independence from the Empire. The Sultan proclaimed him a rebel and invaded Syria.* A battle was fought near the village of Nezeb, on the borders of Turkey and Syria, and once again Ibrahim routed the Turks.

It may have been the news of this drastic defeat that finished off the aging Sultan Mahmoud; more likely it was poison from his vizier. But even more inconvenient for his successor—the sixteen year old Sultan Abdel Mejid—was the sudden defection of the Turkish admiral, who made off with his whole fleet of seven ships of the line and ten frigates and, instead of bombarding Alexandria as might have been expected, simply placed the fleet in the hands of Mohammed Ali. For a while it looked as though the entire Turkish Empire would become the prize of the Pasha in Egypt.

Possibly he was the right man to take over the destinies of Islam and the Khalifate, but Palmerston was not prepared to see Turkey prostrated by a military adventurer. In his eyes, Mohammed Ali was a dangerous and destructive element which must be removed if the Ottoman Empire were to remain and hold the Russians in check. Other people, and France in particular, might talk about the 'sick man of Europe' and his imminent decease, and make plans for the partition of the Ottoman Empire. But not Palmerston. 'It will last our time if we try to prop it up and not pull it down,' he declared. His immediate proposal, therefore, was to send the British and French fleets to Alexandria. 'We ought to support the Sultan vigorously with France, if France will act with us, without her if she declines' he told the British ambassador in Paris. The more he reflected, the more convinced he was that there could be no permanent settlement without making Mohammed Ali withdraw 'into his original shell of Egypt.'

But the French were not so keen on such coercion: they had their own reasons for supporting the Pasha. They were quite happy to concede to Mohammed Ali the hereditary possession of all the territory he now controlled. The possession of Syria, thanks to French intervention, would leave him master of both overland routes to the east—Suez and the Euphrates. This would mean French predominance over both routes, and in the area as a whole.

By the autumn of 1840 the dispute had boiled over to a point where Palmerston was threatening to resign, and Britain and France were on the verge of war. 'Tell Mr. Thiers,' thundered Palmerston, 'that if France throws down the gauntlet we shall not refuse to pick it up; and that if she begins a war she will to a certainty lose her ships, colonies and commerce; that her army in Algiers will cease to give her anxiety, and that Mohammed Ali will just be chucked into the Nile.'

Only prompt action by Louis Philippe in replacing Thiers by Guizot prevented a European conflagration over Mohammed Ali, and Britain was left free to cut the Pasha down to size. A British squadron bombarded Acre and blew up Ibrahim's ammunition dump, the Syrians revolted and rounded on the Egyptians, and Ibrahim, who had so often led his fellahin to victory, was forced, like Napoleon before him, to make a disastrous retreat across the Sinai desert back to Egypt. Of the 80,000 who left Damascus, only 15,000 effective troops got back, of which 5,000 went to hospital. 'Such,' reported the American Consul in Cairo, 'was the result of a few European ships, and a handful of Austrian and British marines, cooperating with a small Turkish army and the maddened revenge of an outraged Syrian population.'

Nor was the defecting Turkish fleet much use to Mohammed Ali. He had to use his own navy to stand guard over its discontented crews, and he must have known the game was up before Commodore Napier anchored in front of Alexandria with six ships and subjected him to some blunt sailor's talk.

'If your Highness will not listen to my appeal to you against the folly of further resistance', Napier told him briefly, 'My God, I will bombard you, and put a bomb right where you are sitting!'

Yet all was not lost, for once his gunboat policy had carried the day, Palmerston did his best for the discomforted Pasha. By a Firman dated 13 February 1841 and the Treaty of London signed the following July 1841, Mohammed Ali was left in effective control of Egypt, under nominal Turkish suzerainty, with rights of succession to the eldest male agnate of his family.

And so, by international guarantee, respectability came to the man who had appropriated a whole country. He might have lost an empire, but he had founded a dynasty. He had, moreover, brought Egypt into the limelight. Once the tension relaxed, visitors began to flow in. One of the first was an enterprising farmer's boy from Preston Capes in Northumberland, who had run away to sea. In 1841 he began to help manage the 'British Hotel' in Cairo, which catered for travelers on the overland route to India. Five years later, Samuel Shepheard had his name on the door. It was one of the first modern landmarks in the otherwise still medieval Cairo, and before long *Shepheard's* with its deep stone baths and European standards of comfort was on everybody's schedule. According to the hotel records, A W Kinglake stayed there during an epidemic of cholera, and marked his visit to the Sphinx with a delightful pen-picture as well as an interesting piece of prophecy:

'Upon ancient dynasties of Ethiopian and Egyptian kings,' he wrote, 'upon Greek and Roman, upon Arab and Ottoman conquerors—upon battles and pestilence—upon the ceaseless misery of the Egyptian race—upon keen-eyed travelers—Herodotus yesterday and Warburton today—upon all and more this unworldly Sphinx has watched and watched like a providence with the same earnest eyes, and the same sad, tranquil mien. And we, we shall die, and Islam shall wither away, and the Englishman, leaning far over to hold his beloved India, will plant a firm foot on the banks of the Nile, and sit in the seats of the faithful, and still that sleepless rock will be watching, and watching the works of the new, busy race, with those same sad, earnest eyes, and the same tranquil mien everlasting.'

Meanwhile the aged bashi-bazouk lingered on in the seats of the faithful for a few more years, maintaining the old order of things intact, but from 1841 onwards Mohammed Ali was clearly a past number so far as the outside world was concerned. His influence in foreign affairs was over; and with the ending of the monopolies his personal state trading collapsed, and dust and desert sand settled over his factories. In the end, even his mind began to fail. In these last days, he made a nostalgic trip to Constantinople, began a barrage over the Nile at Caliub, and constructed the great mosque in the Citadel, whose pencil-slim minarets still command modern Cairo. Perhaps this mosque itself is symbolic of the man: important, rather than beautiful, it is best appreciated from a distance, and in certain lights.

Notes:

The Sudanese troops may in fact have died of plague, or finally have been allowed to go home.

The combination of Mohammed Ali's announcement—made to the French and the British Consuls—that he intended to declare his independence, and the Porte's decision to drive him out of Syria brought Mohammed Ali to war with the Ottomans.

Chapter 6

Pashas and Plunderers

'My grandchildren will reap what I have sown' Mohammed Ali is said to have whispered on his deathbed. To which Sir George Young remarked, 'They reaped all too recklessly and sowed no crops other than wild oats.'

Abbas, his grandson, came first. Morose and tight-lipped, with a pathological hatred for anything foreign or new, he was virtually a recluse who concentrated solely on making money for himself and building a series of sinister palaces in the desert in which, surrounded only by a few slaves and menageries of savage beasts, he shrouded himself like Tiberius at Capri. He was, in addition, a sadist. He had a taste for flogging not only his peasants but his women as well, and on one occasion when a terrified woman convicted of adultery was being sewn into a bag in preparation for being thrown into the Nile (the traditional punishment for girls who have gone astray) he devised a little extra entertainment for spectators. He ordered a cat and its kittens to be included in the sack before the victim was tossed into the water.

His own end was equally *grand guignol.* In a remote palace at Benha he was strangled one evening in July 1854 by two slave boys sent to him from Constantinople by a kinswoman. The startled Pashas in attendance tried to hush up the murder—probably to give his son Ilhamy the chance to return from abroad and seize the vice-regency—and promenaded the body in a closed cab through the streets to give the impression that Abbas was taking his evening drive as usual. But the news nevertheless leaked out, and a particularly vicious heat wave convinced the Egyptians that the gates of hell had opened to welcome their ruler.

A century ago, the rule of thumb method of historians was to label their characters either 'good' or 'bad', and Abbas has always been painted in such somber colors that no one can doubt that he was unspeakable. Appointed regent from the time that Mohammed Ali's mind began to fail, he refused to attend his father's funeral, and immediately set about back-pedaling everything the old Pasha had done. He shut down the factories which still remained, dismissed all the European advisers, dismantled the fleet, and retired behind a smoke-screen of Moslem obscurantism. Yet perhaps the historians have not been quite fair. Abbas had taken part in the Syrian campaign, and had seen for himself the futility of private empire building in the face of European opposition. He had witnessed the total collapse of Mohammed Ali's ambitions, and was convinced that what Egypt now needed was a clean sweep of soaring but bogus enterprises, of unworkable commercial monopolies, and a period of peace and quiet. He found himself surrounded by a pack of hungry Europeans and fawning natives whose only

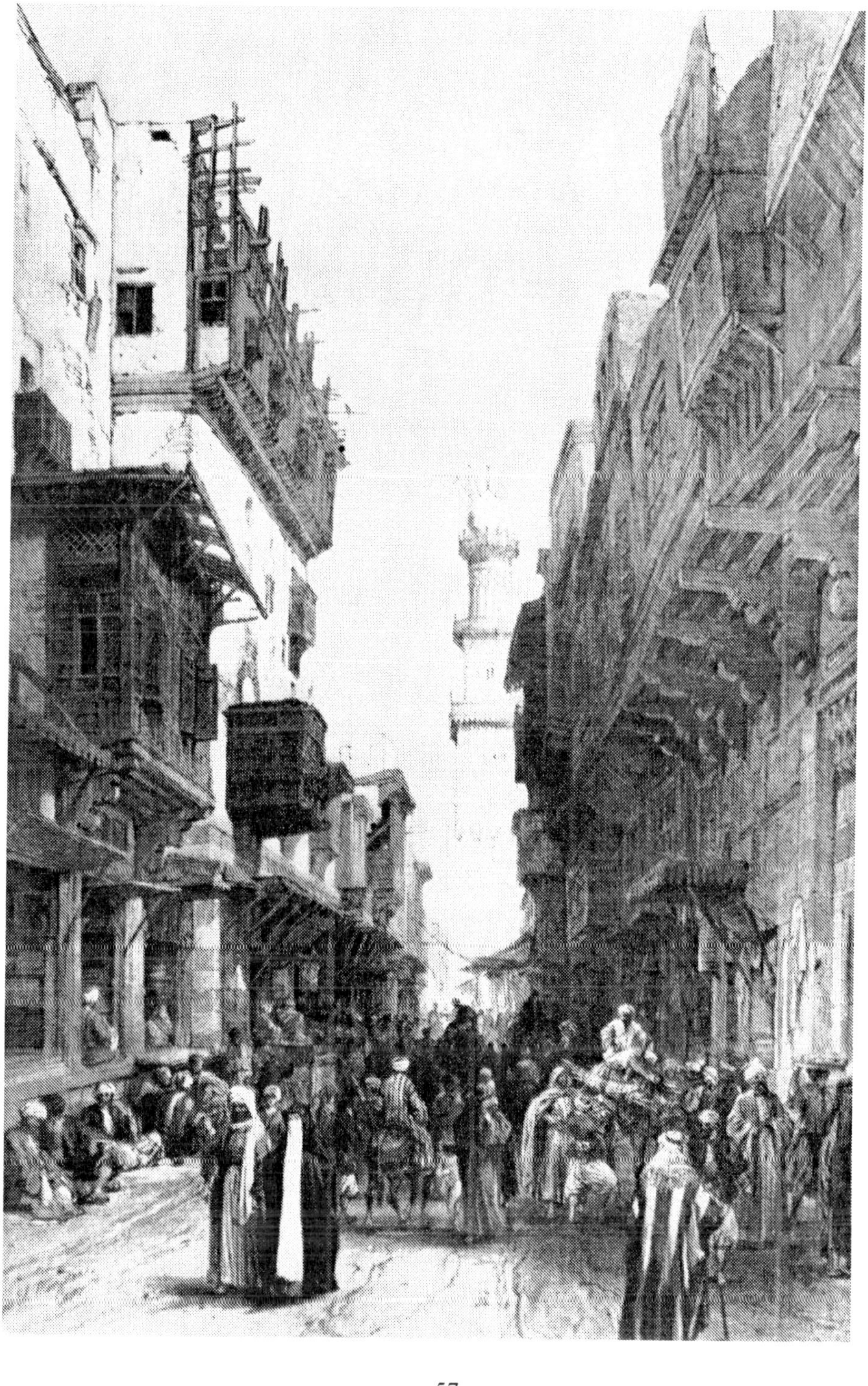

The smoking pavilion at Shepheard's Hotel in the mid-nineteenth centry.

Mansell Colleciton

An English tourist in Egypt in the nineteenth century

Mansell Collecditon

motivation was to enrich themselves at the country's expense. So he took refuge in medieval seclusion. If he kept any contacts at all, it was with the British (who were rather less venal than the others) and one bright spot of his five years' reign was the construction, by the son of Robert Stevenson, of the first railway line in the east, from Cairo to Alexandria.*

Two anecdotes give a glimpse of the man. On one occasion, it is related, Hassan Pasha Monasterli (his adviser) tried to persuade him to sign a decree prohibiting the sale of hashish. Abbas refused. 'The people must have something to amuse themselves' he said, waving the paper aside, 'if I suppress hashish they will buy rakki instead from the Greeks, who will put revolutionary ideas in their heads. Hashish stupefies: rakki does the reverse. So I prefer them to have hashish.'

And again to a French engineer: 'You are always coming bothering me about your barrage,' he complained one day. 'An idea has struck me. Those great masses of stone, the Pyramids, are standing there useless. Why not take the stone from them to do the work? Is that not a good idea?'

'Pull down the Pyramids?' stammered the amazed engineer.

'Yes' repeated Abbas airily. 'Why not? Are you silly enough to attach any reverence to those ugly useless piles of stone? See if you can't make use of them for the barrage. They have helped build Cairo already.'

He meant it, too. But after a sleepless night the French engineer had an idea. He would play on Abbas's avarice to save the Pyramids.

Taking a large sheet of paper he covered it with figures and calculations and returned to the Viceroy next day.

'What is all this?' asked Abbas suspiciously. 'What rubbish is this you bring me?'

'Highness,' replied the engineer, 'after receiving your orders to remove the stones from the Pyramids for the barrage, I thought it my duty to make a rough calculation of the cost. Here it is.'

'Well,' said Abbas impatiently, 'what will it cost?'

The engineer then named an enormous sum as the expense of taking down and transporting the stones, and finally persuaded Abbas to abandon the idea.

'*Figurez vous, Monsieur*', he told the American Consul later, 'fancy your own feelings that your own children would be pointed out everywhere as those of *the man who destroyed the Pyramids!* '

Abbas's place was taken by a much more sympathetic figure. Nearly everyone (even those who had never read Henry IV) looked on Said as a sort of Oriental Falstaff—a red-faced giant with great bushy whiskers who ate and drank and swore and laughed simultaneously with huge enjoyment. 'There was a Rabelaisian humor about this Gargantua of twenty-five stone, who incorporated all that is most comic to the West in the East, or to the East in the West' says Young in his *History of Egypt*, 'for he was a Khalif of the Arabian Nights, doubled with a *cabotin* of the *Quartier Latin*. He jovially decapitated misbehaving sheikhs, and made a jolly bonfire of claims for eighty million piasters of village tax arrears. He entertained foreign sovereigns with funny French stories, and made his pashas wade with him through loose gunpowder, candle in hand, to test their nerves...life with Said was never dull. 'Give him two hundred' he would shout, without explaining whether he meant kurbash or baksheesh.'

From the moment he installed himself on the vice-regal throne, it was obvious that Said intended to enjoy the business of running a country. He began by redecorating the reception rooms in his palace at a cost of ten million francs (two million dollars at the exchange rate of those days). Next he amused himself with the army, dressing the men up in uniforms he designed himself. One of the most striking was a troop of gigantic Nubians, clad from head to toe in the chain armour of the early Crusaders. Another troop appeared to be sheathed in gold, with bright brass breastplates on both the horses and the men, and glittering brass helmets. He liked drilling them himself on a special parade ground covered with iron plates to keep the dust off his Paris clothes, or going on maneuvers in the desert when he won imaginary battles which were so much more agreeable than real and bloody campaigns. To keep everyone happy, he had military service reduced to a year, and the *jeunesse dorée* of the court gleefully tricked themselves up in uniform. He also had connecting railway lines run up to the palaces, so that if he ever felt bored he could slip away in a special coach, designed like a house, and stay on some siding for a while.

His salad days having been spent in Paris, he fancied himself as a man of wit. When in London for the Great Exhibition, the weather was as bad as it often is in the summer. But one day walking round the Crystal Palace, Said noticed a ray of sunshine forcing its way through the glass roof. Turning to Zulficar Pasha who was with him, he said 'You see! The sun is so rare in this country that they are putting it on exhibition.'

Of Wilhelm II, Bismarck once remarked: 'The Kaiser would like to have a birthday every day.' He might have said the same of Said. The Vice-regal palace soon became the most hospitable place in the world. Everyone was welcome, everyone, that is, who was *de famille* among the Turks, or a foreigner, and thus a suitable audience for his displays of munificence. Such restrictive practices which still remained over from the days of Mohammed Ali were quickly swept away. Private ownership of the land was restored. Trade was liberalized. Agriculture began to flourish and, led by cotton, business started booming. Egypt suddenly took on the aspect of a promised land. The trickle of visitors became a flood. 'From every corner of Europe...the manipulators and seekers of gold came *en masse* to fall on Egypt as on a new California' reported the French Consul in Alexandria. An average of 30,000 a year reached Alexandria between 1857 and 1861, practically all of them the scum of the Mediterranean—a mafia-like crowd who were interested in one thing only: the fastest and easiest money they could find.

Engulfed by a sudden plague of speculators who were only too avid to promote any scheme he could think of, Said hardly had a chance. He might just have been able to hold his own through the filter of government administration, but characteristically he preferred personal deals to impersonal market negotiations. Moreover, he was placed at a disadvantage by a curious and archaic arrangement known as the 'capitulations'. These gave an extra-territorial legal immunity to anyone with a foreign passport residing within the Ottoman Empire. The principle of this immunity went back as far as Soliman the Magnificent in the sixteenth century. It was based on the idea that Turkish law was personal rather than territorial, and that Christians within the Turkish dominions should be protected against the possibility of violence or injustice from the local authorities. The legal affairs of foreigners, therefore, were dealt with by their own consular courts.

So long as only a few foreigners were involved, this system worked quite smoothly, but once the riff-raff of Europe came flooding into the country, the capitulations became absurdly abused. Save by the consent of his consul, who invariably protected him, a foreigner was nearly always inviolable, and the diplomatic representatives of some of the smaller countries (themselves businessmen rather than career officers) went to extraordinary lengths to support their 'clients'. Nor were they above some fairly sophisticated duplicity, in return for a percentage of the proceeds, to ensure the transit of the Viceroy's money into their protégés' pockets.

It is true that some degree of protection for Europeans was probably necessary; in the primitive state of Egypt at the time they were unlikely to have obtained fair treatment from Moslem officials who looked back with regret on the old days when the Infidel was a despised and humiliated minority.* Undoubtedly much of the hatred of foreigners sprang from their own abuses, and their arrogant presumption of superiority over the native Egyptian.

Those who know the Egypt of today, with its 'big' government which sequestrates property at will, and sends the ambassadors of the greatest powers packing at the mere clatter of a diplomatic brick, will wonder how Said allowed his treasury to be plundered so openly. The answer, of course, is not so much that the pendulum has swung as the fact that Said could never say 'No' to anyone. It was so much easier to agree, to wave tiresome money matters away with a compliant gesture. The image of a munificent and glorious potentate required that largesse should be showered around with both hands. Whose bright idea can it have been, for example when the court jester came complaining that an estimate made out in Italian lire was too low, to overcome the difficulty by simply changing the Lira sign into £ sterling (the same word in Italian after all)?

The big money, of course, lay in contracts and concessions for public works, services and supplies, which had to be carried out by Europeans: only they—since Mohammed Ali's monopolies had starved the country of local mercantile talent—had the capital and the know-how to deal with the job of westernizing Egypt. And while it would be wrong to suggest that all the contracts were fraudulent, it is certain that they all made the utmost of an exceedingly good thing. Everyone, Said's entourage and the Turkish officials more than most, had his fingers in the honey-pot, and since—through pressure by the consuls—there was profit to be made even from non-contracts, for real or imaginary losses, the most fantastic claims for indemnity were put in on all sides, and, moreover, paid. Surrounded by a fawning pack of sycophants, Said laughed at his troubles. Only occasionally did he show a hint of vexation, as when he interrupted a conversation with a French entrepreneur and told a servant to close the window. If this gentleman catches cold,' he quipped, 'it will cost me £10,000'. But otherwise he cheerfully went on burning the candle at both ends, his European experiments and Oriental extravagance adding up to a plunderer's dream.

And the biggest plunderer of all was about to appear.

Notes:

Opened in 1856, the line from Cairo to Alexandria was the first in Africa. Cape Colony followed in 1860. Switzerland and Denmark opened their first lines in 1844, Spain in 1848, Swede in 1851, Norway in 1853, Portugal in 1854. Turkey and Greece came after Egypt (1860 and 1869). The Union Pacific transcontinental line across North Africa was completed in 1860.

By the nineteenth century the balance of power between West and East had changed so completely that Europeans now had far greater possibilities for interference.

Chapter 7

The Canal at Suez

As an *élève consul* Ferdinand de Lesseps had been posted to Alexandria, where his father was already the French diplomatic representative. Reaching Egypt he found to his disgust that he had to go through a period of quarantine, and to while away a tedious fortnight he picked up a report which Lepère had made thirty years earlier for Napoleon on the project of joining the Mediterranean to the Red Sea. His imagination was fired by the idea.

He knew that there was nothing new in the notion of a canal across the Isthmus of Suez. It was, in fact, one of the oldest enterprises ever considered by civilized man, and details of the construction of the first waterway linking the Nile with the Red Sea are quite literally lost in the mists of antiquity. By tradition this was built by Sesostris, a Pharaoh of the 12th Dynasty, about 2000 BC. Joining the Pelusiac branch of the Nile not far from the modern town of Bilbeis, it followed the green belt of the Wadi Tumilat eastwards to the Bitter Lakes, and reached the Red Sea at the ancient port of Clysma, near Suez.

For over a thousand years this canal of the Pharaohs linked Memphis and the Nile valley with the Red Sea, but by the time of the Persian invasion in 525 BC it had presumably silted up, because the Stone of Darius records that in 521 BC he had the canal dug again. Herodotus mentions that it could be navigated by two triremes abreast and that the journey took four days. The Romans cut the distance by digging a more direct waterway, known as Trajan's canal, which joined the Nile not far from the site of modern Cairo, then called Babylon. Soon after the Arab conquest it was reactivated under the sonorous title of the 'Canal of the Prince of the Faithful', and the project for a direct canal from Lake Timsah to the Mediterranean was only given up by Haroun el Rashid on the grounds that it was too dangerous to open up the coast of Arabia to the Byzantine army. In the fifteenth century the Venetians had studied the project after Vasco da Gama discovered the route round the Cape, but the Turks had objected. Leibnitz suggested it to Louis XIV. Napoleon's engineers, surveying the ground, came to the same erroneous conclusion as the Graeco-Romans had two millennia previously, namely that the Red Sea was nearly ten metres higher than the Mediterranean, and that there was a danger of flooding lower Egypt. This, they had reported, ruled out any possibility. Even so, against the face of such expert evidence, the Saint Simonians continued to lobby the project.

Canals at Suez and Panama were part of the Comte de Saint-Simon's program for the 'regeneration' of the world, and when Prosper Enfantin and a group of Saint-Simonians came to Egypt in 1833, the exhaustive discussions which went on round the dinner table at the consulate served to increase de Lesseps's enthusiasm.

Neither they—nor any other applicants for the concession—made any headway with Mohammed Ali, who feared that if the waters of the Red Sea and the Mediterranean were joined the identity of Egypt itself would be in jeopardy, and that an invasion by one or other of the European powers would certainly follow. But while refusing to let him dig his canal, the Pasha was personally quite fond of de Lesseps, and the French consulate was the one place outside the Palace he would allow his favorite son, Said, to visit.

Although Mohammed Ali was reputed to have fathered over eighty children, only four of his sons actually survived him, the eldest of whom was Said. Perhaps because he was alarmed at such a heavy rate of mortality, Mohammed Ali had paid particular attention to his upbringing. Even as a child Said was already very fat, and his father put him on a strict diet and a Spartan regime. He was made to spend his days doing physical jerks, climbing rigging, and being chased by a drill sergeant round the Palace walls. For meals, all he was allowed was a plate of beans and some salad. It is hardly surprising that whenever he had an excuse—de Lesseps, for instance, was teaching him to ride—the wretched fat boy would slip off into the French Consulate, where the young Consul and his wife took pity on him and gave him a few extra calories. What he liked best, they discovered, was spaghetti. Over plates heaped high with pasta, a bond of friendship was sealed. Said never forgot the kindness they showed him.

It was on a summer afternoon in 1854, when de Lesseps was busy repairing the roof of his house, an old chateau near Bourges, once the property of Agnes Sorel, that the postman appeared in the courtyard with letters from Paris. Still perched on the roof, de Lesseps learnt that Abbas I was dead, and that Mohammed Said had succeeded to the Vice-regal throne of Egypt.

For an energetic diplomat, who had recently had the misfortune to run foul of Louis Napoleon and was finding his consequent *retraite* monotonous, the news opened sudden and exhilarating prospects.

'I hurriedly descended from the scaffolding and hastened to write the new Viceroy a letter of congratulation', he gleefully told his Dutch friend Ruyssenaers. 'I explained that political conditions at home had given me the leisure which would permit me to present my respects to him in person as soon as he would let me know the date of his return from Constantinople.'

Mohammed Said replied immediately, inviting de Lesseps to join him in Alexandria early in November. He little suspected what he was letting himself in for.

The hallmark of a successful entrepreneur, we are led to believe, is the joy he feels in putting something together and seeing it grow. His motivation, it is explained, is not so much materialism as a pure, creative urge. 'If artists give up the world's pleasures to pursue their calling, people understand it' said a

Manhattan millionaire recently, 'What they don't understand is that many businessmen have the same creative drives, and derive the same satisfaction as artists...taking a business idea and making it work is creative.' *(Time* Magazine 3 December 1965).

Viewed from this standpoint, Ferdinand de Lesseps emerges as one of the greatest artists of his time. Certainly he was its greatest entrepreneur. The magnitude of his achievement was phenomenal. Yet the belief has steadily grown stronger that in an age not remarkable for its honesty, he was also the father of all confidence tricksters. Certainly from the moment he planned his voyage to Egypt, he had only one object in view—to wrest from his unsuspecting friend a concession which had hitherto been refused to all applicants.

His own papers, which should be compulsory reading for sales executives, show the circumspection with which he acted. During the first few meetings with Said, not a word was mentioned about the subject in the forefront of his mind. Many topics were discussed, including a number of government matters, but not a whisper was heard about the canal. De Lesseps was determined not to broach it until he was absolutely sure of his ground and until, as he says, 'it will be so ripe that the Prince will adopt it as his own idea'. Gradually, combining flattery with the crossing of palms, he won over the Viceroy's entourage: they in turn prepared the way with Said. At length, as they were travelling through the desert from Alexandria to Cairo, it was intimated to de Lesseps that the climate was favorable. The date was 16 November 1854.

'At about five in the morning' he relates in his *Souvenirs,* 'the camp was all astir...when all of a sudden a rainbow of extraordinary beauty charmed my vision...I saw in this manifestation in the heavens that sign of the covenant that the scriptures describe. The day had come for me to discuss matters with Said.'

Throughout the day, as they rode across the desert, de Lesseps waited impatiently for the appropriate moment. Then towards dusk, a halt was called, and Said, as usual, ordered his officers to do some practice shooting at targets. For some reason or other, everyone was marking wide. It was then that de Lesseps saw his chance. Sending for his carbine, he took careful aim— 'the fate of Egypt hung on that second' he recalls eloquently—and squeezed the trigger. The rainbow did not let him down. His shots were plumb on the target.

'The Pasha's face was wreathed in smiles', he wrote triumphantly later, 'He seized my hand and held it for a moment; then he asked me to sit beside him on the divan. We were alone...I set forth my ideas without going into details. Said followed what I had to say with interest and attention...then he turned to me and said: "You have convinced me. I accept your plan. During the remainder of our trip we shall work out ways and means for carrying out your idea. The matter is settled. You may count on me".'

It was dinnertime. Said clapped his hands for the meal to be served, and as the massive silver tureen was placed on the table, the Viceroy, delighted at the surprise he had up his sleeve, told the entourage what he had decided. 'I have given my friend, Monsieur de Lesseps, a concession' he announced happily. 'That is our plan, is it not?'

It never seems to have occurred to him that he was selling the birthright of Egypt, as de Lesseps might have put it.

And indeed, as he listened, the persuasive Frenchman's smile was for once quite unfeigned. But although success is sweet, it is twice as palatable when safely signed, sealed, and tied up with red ribbon. A fortnight later, de Lesseps had drawn the concession up into an official Deed as remarkable for its impudence as for the one-sidedness of the various heads of agreements which followed. Said, it was said, signed the document without ever having read it. How else, it was argued, could he ever have allowed himself to be fooled so blatantly, and have tossed away so light heartedly the welfare of his people, and the rights of his country?

If Said read anything at all, it was probably the covering note which his 'good friend' had sent with the agreement:

'The names of the Egyptian rulers who built the Pyramids, those monuments of human vanity, remain unknown. The name of the Prince who will have opened the great maritime canal will be blessed from century to century until time shall be no more.'

However devious the means by which he pursued his ends—and however questionable these ends were—the verve with which de Lesseps set about the creation of the *Compagnie Universelle* must rank him as one of the greatest organizing geniuses of the nineteenth century. From the beginning, he found himself practically alone, a commercial David battling against the amorphous Goliath of contrary interests. England was determined to stop him; France was by no means on his side; the Turkish Sultan vacillated between threats from London and reassurances from Cairo.

But for another stroke of luck he might never have succeeded. His cousin, Eugenie de Montigo, married Napoleon III. With the Empress working for him behind the scenes, and a rapacious entourage round the Emperor, it was comparatively easy to buy his way in. Having bribed the little clique which ran the inside politics of the Second Empire, he announced to the Paris Bourse that the Viceroy had guaranteed the shares, while assuring the ever-gullible Said that the public had taken up the subscription. Even so, when subscriptions to the *Compagnie Universelle du Canal Maritime de Suez* were opened in Paris in the autumn of 1858, only a little over half of the 400,000 shares were taken up by the public. But with a prince of the blood and some of the most influential names of France on his board, he had few qualms in misrepresenting the position to the authorities, and in the end Mohammed Said found that 'our friend M. Ferdinand de Lesseps' had saddled him with financial commitments far beyond anything he had ever envisaged. Persuaded by the fluent tongue of this master salesman that the canal would bring him immortality as the Pharaoh of Suez (and the even less justifiable hope that it would be a means to secure independence for Egypt) Said found himself saddled with 44 per cent of the total capital.

Almost overnight, the question of the canal now became an international issue. In London, Paris, Cairo and Constantinople, the chips were stacked. Whitehall opposed the project, preferring, for strategical reasons, the slower but surer route round the Cape. The overland haul from Alexandria to Suez, which was working very nicely, was felt to be quite adequate as a rapid postal service and military transit means to India. The canal would upset the status quo and as likely as not blow up into another 'Egyptian Question'. Constantinople, moreover, would be nearer to India by sea than London. All this would not do. When de Lesseps broached Palmerston in the hope of talking him round, he was quickly disabused.

'Let me tell you of my fears', explained Palmerston. 'They are that this project may completely upset the commercial and maritime relations of Great Britain, and that the creation of a new avenue of trade may cause us to lose the advantage we now possess. I fear also what our future relations with France may be. I think it is my duty to do what a statesman should do. This is to consider what may be in the womb of time.'

These mildly expressed views concealed an inflexible determination to stop the construction at all costs, and such was the pressure exerted by Palmerston on the Porte that Mohammed Said, perplexed by the passions which his concession had unleashed, became convinced that England was determined to have him deposed. Faced with such an unpalatable prospect, he was even prepared to forgive de Lesseps for having tricked him over the shares, if only his friend could save him from the English. Anxiety, in fact, soon did more to his figure than all the gymnastics of his youth. The worry began to make him thin. When de Lesseps walked into the audience room at Ras el Tin palace, Said pointed to his coat, now several sizes too large. 'See what these English have done to me!' he said sadly, adding that he hoped his 'good friend' would be able to help him in his predicament. Meanwhile, he told de Lesseps the digging on the canal would have to be postponed until the international climate had cooled down a bit.

De Lesseps knew exactly how to exploit such a display of weakness. There was no reason why he should require any further favors from Mohammed Said. The Viceroy had been bled white when the concession was granted. He had then given away the right to dig the canal. He had made invaluable grants of land along with the franchise. He had promised corvée labor, in other words, labor which did not have to be paid. He had, besides all this, agreed to take up a quarter of the shares and then had a further 85,000 foisted on him by methods which would have landed most people in jail. De Lessep's only concern now was to consolidate the advantages he had gained.

The Viceroy was not present at the elaborate ceremony which was staged when digging began on 25 April 1859. Although de Lesseps had openly defied him, Said realized that the Emperor was backing the canal, and dared not use force to stop him. All he could do was sulk in Cairo and put spokes in the wheels.

Under the terms of the contract the Company had requisitioned 50,000 men. They needed such a vast army of laborers because their equipment was rudimentary, and it was more economical to use flesh and blood than steam and metal. Said sent only 12,000 men.

His compromise upset both Palmerston and de Lesseps. The American Civil War had focussed attention on slavery. The laborers Said sent to dig without pay were neither criminals nor slaves: they were fellahin who had been dragged from their fields. The British (conveniently forgetting that similar corvée labor had been used when building the Suez railway financed by the P & O Company, a few years previously) accused Said of inhuman practices. And de Lesseps had his board of directors pass a resolution holding Said responsible for damages should digging be delayed.

Trapped in the contending rage of both England and France, Said grew more and more desperate, alternating between anger and pleading, compromise and procrastination. His weight diminished still further. Early in 1863 his dilemma was solved. He died.

Chapter 8

The High Cost of Magnificence

Until quite recently, an old Pasha sat almost every evening in the corner of the bar on Shepheard's Hotel roof, and talked about bygone days in Egypt. He was no longer a Pasha, of course, since the title had been abolished in 1952, but although most of his property had been confiscated by the revolutionary regime he still had the air of a *seigneur,* and his manner and appearance were those of his forbears intriguing gently on the terrace of Shepheard's a century before. The formal clothes, the gold-topped cane, the small cup of coffee (sa'da, well spiced), the flat cigarette in the ivory holder, and the small string of amber beads, but most of all, the parchment face with its kind, cunning eyes, and the soft speech blending distinction with roguery, symbolized the always haunting wisdom of the East.

'The Westerner imagines the Oriental mind to be inscrutable', he would say, 'that there is a barrier, so that he can never really understand the Egyptian. But this is not so. There is nothing so very mysterious about the way we think. It is simply that you should not try to judge the Orient in terms of the West, or look at Egypt through European eyes.'

'We are a very old people, you know,' he would go on, with a slight smile. 'There is a matter of traditions. For example, the Moslem law of succession. It was dangerous, in the Ottoman Empire, to be heir to the throne. If you look at the family of Mohammed Ali, you will see that the heir to the throne rarely succeeded, Ibrahim, for instance, and Prince Ahmed. This is one of the reasons why Ismail was so anxious to get the Firman of Primogeniture...'

Ismail himself, he would remind one, had not been the heir apparent. During the reign of Abbas, Ismail had in fact led a prince's opposition movement, and had found it safer to do his plotting outside the country. With Said he had been on friendlier terms, and ran the High Council of Justice. But the next in succession to the vice-regal throne had been Nabil Ahmed, a miserly man, who was known to be clever at business.

At Bairam in 1858 Said gave a great fête in Alexandria to which he sent invitations—tantamount to a command—to all members of his family. Ismail, who was ill, was the only absentee. A special train took them back to Cairo. Midway between Alexandria and Cairo at Kafr el Zayat there is a bridge built by Robert Stephenson, with a central span that opens and shuts to allow the passage of steamers and fellucas. As the train came steaming up, the driver saw to his horror that the bridge was open. But it was too late to avoid disaster. The carriages, with the Princes in them, crashed into the Nile. In the instant that they were suspended in the air above the river. Prince Halim managed to dive clear into the water, but the fat and awkward Ahmed was drowned. Thus Ismail became the new heir apparent. Although no one ever discovered whether it was an accident or not, it was assumed in palace circles that Ismail had a hand in the deed. In any event, it altered the destiny of Egypt. Had Ahmed ruled instead of Ismail, things might have been quite different.

Yet Ismail (continued the old Pasha) was not really such a puzzling figure as is often made out. As a young man, he was a successful landowner. His cotton was the best grown, his sugar factory was efficiently run, and in quite a short time he doubled the value of his estates. He owed money to no one, and, if anything, people noticed that he lived rather simply and was inclined to be mean. In his Paris hotel, for instance, he refused to give any tips. But the day he became Viceroy all this was changed. Psychologists may be able to explain what turns an avaricious princeling into a spendthrift ruler. Perhaps it was just that the power went to his head. More probably it was that, like his grandfather Mohammed Ali, he looked on Egypt as the Viceroy's personal property—a vast private estate to be exploited as he thought fit. He saw himself as the embodiment of Egypt, and he determined to achieve the aggrandizement of his country through the aggrandizement of himself and his dynasty. Only instead of doing this by war, he chose to do it with money.

In the fifteenth century, Lorenzo d'Medici was known as Il Magnifico not because of the ostentation of his private life, but because of his humanity and the splendor he brought to Florence. Ismail was the reverse. If Ismail was also called 'The Magnificent', it was because of the splendor he invested in himself. The more sumptuous his state, the greater his personal extravagance, the more impressive Egypt would seem in the eyes of Europe. This was his reasoning. To gain the independence of his country, he must first raise Egypt into a position of international eminence—in appearance, at least. He must equal, if not outdo, the great nations in their own status symbols, in the creature comforts and trappings of power. And since he had discovered that the civilized countries of Europe made a free use of their credit for raising loans, he did the same. Money was easy: it was vision that counted.

But for all the vision with which he prided himself, he had no sense of proportion. His capacity for self-delusion was unlimited. He fooled himself more than he fooled anyone else. He believed his own bluff. And when bankruptcy came—as inevitably it did—he still cherished the illusion he was Khedive by a sort of divine right, and that 'There's such divinity doth hedge a king, that treason can but peep to what it would', so that the *coup d'etat* of the Powers took him by surprise and he surrendered without a blow.

He began well. His inaugural address was a model of modest good sense: '...the basis of all good administration is order and economy on finance; I shall seek this order and economy by every possible means, and to give an example to all...I have decided...to abandon the system followed by my predecessors, and to set myself a civil list I shall never exceed.' That the civil list he proposed was twice that of Queen Victoria was unimportant: it was the intentions that counted.

But matters were not as simple as he thought. Said had not only left him an impoverished throne; he had left affairs in an appalling mess.* There was the question of the Suez Canal; there were a hundred and one leeches in the anterooms of the Palace itself, with their consuls in attendance, pressing the most outrageous claims; and there was the Porte, sharpening its claws as usual, which had to be bought off with lavish bribes. But for the guns of Fort Sumter, Ismail might have found himself bankrupt before he started. As it was, the American Civil War created overnight an unprecedented demand for Egyptian cotton.

Up until 1860, the USA had supplied over eighty per cent of Europe's cotton. But the Union blockade now drove brokers into the hands of the Indian and Egyptian growers. Of the two, India produced by far the greater quantity—practically six times as much as Egypt—but the quality of the Egyptian long staple was immeasurably superior. And so, suddenly, Alexandria found itself rolling in gold. The price of cotton rose from 7½,d per pound in 1861 to 29¾ in the summer of 1862 and 29d in 1863. As the largest landowner (after his accession his appetite for land became insatiable and soon he possessed fully one-fifth of the country's cultivated land) Ismail was in the center of the boom, and the frenzy of the speculators was only matched by his own fever to build. For Ismail, it was the chance of a lifetime to indulge in an orgy of public works, aimed at bringing Egypt right up to date and turning Cairo into as fine a capital as any city in Europe. Overnight he embarked on a vast scale of expenditure, and in the comparatively short period of his reign, he did more in the way of public works than any monarch in modern times. Even by today's standards, the list is a prodigious: to mention just a few projects, by 1879 Egypt had 8,400 miles of Nile canals, 450 bridges, 64 sugar mills, and nearly 1,000 miles of railways. Ismail built the largest harbor in the Mediterranean at Alexandria, and a string of lighthouses along the coast. He became one of the original signatories of the General Postal Union, and stretched telegraph lines right down into the Sudan. He started shipping companies and opened nearly 6,000 schools, teaching every conceivable subject, including music, languages, agriculture, law, medicine and military science. There were even girls' schools, under the patronage of one of his wives. He inaugurated the Suez Canal and the brand new city, Ismailia, midway along it. He modernized Alexandria, and to a certain extent Port Said and Suez.

But dearest to his heart was the beautification of Cairo. When he began, the city had barely spilled out beyond its medieval walls, and more than a mile of wasteland lay between the café-fringed Esbekiah gardens and the Nile. Ismail thrust arcaded boulevards modeled on the Rue de Rivoli through the labyrinth of alleys in the old native quarters, and developed all the area towards the river which is now the center of modern Cairo. He had a wide thoroughfare made leading to the apricot E-shaped palace on the banks of the Nile—later notorious among Allied troops in two wars as the most bug-ridden barracks in the world. (British soldiers, looking out from the barracks, used to assert that the huge bronze lions roared each time a virgin passed—which hadn't happened for years, they added.) Today the Nile Hilton Hotel stands on the site of Kasr el Nil palace hard by Ismail's great bridge to Gezira Island. All the present downtown center of Cairo was laid out by Ismail, who parceled out the land and payment facilities to those who wished to build houses. Apart from the vast new Abdin with its Italianate frontage which became his official residence, he dotted the landscape with palaces—including the famous one on Gezira Island which was completed in under six months for the visit of the Empress Eugenie, and twice in a hundred years (in the 1890s and today) was to become a favorite tourist hotel.

He even built out into the desert, creating a watering spa at Helouan, complete with a Grand Hotel des Bains in the approved European pattern, and served by a railway of its own from Cairo. And in three months, employing a labor force of 30,000 men, he constructed a new raised road to the Pyramids so that the distinguished guests coming for the opening of the Suez Canal could go sightseeing in comfort. His energy was astonishing. Everywhere there were suddenly new buildings and statues and avenues and fountains. 'Most people have a mania for something,' he once remarked, 'mine is for stone and mortar.' What Louis XIV did for Paris, Ismail did for Cairo; and it is curious to think that Cairo had gas lighting in the streets before Paris did. Ismail had made up his mind that when the Royal visitors came for the opening of the Canal, they should find themselves in a capital worthy of its magnificent ruler.

The question of the Canal preoccupied him from the start. He had not originated the project: it had been left to him by Said as an expensive legacy. Had Ismail wished to do so, he could probably have refused point-blank to recognize the validity of the concession under which de Lesseps was operating. The ratification by the Sultan, after all, had never been given. But Ismail was not prepared to go against France (a country he admired intensely) to this extent. He liked the idea of the Canal; what he disapproved of were the terms—in particular the handing over of a strip of land each side of the waterway, and the use of forced labor to construct it. He told de Lesseps that he was as 'canaliste' as himself, but that the land concession must be revoked, and the corvée must stop. 'Egypt should own the Canal, and not the Canal own Egypt' he insisted.

De Lesseps hid his feelings, but his papers show clearly what a blow this was. The finances of the company were shaky, and all his calculations had been based on the use of unpaid labor. Turkey was not in favor of the project; the Foreign Office was determined to stop it. His only course was to persuade the French Government to back the Canal as a matter of national interest. Before long a diplomatic battle flared up between London, Paris, Constantinople and

Cairo. Eugenie was once again pressed into service, and in the end Ismail agreed, ingenuously enough, to refer the affair to Napoleon III for arbitration— 'as one gentleman to another'. He could not have realized, of course, that the Emperor did not recognize him as falling within the category, in the European sense at least; and he certainly never expected that the imperial code of honor would permit Napoleon III, in a remarkable fit of judicial skullduggery, to award damages of eighty-four million francs—almost half the original capital of the company—in compensation for the loss of corvée labor and the desert land bordering the Canal. But his own code of honor, or at any rate his pride, forbade him from refusing to accept the Emperor's verdict.

Thus re-financed at the expense of Egypt, the company was able to purchase dredging machines and push ahead with the work. But for Ismail, coinciding as it did with the collapse of the cotton market, this additional financial burden was crippling. He had been out-smarted by the French at a time when he was over-extended with his own vast projects; the fuzzy white fibers were no longer the golden harvest they had been, and the more money he raised the more he needed. From now onwards, it was open season in Cairo for the pawnbrokers and the Jews.

Fortunately, Ismail could reflect, as he sat cross-legged on his divan, occasionally playing with his toes as he conversed with a visitor, his credit was good. There was no lack of candidates to lend him the billions of piasters he was spending so lavishly. The bankers might be more impressed with the pomp of the surroundings than the personal appearance of the Viceroy, sloppily dressed in the Turkish style *stambouli* (a sort of curate's coat) with large baggy-kneed trousers and elastic sided boots he often took off; they might be surprised at the ugliness of his rough face marked with eczema, and with its tufts of red whiskers, and the eyes, one of which was almost always closed while the other revolved, but they never failed to be won over by the fez worn jauntily on the side of his head and the warmth of his smile, the cleverness of his conversation and his prodigal hospitality.

This lavishness was part and parcel of his mystique. Money was the tool with which he sought to buy international status and eventually the independence of Egypt from the Sultan. In 1866 for a million sterling in cash and a doubling of the tribute (as well as a jeweled gold dinner service for the Sultan and a hundred thousand pounds extra in bribes) he finally succeeded in securing a firman which gave him a large degree of autonomy and the title of Khedive. Bankrolled by usurers, 'Effendina' was now ready to dazzle the crowned heads of Europe, and at the same time impress the money-lending world with his incredible wealth—and so entice them to go on lending to him.

The opening of the Suez Canal was his chance. Ismail had intended it to be quite a show; and so it was. First, the fireworks dump blew up and nearly demolished Port Said. Then, on the eve of the opening, a fifteen-foot rock was

Napoleon To Nasser

Raymond Flower

The World leaders of political non-alignment in Cairo: l - r Nehru, Nkrumah, Nasser, Sukarno and Tito.

   Egyptian Tourist Center.

President Nasser welcoming Khurshchev to Cairo I 1964. The Russina premier made Nasser a Hero of the Soviet Union – the most prestigious honour the USR can award.

   Bruno Barbey/Magnum

President Nasser and his successor-to-be, Anwar al Sadat, taking the Constitutional Oath in the National Assembly in Cairo, 1969.

   J. Allen Cash

discovered just below water level, and when it was dynamited, the banks collapsed. Finally, as the glittering cortege moved towards the entrance of the Canal, a police launch ran aground and would have ruined the whole proceedings had de Lesseps not galloped off and blown the vessel up. Even Verdi failed to complete his 'Hymn', in time for the inauguration of the new Opera House Ismail had built for the occasion, which opened on 1 November 1869 with Rigoletto instead.*

But no one minded—it was too lavish a spree. Heads of State had been arriving in Cairo from all sides since the beginning of November, to be conveyed at their host's expense first to Upper Egypt to see the sights at Luxor, and thence to Port Said, which by this time was a stupendous scene, the sun-bathed harbor crammed full of beflagged ships from a dozen nations.

On 13 November 1869 Ismail arrived aboard the Mahroussah. He was followed by the Emperor of Austria, the Crown Prince of Prussia, the Prince and Princess of the Netherlands, members of other Royal families, ambassadors, and distinguished guests of every description. Finally, at eleven o'clock on the morning of 16 November, the guns from the warships and the shore batteries began to boom as the French Imperial yacht, L'Aigle, with the Empress Eugenie on the poop-deck, steamed slowly in. 'Never have I seen a sight so lovely!' exclaimed the enraptured princess, and observers saw that Europe's most beautiful woman had tears in her eyes. The passage through the forty-mile long canal to Lake Timsah took twelve hours, and at sunset the following day the Royal flotilla met up with a convoy of Egyptian ships which had sailed north from the Red Sea. Under the brilliance of ten thousand lanterns Ismail and Eugenie sat down in the new Khedevial palace at Ismailia to a banquet which has gone down in history as one of the most sumptuous ever known, while the news flashed round the world that the union of the two seas was at last an accomplished fact.

Among all the celebrations, it was left to Ernest Renan, in a speech welcoming de Lesseps to the Academic Francaise, to be a prophet of doom. 'The isthmus now cut will become a battlefield' he declared with astonishing foresight, 'a single Bosphorus has hitherto sufficed for the troubles of the world; you have created a second and much more important one. In case of war...it will be of supreme interest, the point for the occupation of which the whole world will struggle. You have marked out the field of the great battles of the future.'

It should have been fairly obvious at the time that Ismail's great public works, his bribes to the Sultan, and his entertainment of royalty were costing a great deal more money than either the Khedive or Egypt had got. In the long run, the country could perhaps have been made to pay—as indeed it eventually did, for Egypt is basically an extraordinarily rich land—but at the moment Ismail's extravagance had far outstripped the means of his treasury. He had got Egypt into the position of a sound private business which, to finance its growth, has to borrow too heavily from the banks. Yet loan now succeeded loan at dangerously short intervals, and the most distinguished as well as the most scurrilous moneymen of Europe fell over each other in their efforts to cheat him, as Emile Ludwig remarks; 'With their interests, their brokerage, their commissions and fictitious payments, and all the tricks of the Paris and London stock exchanges, in a way which would have sent a small man to prison. An Englishman of that day called the big bankers the scum of Europe, for they actually paid over to the cheerful King only sixty per cent of his loans on paper.'

Certainly the State loans placed with Goschen's (1862/64/66); Bischofsheim's (1870); Oppenheim's (1873) and Rothschild's (1879) show that for a liability of 77 million pounds Egypt actually received about 50 million pounds. In the Oppenheim loan of 1873, for a liability of 32 million pounds involving an annual charge of 3½ million pounds, Egypt received less than 18 million pounds. The unfortunate Jews who were chased out of Egypt in the wake of the Suez crisis may be tempted to moralize about the sins of their fathers, for, as George Young tartly remarked; 'Never was there such a spoiling of the Egyptians by the chosen people.'*

Nor was it only the Hebrews; in Ismail's frenzy to build he allowed contracts to be awarded at absurdly high prices—the profits of which went abroad. For example, the Alexandria dock was constructed by a well-known British firm. The contract price was 3 million pounds, but in the opinion of Sir Rivers Wilson (subsequently the British financial representative) half of this figure would have been enough.

When the crash came, there was a good deal of talk about injustice by both creditors and debtor. Yet neither the bankers nor the Khedive have much call for one's sympathy. If injustice there was, it was surely to the ordinary citizen of Egypt. For, as always seems to happen, it was the unfortunate fellah who had to pay in the end. 'The sufferings of the Egyptian fellahin' to quote George Young again, 'both in the years of forced labor and in the subsequent fiscal exactions to meet interest on the Canal debt, put Europe heavily in their debt, a debt of honor of Europe to Egypt as to which we have not heard so much as we have of the less worthy liabilities of Egypt to Europe.'

The Suez Canal, for example, although largely built by Egyptian labor and paid for by Egyptian money, was virtually a dead loss to the country for the next eighty-eight years. Apart from the political problems it caused—and under the heading of imperial communications the waterway was one of the basic reasons for seventy years of British occupation—it also put an end to the overland transit trade which had hitherto meant revenue and employment. Moreover, within six years of the opening of the Canal, Ismail's insolvency caused Egypt to lose even its minority shareholding in the enterprise.

The British government's attitude towards the Canal had swung from one extreme to the other. At first, Palmerston did all he could to block the project. It is an undertaking' he told the House of Commons, 'which I believe...to rank among the many bubble schemes...founded on remote speculations with regard to easier access to our Indian possessions. A scheme which is in every way hostile and adverse to British interests. For fifteen years Her Majesty's Government has exercised all its influence at Constantinople and Egypt to prevent the execution of the project.' But once the Canal was built, and was a part of the world's physical and political geography, it was a different story. The Earl of Clarendon, Secretary of State for foreign affairs, wrote to de Lesseps that 'The successful opening of the Canal has been received with great and universal satisfaction', and went on to extol 'the political and commercial advantages we may confidently expect will result from your efforts'. British policy was now inevitably directed at controlling the waterway which so significantly joined two seas and divided two continents. The opportunity to do so came six years after the opening of the Canal.

For a full decade Ismail had been running recklessly into debt, mortgaging every asset to raise fresh loans, and in 1875 he was finally on the verge of bankruptcy. His only really valuable remaining assets were his Suez Canal shares. Stanton, the British Consul in Cairo, reported that a group of French financiers were negotiating to purchase them. Disraeli told Lady Bradfield and Lady Chesterfield privately that if the deal went through 'the whole of the Suez Canal would have belonged to France and they might have shut it up.' Be this as it may, he cabled Stanton on November 17 that the British government were in the market to buy the shares. On 23 November Stanton reported back that Great Britain was offered the shares for four million pounds and that the offer was valid for forty-eight hours only.

This put Disraeli in a quandary. Parliament was in recess until February and therefore there was no way of having the necessary credit voted. Only one man in England could write a cheque on the spot for such a sum. Disraeli's secretary was shown in just as Lord Rothschild was finishing his lunch.

'How much?' asked the banker, passing him the port.
'Four million pounds.'
'On what security?'
'The British government.'
Rothschild sniffed his port, smiled, and drained the glass.
'You shall have it' he replied quietly.

The shares safely secured, London henceforth took a proprietorial interest in the real estate it had acquired, and consequently in the government and affairs of Egypt. Kingslake's prophecy was coming true; and Renan's too.

Raymond Flower

Notes:

A month before he died, Said confided to Sir Henry Bulwer in Constantinople his remorse at having dilapidated his country's fortune. (F. O. Bulwer—Russell 15 December 1862).

The draft of a letter written by Verdi's wife in August 1969 makes it clear that Ismail's request was for a 'hymn' and not for an opera. So the usual story about the origins of 'Aida' is in fact wrong (see Frank Walker **The Man Verdi** p 278). Nevertheless the Khedive did have the intention of commissioning a national opera—as Draneht Bey wrote to Verdi—which would 'in the future become one of the happiest memoirs of his reign'. At first Verdi refused, but when Mariette Pasha wrote, through the intermediary of Camile du Locle, that Ismail had suggested 'knocking at another door...there are ideas of Gounod, even Wagner. If the latter would do it he might produce something grandiose,' the composer had a change of heart. The terms were certainly princely: a down-payment of 150,000 francs, with Verdi reserving all rights of performance outside Egypt The first performance of Aida finally took place in Cairo on 24 December 1871 in the presence of the Khedive. Unhappily the Opera House was totally destroyed by fire on 29 October 1971 on the very eve of its centenary.

The figures have been taken from Sir George Young's **Egypt** p 84, but excluding the 1879 loan for which Ismail was not entirely responsible, the figures for moneys borrowed and received are usually put at £68 million and £47 million.

Chapter 9

Blunt Talk

His daughter wrote that Wilfrid Blunt was a born agitator at the mercy of Oriental deceit and Irish blarney, and a cynical intriguer with women. But quite recently Dr Sayed Mahmoud, a former minister of external affairs in the Indian government, declared that 'England's greatness will hereafter be remembered by Blunt's ideas and work.' Previously he had written; I learnt honesty in politics from him long before I met Ghandi.'

Wherever the truth may lie between these two judgements, Wilfrid Scawen Blunt, who died in 1922 at the age of eighty-two, has left posterity with a well-documented picture of the disreputable sequence of British imperialist designs on Egypt. A Tory landowner, rich and grand enough to do what he liked, he was also a painter and a sculptor, and even more of a poet— 'wholly by temperament, but only partly by achievement' as E M Forster once remarked—but above all he was a political propagandist and an anti-imperialist at a time when to be one needed courage. A champion of lost causes in the aristocratic tradition of Byron and Shelley, he must have been an unmitigated nuisance to his friends who were directing the policies of England; yet his hatred of humbug and imperialism in general seems to have sprung not from any lack of loyalty to his country but rather from a deep feeling of sympathy for the exploited.

Joining the diplomatic service at eighteen, and attached to British legations in various parts of Europe, he had soon been disillusioned to find that the role of a junior secretary was to move in society and amuse himself decorously, but under no circumstances to take an interest in current affairs. For a while he wrote poems rather than dispatches, assisted at some of the contemporary dramas in Europe as a spectator, and then retired to breed horses on his estates in Sussex. It was not until 1873, to escape the English winter, that he and his wife—the granddaughter of Byron—made a trip to the East. They went by way of Belgrade down the Danube to Constantinople, and while at the Embassy there bought half a dozen horses at the Al Maidan market and spent some pleasant weeks wandering in the hills and poppy-fields of Asia Minor. They were impressed by the honesty and friendliness of the people and the badness of their government. 'Yet', remarked Blunt in a comment which has a modern, almost ecological ring, 'it was clear that with much fiscal oppression a large personal liberty existed in rural Turkey for the poor, such as contrasted not unfavorably with our own police and magistrature-ridden England.'

The following winter they went to Algeria. It was the time of the Arab uprising which was viciously crushed by the French, who, in Blunt's opinion, took advantage of the rebellion to confiscate native property and hand it over to the French *colons*. 'Here we assisted at another spectacle which gave food for reflection: that of an Eastern people in violent subjection to a Western' he wrote, 'with all my love for the French (and I had been at Paris during the war, and had been enthusiastic for its defense at the time of the siege) I found my sympathies in Algeria going out wholly to the Arabs.'

On New Year's Eve, 1875, passing through Lake Menzaleh down along the Suez Canal, Wilfrid Blunt had his first glimpse of Egypt. In those days the lake was still an almost virgin region, and he was enchanted by the flocks of flamingoes, ducks, pelicans and ibis which covered it, and the quantities of fish which swarmed around the bows of the ship. When they reached Suez they were greeted with the news of a disaster which had overtaken the Egyptian army in Abyssinia. The rumor—afterwards disproved—was circulating that Ismail's own son had been captured and mutilated. It all sounded most unpleasant, and the Blunts decided, instead of continuing to Kassala, to alter their plans and stay in Egypt.

They had no desire to follow the usual tourist rounds, so having camping equipment with them, they hired camels at Suez and rode across the desert to Cairo. It must have been a nasty moment when, camping by mistake behind the targets of the Khedivial ranges, they were woken by a whistling of bullets; but luckily the recruits were poor marksmen, and they reached Cairo without mishap—pausing only to collect their letters at the Consulate before going on towards the Pyramids. At sunset they made a halt at the little village of Tolbiyah where—surprisingly enough, since it was on the sightseers' route to the Pyramids and all foreigners were considered as legitimate prey—they were received with the greatest hospitality. The fact that they had stopped at the village for a night's lodging established them as guests. Of all the Europeans who had passed that way, no one had ever stopped to stay the night. It was the first contact between the poet and the fellahin.

The peasants Blunt saw were in a desperate state of poverty. Ismail was tottering on the edge of bankruptcy: Ismail Saddyk, his notorious Muffetish, was in power. The European coupon-clippers were clamoring for their dividends—and the fellahin were made to pay. With the tax collectors everywhere, whip in hand, the provincial towns were full of women selling their silver ornaments and even their clothes to the inevitable Greek usurer. Blunt bought their trinkets, listened to their stories, and joined in their curses against a government that was laying them bare. He did not as yet understand—any more than the peasants did themselves—the financial pressure from Europe, which was the real cause of their misfortunes; it was only later that he realized that his own country had a share in the blame.

Certainly the villagers were outspoken enough. Englishmen in those days were popular in Moslem countries; they were looked upon as free from the political designs of the other 'Franks' and individually honest in their commercial dealings. In Egypt especially they stood out in sharp contrast to the seedy carpetbaggers from the Mediterranean—the Italian, Greek and Maltese money-lenders—who were literally sucking the life-blood of the Moslem peasantry. Already there were whispers of a possible European intervention, and to the peasants the idea of it (if it were to be English) was not unpopular. The existing state of things was so unendurable that any change would be welcomed with joy. To the fellahin in their actual condition of beggary, robbed and beaten and perishing of hunger, England seemed a sort of bountiful, friendly providence, very rich and quite disinterested, a redresser of wrongs and a friend of the oppressed—just as individual English tourists who went around with open hands and expressions of sympathy so often were. Blunt became bitterly ashamed that these simple people should feel like that, little suspecting the commercial selfishness which had led his countrymen to so many aggressions on the weak races of the world.

'The fellahin,' he wrote in his journal, 'have every virtue which should make a happy, well-to-do society. They are cheerful, industrious, obedient to law and pre-eminently sober...kind to old men, beggars, idiots...Their chief fault is their love of money, but that is one that political economists will readily pardon...It would be difficult to find anywhere a population better fitted to attain the economic end of the greatest happiness for the greatest number. In politics they have no aspirations except to live and let live, to be allowed to work and keep the produce of their labor, to buy and sell without interference and to escape taxation. They have been ill-treated for ages without losing thereby their goodness of heart; they have few of the picturesque virtues, they are neither patriotic nor fanatical nor romantically generous. But they are free from the picturesque vices. Each man works for himself—at most for his family. The idea of self-sacrifice for the common good they do not understand, but they are innocent of plots to enslave their fellows...in spite of the monstrous oppression of which they are the victims, we have heard no word of revolt, this not for any superstitious regard for their rulers, for they are without political prejudice, but because revolt is no more in their nature than it is in a flock of sheep. They would hail the Queen of England or the Pope, or the King of the Ashantee with equal eagerness if these came with the gift for them of a penny less taxation in the pound.'

Such were the poet's first impressions. He was still, of course, unaware of the political ideas which were already being heard in the towns, and the nationalism which was beginning to stir, and he had yet to realize the full influence of international finance in the hardships the peasants were suffering. On his return to Cairo he soon got an idea of the country's economic predicament, and the enormity of the disaster which Ismail had caused. Already the interest on the Foreign Debt amounted to four million pounds a year, and it was generally reckoned that the cost of his reign exceeded 400 million pounds—a prodigious sum at that period. The whole of the fellahin's savings over a number of prosperous years had been seized, together with all their agricultural stock, and furthermore they were now privately indebted by something like twenty million pounds to the Greek and other local usurers.

Before leaving Cairo, Wilfrid Blunt was guest at a sumptuous banquet given by Ismail to members of a financial mission to the Pyramids. As they feasted elaborately and drank their champagne literally under the eyes of a starving crowd of fellahin, he saw the scene for what it was worth, with its waste and surrounding misery; 'A true presentiment of the twin causes of the coming revolution.'*

Soon after this, a curious quirk of international diplomacy had its repercussions on Egypt. As a young man, Disraeli had advanced half jestingly in his novel *Tancred* the idea of a great Asiatic empire under an English monarchy, with Cyprus as its center—recalling, perhaps, the historic fact that Richard Coeur de Lion had been its ruler. He must have had a quiet chuckle when early in 1878 he ratified a secret convention with the youthful Sultan Abdul Hamid of Turkey, by which Cyprus was leased to England in return for a guarantee to the Sultan (at that time hard pressed by the Russians) of the integrity of all his Asiatic provinces.

Cyprus itself was of no particular use to England: at best it was a whim of Disraeli's based on a somewhat spurious report about the wealth of the island put in by a consul who had interests there. Disraeli's real purpose was to establish, informally but effectively, a British protectorate over Asiatic Turkey. A month later, at the opening session of the Congress of Berlin) held to determine the fate of European Turkey, it was proposed that each government should solemnly affirm that they had no secret engagements in the matter. Taken by surprise, Disraeli and Lord Salisbury gave their word with the others—to be greatly embarrassed when the next day the whole text of the Cyprus convention was published in a London evening paper. It was bad luck, of course; (a translator had sold the information to the *Globe* for £5) but the shock was corrosive. Convicted in front of the assembly of a direct lie, Disraeli took to his bed, leaving Salisbury to wriggle out of the mess as best he could. The French and Russian delegations made the most of it, walking out with a great show of dudgeon, and all Bismarck's skill was required to placate the French and achieve a compromise whereby, to compensate for England's acquisition of Cyprus, France would be allowed to occupy Tunis and even, it is alleged, have her claims on Syria recognized; moreover—most significant of all—in the financial arrangements being made in Egypt, France would have an equal say with England.

The price thus paid to France, Wilfrid Blunt pointed out to his friends on the *Messagerie Maritimes* steamer that was taking them from Marseilles to

Alexandria, enabled Disraeli to return to London and boast publicly that he had brought back 'Peace with Honor'.*

'Peace with Plunder' would be a more appropriate epithet he thought, appalled at this revelation of unprincipled imperialism. To the Cyprus intrigue, would later be traced a long string of crimes against Oriental and North African liberty: it put Tunis under the heel of the French and triggered off the great partition of Africa among the European powers, embittered Moslems against England, and was the determining cause, a year later, of the Anglo-French Condominion in Egypt.

In the autumn of this same year, Blunt found himself once more heading eastwards, in search of Arab mares for his stud at Crabbet. Sitting on the boat deck with Sir Rivers Wilson, (who had been established as Finance Minister to camouflage a foreign receivership) he heard what had been happening during the past two years in Cairo. It was mainly a catalogue of the crimes of Ismail, but nevertheless Wilson had high hopes of restoring Egypt to prosperity and rescuing the fellahin from their financial bondage. He knew Ismail to be an astute and unscrupulous opponent, but he counted on his own ability to be able to come to terms with him. Despite the old saying; 'An Armenian vizier and ruin is near', he had confidence in Nubar (the new Prime Minister) and believed he had behind him not only the support of the Foreign Office but more important still, the backing of the Rothschilds. He had just persuaded them in Paris to advance a loan of nine million Egyptian pounds on the Khedivial domains—a fatal move, it turned out, which precipitated the crash in Cairo.

Sir Rivers Wilson's brief career as Finance Minister failed, mainly because he had to contend with the greed of the European money-lenders and relied too much on Nubar—whose reputation as an Armenian who had grown rich as agent of the loan-mongers of Europe made him a weak reed to lean on. If by an act called the Rescript of 1878, Ismail had surrendered his personal control of revenue to the Nubar—Wilson ministry, it was only as an alternative to actual bankruptcy, and he had every intention of getting rid of them as soon as he could. It was not difficult to rouse Moslem opinion against Wilson, a Christian alien, particularly when, with his accountant's mind, he began a series of crude retrenchments among the Egyptian officials, while increasing the Europeans' salaries. Nor, for all his good intentions, did Wilson succeed in relieving the peasants of their burdens; it was essential that the Khedive should remain solvent, and this meant that the interest on the enormous debt had to be paid punctually. The regime of the whip continued as mercilessly as ever in the villages, and a badly managed revenue survey—interpreted as the prelude to even heavier land taxes—only made matters worse. When Wilson went on to suggest rescinding the Moukabalah arrangement (which would have meant, in effect, the confiscation by the government of about 9,500,000 Egyptian pounds paid by landowners in the form of advance taxation on landed property) the belief grew that even worse things might be expected of the English accountant than before. To Blunt it seemed absurd that anyone so intelligent and well-meaning as his friend should make such a mess of things. The thought crossed his mind that some of the measures that Rivers was taking must have been suggested by the Khedive himself to discredit him. The climax of his foolishness was to reduce the army, including a large number of officers, without meeting their arrears of pay.

'Let pigs at sea cut their own throats' says the Oriental proverb. A demonstration of students was stage-managed by the Khedive to reach the government offices just as the ministers were leaving. As Nubar got into his carriage he was surrounded by shouting youths who pulled his moustache and boxed his ears. The Khedivial guard, who had been hiding behind the scenes, fired a few shots over the heads of the crowd; the Khedive made an appearance and ordered the demonstrators to go home. By such *opera bouffe* stuff Ismail seems to have persuaded the English and French Consuls that, but for his intervention and personal authority, much worse might have happened. Nubar was advised to resign and Ragheb Pasha, the Khedive's nominee, was named Prime Minister in his place. Shortly afterwards it was Wilson's turn. On 30 April 1879 he wrote to Blunt; 'You will daresay have heard that I have been upset by that little scoundrel the Khedive. He didn't quite have me assassinated but he had me attacked in the street and very roughly handled...HMG with their usual loyalty to their agents have left me to my fate.'

But Wilson also knew the Oriental proverb. Crestfallen and left in the lurch by his own government, he traveled home via Paris and warned the Rothschilds of the danger their money was running in Cairo. The Khedive, he told them, intended to repudiate his whole debt, and cover himself by proclaiming a constitutional government in Egypt. If they did not prevent this, they would be lost. The Rothschilds acted on the tip and began lobbying for an active intervention by the Powers. But the British government, who had their own troubles in South Africa, were no longer in an intervening mood, and Paris was equally unwilling. In desperation the Rothschilds finally turned to Bismarck, who ever since his Frankfurt days had given them his rather condescending support. The British and French governments were made to understand that if they could not protect the bondholders' interests in Egypt, the German government would. This settled the matter.

On 26 July 1879, a telegram from the Porte was handed to the Egyptian Prime Minister. It was addressed to 'The ex-Khedive, Ismail Pasha'. For a moment, the Minister's nerve failed. Then he pulled himself together and entered the Khedive's study.

Without twitching a muscle, Ismail read the sentence of his deposition. Then he turned quietly to the Prime Minister.

'Send for Prince Tewfik', he said.

When his son entered, he stood up, walked across the room, and with a dignified gesture raised Tewfik's hand to his lips.

'I salute you, my Khedive' he said. Then placing his two hands on his shoulders, he kissed him on both cheeks with the words, 'May you be more successful than your father', and left the room.

'I shall be the first to call and inscribe my name in the books of the new sovereign of Egypt', he said to the Prime Minister outside. 'Now we will go and have a game of tric-trac.'

A few days later he boarded the yacht Mahroussa and sailed for Italy as his grandson would do seventy-three years later. His last act before leaving was to pocket the cash that was still in the Treasury.

Raymond Flower

Notes:

Ten years earlier, in January 1865, Lady Duff Gordon had already written (letters from Egypt 1863-1865): 'Last week the people were cussing Ismail in the streets of Aswan, and everyone talks aloud of what they think...the kurbash has been going on my neighbors backs and feet all the morning...the system of wholesale extortion and spoliation has reached a point beyond which it would be difficult to go.' Lucie Duff Gordon lived for several years at Luxor in a house built by the English Consul-General, Salt, on top of the Temple of Khem, and her observations are significant because she was the only English person who actually lived in the countryside and described what was going on. In 1867 Last Letters from Egypt) she said: I cannot describe the misery here now—every day some new tax. Every beast, camel, cow, sheep, donkey and horse is made to pay. The Fellaheen can no longer eat bread; they are living on barley meal mixed with water and raw green-stuff, vetches, etc...The people in Upper Egypt are running away by wholesale, utterly unable to pay the new taxes and do the work exacted. Even here (in Cairo) the beating for the year's taxes is awful.'

Queen Victoria offered Disraeli the Garter, a dukedom, and the settlement of a peerage on his brother or nephew. He declined everything except the Garter. Gladstone, however, was not so pleased and denounced the Cyprus convention as an 'insane covenant' and 'an act of duplicity'—to which Disraeli responded with his celebrated piece of invective, made at a public banquet, calling Gladstone 'a sophisticated rhetorician inebriated with the exuberance of his own verbosity', cf Blake's Disraeli pp 649-50.

Chapter 10

The Subduing of Arabi

Egyptians all. Awake,
Defend your faith and your land.
Your wealth is looted and
Your sons are nothing but slaves.
Your knowledge was the sun
That illuminated the world;
Today you are in eclipse...
               (Salih Magdi, *Divan*)

With his thin ascetic face, his stringy black beard, and the passion in his stomach, the slight, turbaned figure from Afghanistan was every inch a revolutionary. Night after night in Fashawi's coffee-house near Al Azhar, surrounded by an enraptured audience of poets, grammarians, students and journalists, Jamal al-Din al-Afghani crystallized their feelings into words.

His message was clear. It was to 'arouse the Moslems to strength and leadership, so that the Islamic community might catch up with the civilized nations of the world.' He was convinced that the native Egyptians had all the ingredients that make up a nation: a deep sense of religion, a language with its roots in the soil, and a character and customs which had been built up over the centuries. But, he maintained, they lacked a sense of pride; they had no thirst for adventure. 'From fear of death' he told his audience, 'you have succumbed to death. Years of submission...have made Egyptians purposeless, apathetic, timid, lacking in perseverance and unendurably humble.'

As the country's plight worsened in the last disastrous years of Ismail's rule, al-Afghani sowed the first strong seeds of nationalism, and indeed began a systematic attempt to incite youth against authority. Young patriots started littering the streets at night with anonymous sheets attacking the Khedive and the Turkish ruling class. Their frustrations found an outlet in verses such as those of Salih Magdi:

Your country has been hurled into the abyss
And why? To amuse Jasban.
Your money is squandered on pimps and prostitutes.
Normal men take a woman for a wife: he wants a million wives.
Normal men take a house for a living: he takes ninety.
O Egyptians, there is disgrace all around. Awake, awake!

Of the various students who studied regularly under al-Afghani, none was won over by the Sheikh's eloquence more than Mohammed Abdou. Later, when he had become the leading philosopher of his time, he described al-Afghani in almost mystical terms, as a saint and a deliverer. And when al-Afghani was finally arrested and expelled from the country, his last words on Egyptian soil were: 'I leave you Sheikh Mohammed Abdou. He is sufficient for Egypt.'

In September 1880, Mohammed Abdou was appointed editor of the official gazette, Al Waqa'i al-Misriyyah. Within a short time he managed to transform this dreary government organ into an instrument for guiding opinion, and, insisting on a high literary standard from contributors, gave an articulate and mature expression of the new generation of Egyptians. It was essential, he preached, that Egypt's internal reforms should be achieved by her own efforts. His yearning for change ranged from the idea of a dictatorship ('Should a benevolent despot arise in the East?') to an enunciation of the requirements for democracy. 'The first step towards a certain measure of freedom being the formation of rural councils,' he wrote. 'After a number of years, municipal councils would follow, provided that they be not instruments that are swayed this way and that, but sources of ideas and opinions. After that will follow representative parliaments.' When necessary, he did not hesitate to criticize the government itself. The army he described as commanded by 'feeble-minded' soldiers.

This was meat and drink to certain of the native Egyptian officers. Not only were they indignant at the behavior of the foreigners; they were exasperated by the blatant luxury of the Turkish ruling class, particularly the princes and landowners, and the favoritism that was quite openly shown to Turks and Circassians. When a humiliating defeat in Abyssinia was followed by Rivers Wilson's economy measure which put 2,500 officers on half pay and dismissed scores of others, and on top of all this Osman Rifki, a notoriously unpopular Turk, was made minister of war, their resentment boiled over. A group of young colonels had been meeting for some time in each other's houses, tentatively plotting to put an end to the Turkish favoritism in the army, and if necessary even to depose the Khedive. When news reached them one evening that they too were scheduled to be dismissed, they decided that their leader, Lieutenant-Colonel Ahmed Arabi,* should go directly to the Prime Minister with a petition.

The premier's reaction was hardly encouraging. Such insubordination, he told them roughly, was a hanging offence. Was their intention to change the ministry? And if so, he added with heavy irony, with whom did they intend to replace it? 'Is Egypt a barren woman who has but eight sons?' replied Arabi (alluding to the Prime Minister and the seven ministers of his cabinet).

Angrily the Prime Minister waved him out of his office, and the drama began.

A few days later the three colonels who had signed the petition were summoned to Kasr el Nil barracks, on the pretext of planning a procession for the wedding of one of the princesses. Once there, they were arrested and disarmed. A summary court martial began: Arabi always maintained that it was intended to put them on board a steamer lying outside and drop them quietly into the Nile with a weight on their feet. But the colonels had taken their precautions. When at a pre-arranged time they failed to emerge, the men of their regiments marched into the barracks and broke up the court martial. The Circassian generals had to beat an undignified retreat, Osman Rifki escaping through a window, and Arabi and his friends were able to march triumphantly back at the head of their troops.

And so, rather ponderously, but nevertheless dramatically, Ahmed Arabi made his bid to anticipate history. A typical fellah, tall, heavy-limbed and slow in his movements, he seemed, in the words of Wilfrid Blunt, 'to symbolize that massive bodily strength which is so characteristic of the laborious peasant of the lower Nile...there was a certain deliberation in his gestures which gave him the dignity one often sees in village sheikhs.' His eyes sometimes had an abstracted, dreamer's look, but when he smiled his heavy-plain face became 'illuminated as a dull landscape by the sun.' To the ruling Turks, Arabi was just another boorish fellah of the type they had dominated for centuries, and at first even the intellectual reformers of Al Azhar discounted him as a political force. But to his own peasant class he was one of themselves, a hero of their own mould.

For the revolution of 1881 was above all a native Egyptian movement, aimed against the Turkish 'palatocracy' which had ruined the country, and directing its hatred also against the Europeans after the Anglo-French control had come out on the side of the Khedive Tewfik. Ismail's attempts to turn the Nile valley into a part of Europe, and the increasing intervention of the European powers after his deposition had led to an instinctive coalition between the liberal politicians of the National Society, 'al-Jam'iyyah al-Wataniyya' and the officers of Egyptian stock in the army. Frustrated by the closure of the Chamber of Deputies—which had gradually become a platform for Egyptian nationalism—the nationalist politicians turned to the army as the only force which could preserve the country's liberties in the face of Europe and the Khedive. Thus Ahmed Arabi emerged as the first leader of the Egyptian nationalists. But his movement represented far more than just a temporary alliance between disaffected army officers and liberal politicians: it was the spark-point of a racial reawakening which drew its strength from the heart and soul of a persecuted, passive and fatalistic land.

At first, Tewfik temporized with the mutineers. He dismissed Osman Rifky and accepted their subsequent oath of loyalty. But the honeymoon between the Khedive and the colonels was brief. As soon as he dared, Tewfik appointed his brother-in-law as Minister of War, and transferred Arabi's battalion to Alexandria and the other two colonels to the provinces.

Arabi saw plainly that it was now or never. If they allowed themselves to be separated away from Cairo, it would be easy to bring them to heel. A quick bullet or a splash in the Nile was the best they could expect.

'I wrote a letter stating our demands and sent it to the Khedive' he recalls of the events which occurred on a September morning of 1881, 'saying we would march to Abdin Palace...to receive his answer. When the Khedive arrived...he found us occupying the square, the artillery and cavalry in front of the west entrance, and I with my troops in front of the main entrance...the Khedive called on me to dismount and I dismounted. He called on me to put up my sword and I put up my sword, but the officers, my friends, approached me to prevent treachery, about fifty in number, and some of them placed themselves between him and the palace.

'When I had delivered my message and made my three demands to the Khedive, he said "I am the Khedive, and shall do as I please." To which I replied, "We are not slaves and shall not from this day be treated as such." He said nothing more, but turned and went back to the palace.'

As a revolutionary, Arabi—from his own account at least—sounds mild enough.

Seen from the opposite side, through the eyes of Sir Auckland Colvin, the British controller, it was more than enough for the timorous Tewfik. Since early morning, Colvin had been urging him to take strong action against Arabi; but the Khedive, like an anxious hen, had spent the day clucking around from one detachment of the royal guard to another to reassure himself of their loyalty. Finally Colvin, a specialist in coping with tricky situations, practically manhandled him out.

'When Arabi presents himself,' he told the Khedive as they finally emerged from the palace, 'tell him to give you his sword, and to order his troops to disperse. Then go the round of the square and address each regiment separately, and give them the order to dismiss.'

The buildings around Abdin Square were crammed with onlookers. Arabi approached on horseback.

'Call on him to dismount' hissed Colvin to the faltering Tewfik.

'Iniz il!'

Arabi dismounted and came forward on foot, followed by a guard with fixed bayonets. The crowd held its breath.

'Now is your chance' whispered Colvin.

'But we are between four fires,' gasped Tewfik, 'we shall be killed!'

'Order him to sheath his sword.'

Arabi saluted and obeyed. Then he stated his demands: the dismissal of the ministers; the convocation of a representative chamber; the raising of the army to 18,000 men. The same evening, Tewfik agreed to them all.

Colvin's memorandum to the Foreign Office showed his own feelings on the matter. 'There seems no reason to believe that anyone but the officers themselves are concerned in the movement,' he wrote, 'It was a purely military demonstration. Nothing so much impressed me yesterday as their profound unconsciousness of the immense danger to themselves they are incurring...they are blinded to the unconsciousness of their act.'

Maybe, but Egypt woke up the following morning to discover that not merely a revolt but a revolution had taken place. 'Throughout Egypt a cry of jubilation arose such as for hundreds of years had not been heard on the Nile' wrote Wilfrid Blunt, 'and in the streets of Cairo men stopped each other, though strangers, to embrace and rejoice together at the astonishing new reign of liberty which had begun for them.'

Arabi was made Minister of War, under a Prime Minister of his own choice, and there could be no doubt that he was now the real power in Egypt. Towards the Khedive he professed perfect loyalty 'so long as he kept to his promises'. His own position he saw as being the representative of the army, which itself—as the sole national force standing between Egypt and its Turkish rulers—was the guardian of the people's interests. 'We soldiers' he explained, 'are in the position of those Arabs who answered the Caliph Omar, when, in old age, he asked whether the people were satisfied with his rule, whether he had walked straightly in the path of justice. "0 son of Al-Khatteb" they replied "thou hast indeed walked straight and we love thee. But thou knowest that we were at hand and ready, if thou hadst walked crookedly, to straighten thee with our swords".'

For all his good intentions, Arabi had no program beyond the general and rather idealistic aspirations of the nationalists. Towards the end of the year, therefore, Mohammed Abdou and Wilfrid Blunt drew up with him a document which was called the Program of the National Party of Egypt. This recognized the services rendered to Egypt by the Governments of England and France, and even acknowledged that all freedom and justice obtained in the past had been due to them. 'The National party recognizes European control as a necessity in our financial position, and the continuance of it as the best guarantee of our prosperity' it declared. 'We declare it as our hope gradually to redeem our country out of the hands of its creditors. Our object is, some day, to see Egypt entirely in Egyptian hands.'

This document was sent by Wilfrid Blunt to Gladstone, in the hope that with his well-known sympathy for young nationalists struggling for independence, he would give them his blessing. But the question was not as simple as all that. Wherever Gladstone's private sympathies might lie, there were outside pressures which could not be ignored. The Sultan was rumbling in Constantinople; the creditors were lobbying for action. And some horse-trading was being done with the French.

Faced with a Moslem revolt in Tunis and Algiers, Gambetta was sharpening his knives. He was alarmed at the pan-Arab character of the movement, and he saw the same influences at work in Egypt. England, he said, should join in a 'crusade of civilization', as he called it, to safeguard the status quo in Egypt—by which he meant, of course, the existing financial arrangements. (Through his Jewish origins, Gambetta was closely connected with the Rothschilds and others.) The form of intervention he had in mind was that the English should send a fleet to Alexandria, while the French landed troops.

Whitehall, on the other hand, was anxious to renew the commercial treaty with France, which was about to expire. Sir Charles Dilke, who was conducting negotiations, cheerfully told Gambetta that he was quite ready to 'trade Egypt for his commercial treaty'.

Had Gambetta not fallen shortly afterwards as a result of an adverse vote on quite another matter, the French might have invaded the Delta and the history of Egypt been radically different. As it was, Dilke got his Treaty, and Gambetta his crusade—in the shape of a joint Note. This stated flatly that the two governments 'considered the maintenance of the Khedive on the throne...as alone able to guarantee the order and prosperity of Egypt', and that they intended to 'guard by their united efforts against all cause of complication, internal or external, which might menace the existing order in Egypt.'

What Gambetta meant by this was clear: an expeditionary force was already being formed up at Toulon. What Gladstone meant was anyone's guess, since he ambiguously added a postscript that 'HMG must not be considered as committing themselves thereby to any particular mode of action', but the depressing similarity to Mollet's bludgeoning and Eden's vacillating under such similar circumstances seventy-four years later is only too obvious. Except that in 1882 both Britain and France were in the high noon of their imperial power.

In Egypt, the effect was disastrous. The morning the text became known, Wilfrid Blunt called on Arabi at the ministry. For the first time, and indeed the only time he could recall, he found Arabi in a fury. 'His face was like a thundercloud, and there was a peculiar gleam in his eye.' The declaration that English and French policy were one, snapped the fellah soldier, meant that just as France had invaded Tunis, so England would invade Egypt. 'Let them come' he added grimly, 'every man and child in Egypt will fight them. It is contrary to our principles to strike the first blow—but we shall know how to return it.'

A big bang was obviously not far off. In Cairo the rift between Egyptian revolutionaries and Turkish palatocracy was stirring up the dust as grittily as any khamseen (that uncomfortable south wind which percolates into every pore) and apprehensive Europeans were expecting a campaign of atrocities at any moment. In London, the Press began a concerted blast against Arabi, painting him as a blood-thirsty mutineer and a treacherous fanatic. When Englishmen read over their toast and marmalade that Arabi, now a Pasha, had stamped down an assassination plot by some Turkish officers, and was raising fresh battalions for national resistance against British intervention, it took little to convince them that another Indian mutiny and a British massacre was being prepared. 'Arabi...should be blown from a gun', preached a country clergyman. An elderly peer proposed going out with a party of big game hunters to hang the scoundrel. Wilfrid Blunt found that he was always 'quarrelling fearfully about Egypt' with his friends, and he did, indeed, put Arabi's case personally to Gladstone.

But not all public opinion was unfavorable to the Egyptians. The Anti-Aggression League published a circular pointing out that while it was not the duty of private citizens to interfere in public affairs, they should 'insist that the government should not drag the nation to the verge of war and embroil it with a foreign people without adequate cause', and an ex-governor of Ceylon sent a lengthy letter to *The Times* pleading for fair play for the nationalists, saying: 'I believe the leader Arabi to be honest and patriotic...I believe that no policy can be more clear than for England to support the present Egyptian government, and to be sorry for our own sakes if it fails.' In fact, as plots and rumors and incidents multiplied, feeling built up for and against Arabi almost as much in England as in Egypt. Finally the Powers resorted to the traditional ploy: a joint fleet under the command of Sir Beauchamp Seymour was sent to Alexandria, and Arabi was told to resign and leave the country.

On 27 May the nationalist ministry complied, meekly enough, only to find itself re-instated by a spontaneous public rising in Cairo. With the normal machinery of government in pieces, in the sense that cooperation with the Khedive and the Palace men was virtually at an end, Arabi became not only a military dictator, but a national hero as well. The Cairo Press screamed for a regeneration of Islam, and the independence of Egypt; the European community, panic-stricken, fled to Alexandria and the safety of the allied warships. Engulfed by frenzied acclamations wherever he went, Arabi began to prepare for war. The fuse was now lit: the explosion was purely a matter of time. On 10 June, savage riots broke out in Alexandria.

In 1882, the city was more Greek than Egyptian, inhabited by large colonies of Mediterranean business people, many of them money-lenders. Little love was lost between the Europeans and the Egyptians, and the arrival of the allied fleet to protect European interests naturally heightened the ill-feeling. In this charged atmosphere, a street incident between a Maltese and a donkey-boy over a piaster was enough. An hour later the exasperation of the city blew up. Mobs rushed through the streets, screaming and looting: by the end of the day, when Arabi firmly restored order, several hundred people were either dead or wounded. The British consul was seriously hurt, and the Greek and Italian consuls roughed up. It only went to show, said the wiseacres in Whitehall, that Egypt was in a total state of anarchy. Something drastic would have to be done; the diplomatic defeat of the Foreign Office was only too glaring. Arabi had been ordered to leave and he had not gone. Instead, he had organized the riots and then put them down as an ostentatious demonstration of his strength. He was gaining a reputation in the East at Britain's expense. If he were allowed to go on, there might be a pan-Islam revolt in India. The position was intolerable. Strong measures were absolutely necessary.

By now Gambetta had resigned, and the French were back-pedalling. It was up to England on her own. Torn between his private convictions and the jingoism of his colleagues, Gladstone did his best to avoid taking a decision. He decided to leave it to the man on the spot'.

In Alexandria harbor, Sir Beauchamp Seymour's guns were alert. An elderly Swiss resident remembers watching the admiral appear on deck at dawn each morning somewhat unmartially clad in a jersey, his bare feet emerging from his pajamas, to scan the Egyptian fortifications. 'Sir Beauchamp' said the Berner-bunder crustily (as a landlubber, he could hardly be expected to know quarterdeck protocol) 'was playing *Au Jupiter tournant,* and frightening everyone with his oaths'. In fact, the admiral was waiting until all Europeans had been evacuated before blowing the fortification to bits.

On 10 July he sent an ultimatum to Arabi: surrender the fort within twenty four hours, or we fire. To which the Khedive, prompted by Arabi, replied with a polite but firm protest, before withdrawing from the danger area (where he spent the next two days debating whether his honor permitted him to take refuge on a British man-o'-war which might, of course, be sunk). Foreign shipping in the harbor got up steam and put out to sea, ceremoniously saluting the British flagship, while the admiral's band played the appropriate national anthem as each ship sailed past. The last to leave were the French.

At dawn the following morning, the bombardment began.

From Fort Agami (where the local jet-set now have their week-end pads) to Silsileh (where the palace of the Ptolomys once stood and the Alexandria Hilton is scheduled to be sited) the shells pounded down. As energetically as they could, the fifteen forts fired back. But there was never any doubt about the outcome. 'The Egyptians fought with determined bravery, replying to the hot fire...from our heavy guns until they must have been quite decimated', Seymour reported to the Admiralty. By five-thirty in the afternoon, more than 2,000 Egyptians were dead, and the forts were a shambles.

Not only the forts: Alexandria itself was in flames. Fires started by the shells had fanned out, and the mobs had taken over, feverishly burning and looting everything in sight. Soon the whole European quarter was burning. Bands of cut-throats rushed from building to building, ripping out everything they could lay their hands on, and then spreading the flames with paraffin-soaked cotton. Early the next morning, a melancholy procession of carts started rumbling towards the cemeteries, piled full of bodies, each followed by a crowd of wailing women-folk. The Greek consul was the first to come ashore after the bombardment had ceased. 'At each step we were afraid of being engulfed under the ruins of burning houses which were crashing into the road with a tremendous noise' he recalls. 'All the shops had been looted and sacked, and the road was full of empty cases and boxes which the pillagers had abandoned as they went. Five or six houses in this road were full of holes from the cannon-balls of the British fleet.' Eye-witnesses were aghast at the extent of the damage. 'Many of the principal streets were quite impassable', declared the English manager of the Alexandria waterworks. 'Even to a person knowing the town well it was not at all easy to find one's way around.' Almost the only thing in the center of the town which remained unchanged, he said, was the statue of Mohammed Ali. Otherwise it was nothing but blackened ruins. Even the trees had been burnt.

The bombardment resulted in a clear-cut rift between the Palace party and the Nationalists. Until now, Arabi had been acting, at least nominally, under the Khedive's authority. But when from his rooftop in Ramleh, Tewfik saw for himself that the British meant business, he lost no further time in placing his person under British protection. Guarded by a company of Marines, he issued a proclamation declaring Arabi a rebel, and sat back to wait for his subjects to be defeated.

Arabi, meanwhile, had withdrawn with the army to a position near Kafr el Dawar, which now became the headquarters of the nationalist regime. Most of his time seems to have been taken up with receptions. A continuous stream of Ulema, sheikhs and notabilities of all kinds flowed into the large tent which had once belonged to Said and had been presented to Arabi by the viceroy's widow. Ninet, the Swiss, who was there in a Red Cross capacity, noticed visitors from as far afield as the Hedjaz and Yemen. Presumably Arabi hoped to enlist their support. But although during August a British force advancing under General Allison from Alexandria was repulsed, remarkably little preparation was made against the attack of the main forces under General Wolseley. Arabi had been warned that the British might come through the Canal and outflank his position. But when de Lesseps promised that the Canal would be kept neutral, he believed him and refused to give the final order to block it until too late. This was his great mistake. If Arabi had blocked the Canal as he intended to do' Wolseley went on record as saying, 'we should be still at the present moment on the high seas blockading Egypt. Twenty four hours saved us.'

Ninet, wandering around the Egyptian positions during the hot months of July and August, was struck, in fact, by the nonchalance and rather fatalistic attitude of the fellah army. Beyond building a few earthwork defenses, the Egyptians took little initiative. True, they did sometimes slip behind the British lines at night—but only to see what they could lift. Once they came back with some hussar uniforms and spiked white helmets, roaring with laughter as they dressed themselves up in them. What amused them most was the idea that the

British removed their clothes to sleep. But on the whole they spent the summer nights listening to the Koran or squatting in a circle telling jokes.

On 12 September, their laughter was abruptly shattered. Stealing up by night through more than seven miles of pitch darkness, General Wolseley's army, which had come up through the Suez Canal, caught them completely by surprise. The battle of Tel el Kebir, which determined the fate of Egypt for two generations or more, was the briefest on record. 'We fell on them like a thunderbolt on a man asleep' recounts Sir William Butler. It was all over in thirty five minutes.' Probably the first the Egyptians knew of an attack was the sudden onrush as men of the Black Watch, their heads down, charged the earthworks with fixed bayonets. Although taken unawares, the defenders fired back furiously. 'The 42nd...sprang into the trenches like tigers' recalls a British NCO, 'while the bullets were whirring, whizzing and pinging like bees when they are casting.' For a brief moment it was bayonet to bayonet. The Egyptians fought like maniacs. 'So earnest were the Egyptian artillerymen' marvels General Allison, 'that they were actually bayoneted from the rear while still working their guns'. Then suddenly, through the dust and confusion and noise, the British cavalry came galloping in. This settled the matter. Almost before it had begun, the battle was over, and Arabi's army was no more than a mob, streaming across the desert in every direction.

Arabi himself was asleep when the firing began. Without even stopping to put on his boots, he flung himself on to a horse and, commandeering a steam engine at Bilbeis, reached Cairo in the fireman's compartment in time to witness, if not actually take part in, the celebrations which the Khedive gave in honor of the victorious British army. 'Tewfik in state takes the salute from the 18,000 British who have replaced him on the throne', reported *The Times*, 'while Arabi from his prison window in the same square, watches the defile of the army which scattered to the winds, in twenty minutes, his ambitious labor of the year.' Lavishly Tewfik heaped honors on the British generals. Less lavish was his treatment of his own army. In exactly four words, its existence ceased. *'L'Armée Egyptienne est dissolue'* decreed Tewfik. Briefer than this, he could not have been. What Wolseley accomplished in the field, Tewfik consummated in the orderly room. Indeed, he did more. He tried to extinguish the very nationality of his people. Before long the nationalist movement would be almost forgotten and the Egyptians would have accepted, fatalistically, to be ruled by the British. Meanwhile, shopkeepers hastily replaced pictures of Arabi by ones of Tewfik. The Coldstream Guards took over the Citadel. Europeans in Cairo and Alexandria went mad with joy.

As for the Egyptians themselves, 'God knows what they feel', shrugged Baron de Kusel. But Tigrane Pasha, the Armenian under-secretary for Foreign Affairs, voiced the sense of defeat and futility. 'We drift down the stream like a log', he said sadly. It was left to Al-Afghani and Mohammed Abdou, in exile in

Paris, to keep the flame of nationalism alight with their periodical 'al-Urwah al Wuthqa'.

Since Napoleon had jerked the country from its lethargy eight decades previously, Egypt had known both regeneration and frustration: Mohammed Ali had made it a Mediterranean power, but at the expense of the fellah; in sixteen years of feverish activity Ismail had consolidated his grandfather's ambitions, but his mismanagement of foreign 'financial imperialism' had precipitated a European occupation. For several months Arabi had been the spokesman and the symbol of an Egypt that hungered for justice and dignity. 'The collapse of his movement when faced with British power, and the distorted way in which it was represented by the European press of the time, have perhaps made him seem a smaller figure than he was' affirms J. M. Ahmed. Perhaps the most striking feature of the 1882 events was not so much that the army had emerged as a revolutionary force, but that it was simply the spearhead of a collective movement to which the British presence would deny fruition for a further seventy years. This foiled revolution was a preface for the 1919 upheavals and Gamal Abdel Nasser's final break-through in 1952.

Raymond Flower

Note:

Although traditionally written Arabi in English, in the Arab world he is known as Orabi.

Chapter 11

Aldershot on the Nile

The Victorians were a preposterous lot, of course, with their 'Piccadilly weepers', their fads, and their curiously over-stuffed conventions, but no doubt today's Beautiful People will look just as ridiculous in fifty years' time. So it is only fair to consider Lord Cromer, the British representative, in the context of his age, and undoubtedly in a hero-worshiping era he was every bit of a Great Victorian, a capable administrator, and a portentous pro-consul. But even as a young official in India, as Major Evelyn Baring, he had achieved a reputation for rudeness and was known to his colleagues as 'Over-bearing'. Once installed in the Residency at Cairo, and 'hiding dictatorial powers under the modest title of Consul-General' as H. A. L. Fisher describes it, Cromer quickly made it clear that he was a no nonsense man in a country where a little nonsense, or at any rate a few 'simpatico' gestures, might have acted as balm to wounded national feelings. In the Orient, an almost adolescent susceptibility goes hand-in-hand with the dignity of age-long culture. An injury may be forgiven; an insult never. Cromer, with his frosty, disapproving look, his walrus whiskers covering a tight mouth, and the soul-corseting smugness of a Victorian in an alien land, seemed to symbolize the patronizing superiority of an industrious and mercenary West over the untidy, easy-going and holy East. Yet for all his lack of tact, Cromer was an honest public servant doing his best in a difficult job. Born of a well-known banking family, he had been trained in the inner ring of international finance and it was with a money man's expertise that he now sat down to tackle what Lord Milner described as 'the race against bankruptcy'. The main reason for the British occupation was to see that Egypt paid its debts. It was, to all intents and purposes, a receivership, and the skill with which Cromer handled the financial situation paved the way for a minor economic miracle which pulled Egypt out of the red, despite a good deal of under cover maneuvering by the French to obstruct the recovery. Up until the *Entente Cordiale* of 1904 French policy was so much at daggers drawn with the English that, although owning two thirds of the debt, France was prepared to force Egypt into bankruptcy merely to undermine the British occupation—which was all the more resented in Paris because it was so obviously a self-inflicted wound.

However, by the end of 1886 the Budget was balanced (admittedly through some legerdemain with the contra-accounts) and the 'convalescence of a hard-working people after an imported sickness' as George Young neatly puts it, had begun to take place. Trade was again flourishing, and the boom, supported by British bayonets, brought Europe to Egypt. In the nineties, wintering in Cairo became the smart thing to do. Shepheard's, Mena House, the Gezira Palace (which Ismail had built for Eugenie) and a score of other great hotels were thronged with royalty and pace-makers of Europe, along with quite a number of ordinary people intent on escaping the English winter. It was fashionable to take a villa on Gezira Island or charter a houseboat on the Nile; alternatively one could be conveyed to Upper Egypt by Mr. Thomas Cook, who had begun to organize trips up the Nile. (In doing this, of course, he was cashing in on an ancient tradition. Tourists in Greek and Roman times had left their marks on the Colossus of Memnon at Thebes, and on the polished granite of Abu Simbel. So that Mr. Cook's guests were following much the same program as Herodotus and Strabo had done). Undoubtedly for anyone who had a month or two to spare, there could be no pleasanter region in winter than the Upper Nile, and the temples and tombs offered an excellent excuse for long rides and picnics in the desert. Back in Cairo was the Khedival Sporting Club which in due course as 'Gezira' became the finest sporting club in the world. One could dance all night and as dawn came up ride out to Mena House for an early morning swim followed by a large breakfast before going out into the desert to shoot; and after a siesta, spend the afternoon at the Club in preparation for dressing for dinner and starting the whole thing over again. All this pleasant routine, of course, hardly added to the wealth of Egypt or benefited the Egyptians who were not so much cold-shouldered as quite simply ignored. Although a great deal of money was spent during the season, most of it returned to Europe as dividends to the tourist agencies, steamship companies and hotels run on international capital. The hotels were almost entirely staffed by Swiss managers and German waiters, and the money spent in the fashionable Cairo shops went into the pockets of Greeks, Italians and French, but not the Egyptians.

Indeed, most of the visitors who wintered in Cairo imagined that Egypt belonged to Great Britain. With Lord Cromer as the Cromwell of Cairo, and British uniforms everywhere, they could hardly be blamed for thinking so. Somewhere in the background, they knew, there was the Khedive, but it was barely apparent that—subject of course to a shadowy control from his suzerain in Turkey—the Khedive was the sovereign ruler of an autonomous state. Yet officially this was the position. Whitehall was quite clear about it. Britain, in the official British view, had bombarded Alexandria merely to save the lives of Europeans threatened by a military rabble. She had sent Lord Wolseley with an army to 'restore the authority of the Khedive' which had been weakened by the revolt of the mutinous colonels. She had been restoring, or maintaining the authority of the Khedive ever since. The regiments stationed at the Citadel and in the Ismailiah Palace on the Nile were not really a British garrison, they were the remains of an army of occupation to enable the Khedive to preserve public order. To have simply withdrawn after the Arabi revolt, in the eyes of London, would have been to have left Egypt to 'stew in its own juice' which, Whitehall felt sure, would have led to further outbreaks, revolts or revolutions and another European intervention of one sort or another. So Britain neither annexed Egypt nor retired. 'The Anglo-Saxon' explained Lord Cromer 'asserted his native genius by working a system which according to every canon of political thought was unworkable'. While officially not interfering with the liberty of the Egyptian government, in practice he made quite sure that the Khedive and the Egyptian ministers did exactly what he told them to do. He apparently found nothing odd about occupying a part of the Turkish Empire with British troops and at the same time punctiliously avoiding to infringe on the legitimate rights of the Sultan. To Lord Cromer, it was simply acting with all the practical common sense (and total absence of any fixed plan) which distinguished most of the British Imperial policy.

Thus British officers in the Egyptian regiments and in the Egyptian War Office were not actually in British service at all. They were temporarily, 'lent' to the Khedive to assist him in the training and discipline of his own army. In the same way the British civil servants were serving under the Khedive to give their aid in the conduct of his administration and the management of his finances. They were employed and paid by the Khedive, not by England. The Khedive remained nominally the supreme power in the state. Every administrative decree or act of legislation was supposed to emanate from him.

In short, to use Cromer's own words, the British did not govern Egypt; they only governed the governors of Egypt. It was a pretty fine point. Each public department had an Egyptian minister as its chief. These officials received not only the pay, but also the perquisites of their office. A visitor would find the minister seated in a large office surrounded by secretaries and ushers. Having drunk a cup of coffee with the Pasha, he would be conducted to a much smaller room where a harassed-looking Englishman sat at a desk covered with files, giving hurried commands to clerks and messengers. This Englishman was the adviser—nominally the subordinate—of the minister, employed to assist him in his work and to supply such good advice as he might consider necessary. He would never command. He would only say 'I think it is advisable that your Excellency should issue this order...' or I hear that such and such has happened and I hope your Excellency will think it proper to do such and such to put it right...' If His Excellency failed to comply, of course, the adviser would report the matter to the Residency who would promptly bring pressure on the Khedive, so it was hardly surprising that the Egyptian ministers resigned themselves to smoking cigarettes and reading French novels in their stately offices, only occasionally rousing themselves to sign, without even reading, the documents prepared by their English mentors.

This elaborate fiction, comparable to the ingenuity of the Hadji Nasredin, who carried his donkey over the stream on his back so that it should not throw him off its back into the water, was conducted largely to avoid a head-on collision with Turkey, and also for the sake of *bella figura* with the Powers, but it was hardly calculated to appeal to the Egyptians, least of all the Khedive. Tewfik, submissive to the end, died suddenly in 1892, and his son, Abbas Hilmy, who had been schooled in Vienna to believe in the divine power of princes, succeeded to a shadow throne at the age of eighteen, and was immediately in conflict with the Residency. 'The Khedive is going to be very *Egyptian*' commented Cromer in a letter to Lord Salisbury barely a month after Abbas's accession, and he lost no time in publicly humiliating the young Khedive. To a man of Cromer's mentality—and Wilfred Blunt says he had very little real knowledge of the East beyond what filtered through the official papers on his desk—it was more important to clip the Khedive's wings than to cultivate his friendship, so that for the remaining years of Cromerism, Abbas was reduced to embittered palace intrigue with the Sultan (who was meditating war with England) and backstairs conspiracies with anti-Christian movements in Morocco and Macedonia. Sir Eldon Gorst, who followed Cromer at the Residency, did his best to patch up the quarrel, but although he established a personal friendship with the Khedive, he was unable to eradicate the deep-rooted antiBritish feeling which Cromer had aroused.*

The same autocratic ways began to stir up hatred among the Egyptians themselves. It would be idle for colonizers to expect to be popular: they think of their jobs as the VDO or the Peace Corps may think of theirs, as interesting, dangerous, rather underpaid and very much in the general interest, but they do not expect to be thanked. Yet it should be remembered that for the first years of British rule the man in the street had little else but gratitude for the English. He recalled the miseries he had suffered under Ismail. The older fellahin had not forgotten the Kurbash and the corvée called at the sound of a whistle, with twenty lashes for whoever arrived last. Such abuses had now been remedied. Things were better, prosperity was round the corner. But it soon became apparent that any golden age would be strictly for the Europeans and their hangers-on: there would be no room in the bandwagon for the Egyptians themselves. On the contrary, social distinction was becoming wider, the rich were becoming richer, and Masri Effendi was being relegated to the position of a second or even third-rate citizen. Moreover, despite repeated assurances that the British occupation was only temporary (and at a conservative count there were forty such assurances in 1883 alone) the suspicion was growing that El Lord in his study at the Residency was methodically planning for the British to stay for good, and for Egypt to be turned into a sort of junior India.* Underground at first, in the cafés around El Azhar, and then more boldly as it felt the support of the people behind it, the nationalist movement which had been dormant for nearly twenty years, began once more to be heard. Mustapha Kamal, through his newspaper *El Lewa*, started to voice the feelings of a new generation and to canvass for support in France.

Reading his tracts today, they seem mild enough in tone, and harp on subjects which have long since been accepted as obvious. In *Le Peril Anglais: consequences de l' occupation de l'Egypt par l'Angleterre* for instance, which was published in Paris in 1899, he declares: 'People ignore the real significance of Egypt, its geographic position...The Power which becomes the absolute master of the Nile Valley becomes virtual sovereign of Africa...the Holy Land and the Red Sea. The Suez Canal is an integral part of Egypt and commands the route to India, China and Australia...England already controls the Mediterranean and it is vital to the Powers of Europe that she should not command also the trade routes of Africa...Thus the British occupation of Egypt is a menace to other Powers in Europe.'

But to Cromer this was anarchy, dangerous vituperative nonsense which only went to prove that Egyptians were not to be trusted on their own, and that Britain's mission in Egypt could not be ended in the foreseeable future. It conditioned likewise his priorities where public expenditure was concerned. Thus, while he was quite prepared to approve a number of development and irrigation schemes, including the great new dam at Assouan, which materially improved the country's agricultural production,* he allotted as little as possible for education—on the principle, presumably, that since Egyptians could not be sent to a public school *á l'Anglaise,* it was better to keep them on the land, where they could produce raw materials economically for the textile factories in Manchester.

Cromer's failure, in fact, was on the human level—a level from which the discomforted Arabi seemed at least to have been striving—which means, as anyone from the East will understand, giving proper importance to the things for which an Egyptian cares most: his religion, his family, his village, his people, his country, his personal dignity, all of which Cromer not so much neglected as totally ignored. Although he ruled Egypt for twenty-five years, longer than most pharaohs, Cromer barely ventured out of the Residency beyond a state visit to the Palace to rap the Khedive over the knuckles, or to patronize the races at Gezira. He ruled from his study according to the dictates of the balance sheet, and it is unlikely, in his heart of hearts, that he ever thought of the Egyptians as people at all.

The emotional gulf between Cromerism and Egypt was finally brought into focus by the Denshawi incident. On a hot June day in 1906 some British officers out shooting were suddenly surrounded by an angry crowd of villagers who objected to the pigeons—of tremendous importance in their meager diet—being shot. In the uproar, a gun went off, wounding a woman, and the officers had to run for it. One of them, who had been hit on the head, fell dead on the road from shock or sunstroke, and angry soldiers from the dead officer's unit seized a young villager, who had nothing to do with the matter but had come over to help, and clubbed him to death. The foreign communities in Cairo panicked, imagining that a general massacre was imminent, and a special tribunal of three British officials and two Egyptians condemned four of the villagers to death, three of them to fifty lashes each, and a number of others to long terms of hard labor. Cromer confirmed the sentences and Egypt simmered with hatred. The positive achievements of two decades were forgotten; from this point onwards most Egyptians were in sympathy with the nationalists, and felt themselves to be resistance fighters, against a common enemy. Even so, Cromer was undismayed. In his valedictory address the following year, he catalogued the benefits of British rule with which Egypt had so providentially been blessed, and dismissed the nationalists with contempt. 'I shall deprecate any brisk change and any violent new departure', he declared. 'More especially...I shall urge that this wholly spurious and manufactured movement in favor of a rapid development of parliamentary institutions should be treated for what it is worth; and gentlemen, let me add that it is worth very little indeed'.

The following day he was driven through empty streets to the station and his retirement in England, which characteristically enough he spent opposing the suffragettes. Egypt's comment on the exit of the latest of her foreign autocrats was in the verse of the poet Showky:

> *Were you born Pharaoh to govern the Nile,*
> *Or despot by conquest of the land of Egypt,*
> *Deferring to no one, never answerable?*
> *Master by might of our necks in servitude*
> *Did you try the path to our hearts meanwhile?*
> *At your departure the land gasped in thankfulness*
> *Freed from a pestilence too nearly fatal...*

Nothing illustrated better the change from Cromerism than the state reception held in the summer of 1907. The Khedive's power might be insubstantial, but the trappings of royalty were carried on with as much pomp as in any European court, and, sweating gently in its regalia of official millinery, the Diplomatic Corps filed slowly past the Khedivial throne and made its bow to His Highness. Envoys went in order of seniority of appointment. First, an elderly Dutch shipping agent, the representative of the Queen of the Netherlands; then the others in due order: Spanish, Austrian, Russian, German, and the rest down to the smaller states which maintained diplomatic contacts. Very nearly last of all came a slightly built Englishman with round gold spectacles. Looking as unobtrusive as it is possible to do so in a lace coat and gold-braided trousers, he took his place far down the line, with Swiss and Belgians in front of him, and only a Swede of still more junior standing than himself behind. Anyone who did not know might have thought him a person of no importance. Yet this was Sir Eldon Gorst, successor to Lord Cromer, the virtual ruler of Egypt, with far more authority and power than the Khedive and all his ministers put together.

Gorst was an exponent of the informal approach, the soft sell. Whereas a tophatted Cromer had swept through Cairo in a carriage with out-riders and running sayces in front, his open-shirted successor drove himself around in a two-seater Wolseley—one of the first batch of cars to be imported by the Cairo Motor Company—and chatted in the vernacular with the bystanders. But this change of approach by its agent did not herald a shift in British policy. The mixture remained as before; it was simply the wrapping that had been changed.

Yet Sir Eldon's easy ways, which puzzled the extremists and infuriated the British community, were very nearly successful in extinguishing the anti-British flare-up in Egypt. Within a short while he had made friends with the Khedive, gratified the intelligentsia by sponsoring the new Cairo university (which Cromer had vetoed the previous year) set free the Denshawi prisoners, and taken the steam out of the nationalists by detaching the most able from their ranks and appointing them to public office. At his instigation, the first Egyptian Prime Minister was sworn in—which by an unhappy incident contributed more than anything else to bring this brave experiment in conciliation into disrepute. Previous prime ministers during the occupation had all been of foreign extraction: Cherif Pasha and Mustapha Pasha Fahmy were Turks, Nubar was an Armenian and Riaz a Jew. But Boutros Pasha Ghali, a great public figure in the country, was a Copt, and moreover the man who had presided over the Denshawi trial. So when Gorst referred to Boutros as 'the first genuine Egyptian who has ever risen to the highest position in his country', which, from the Moslem point of view was more aggravating than accurate, he seemed to be deliberately driving a wedge between the nationalistically minded Moslems and the co-operative Copts. To the nationalists, burning for a break-through like the young Turks in Constantinople, it was a slap in the face, and when Boutros showed his desire to promote European interests by approving a proposal to extend the Suez Canal Company's concession for a further period in return for a higher share in the profits, the nationalist press and Egyptian opinion as a whole went up in arms. Two days later, Boutros was assassinated.

It was now the turn for European opinion to boil over with indignation. Through his attempts to allow Egyptians a say in their own affairs, and by steadily replacing British officials by Copts, it was felt that Gorst had encouraged a dangerous situation to develop. European lives and property were in jeopardy. Even Theodore Roosevelt, holidaying in Egypt, added his voice to the rest. 'Govern, or get out' he growled. But by now Sir Eldon himself was in hospital, dying of cancer. Few people realized at the time the value of what this quiet little man had been trying to do for Egypt. But the Khedive himself traveled all the way to England to say goodbye to his friend, and Sir Ronald Storrs wrote an epitaph to his efforts when he said: 'He had fought his fight, and where the world saw failure he had succeeded.'

In Whitehall's view, however, the time for tact was over, and a Gauleiter was needed back in Egypt. So, upright, stiff and gleaming, with the same pale blue eyes and formidable mustachios which later were to glare down from recruiting posters, Lord Kitchener of Khartoum emerged from Cairo station on a November day in 1910, and the splendor of his cavalcade, the shine and glitter of the escort, the red and gold of the running sayces, were calculated to persuade any Egyptian, nationalist or otherwise, that Ramses and Alexander and Napoleon all rolled into one had arrived. Perhaps the ex-sapper officer imagined that they had. Privately, he had been lobbying for India, and the vice-regal state he imposed at the British Residency—which suddenly burst out in a rash of scarlet liveries, a service of gold plate, and a new ballroom—were possibly to compensate for the disappointment at being fobbed off with Egypt.

The morning of his arrival coincided with the declaration of war on Turkey by Italy. Since what remained of the Egyptian army was still nominally under the suzerainty of the Sultan, who might reasonably be expected to have it at his disposal for operations against the Italians who were invading Tripoli, it was immediately made plain that while Egypt might still keep up the fiction of being *de jure* part of the Ottoman dominions, *de facto* the country was very much part of the British Empire.

By the same token, a flood of decrees—a criminal conspiracy act, a press censorship act and a school discipline act among them—gave the extremists a clear warning of the manner which the new satrap was intending to deal with any trouble. Within a matter of days, prominent nationalists found themselves interned on the flimsiest of excuses under the 'exile act' (which was originally intended to do with brigandage). For writing a few lines of introduction to a book of nationalist verse, for instance, their leader, Farid Bey, was sentenced to a stiff term of imprisonment; while the editor of a literary review which spoke out of turn was chased as far as Constantinople and brought back by Kitchener for trial. Even co-operative nationalists fared little better: Saad Zagloul was dismissed from his job and Soufani Bey—a prominent moderate in the National Assembly—was prosecuted for insisting on a constitution. Nor was the Khedive himself given much latitude; there was no room in Egypt for two bosses. Understandably, the nationalists were cowed and went underground, while Abbas Hilmy was reduced to playing with dubious commercial ventures and arguing with the Ulemas to recognize his new wife, who—as everyone in Cairo knew—had started her career in a night-club in Vienna.

Even Kitchener soon realized that this return to the bleaker forms of Cromerism and police-state coercion was a negative way of dealing with the situation in Egypt, and the harshness of his early actions was balanced to some extent by his efforts to improve conditions for the fellahin, and his genuine affection for the land. Egypt, after all, had given him his chance. It was here that he had risen, like Mohammed Ali, from obscurity to a world reputation as Kitchener of Khartoum (a matter which is dealt with in the chapter on the Sudan) and, like Mohammed Ali, he seems to have understood the workings of the Egyptian mind.

For, along with great organizing ability, Kitchener had a theatrical streak, which enabled him to realize how important it was for success in the Orient to be considered a personage, so that whereas Cromer was an all-powerful name hidden behind the walls of the British Agency, Kitchener was a figurehead that everyone could see.

'He made progresses through the provinces, receiving and replying to petitions in the vernacular with the condescension of an Oriental autocrat' says George Young. 'His own mind had shaped itself into that baffling blend of despotic decision and diplomatic duplicity peculiar to Oriental princes'. His Arabic was often incomprehensible, but he knew how to play to his audience. 'He put his hands on my shoulders' an old sheikh told Sir Arthur Weigall, 'and said to me: "Am I not your father? Will a father ever forget his children?"'

In many ways he was as good as his word, and his five-feddan law, making it illegal to foreclose on land less than five acres in area, together with the creation of an agricultural bank, saved many fellahin from the clutches of the moneylender, and gave a new sense of security to agrarian life. A ministry of Agriculture was formed, and enormous drainage and irrigation projects started which enabled the cotton crop in particular to be greatly extended. Initiatives such as these, together with a fresh constitution in 1913 which gave some degree of power to the provincial municipalities, and a new legislative assembly, brought many Egyptians round to an appreciation of Kitchener's regime despite its brutal undertones. It is something of a paradox that Kitchener, in private life notorious for being morose, surly, and impossibly rude to everyone around him, especially when he had had too much to drink, should in his heavy-handed way have managed to put himself across to the Egyptians with such success that when war broke out in 1914 relations between Britain and Egypt were better than they had been at any time since the occupation.

Raymond Flower

Notes:

'British officials, particularly as they became more numerous, were not invariably efficient and even less invariably tactful...The Anglo-Indian tradition, imported into Egypt, of regarding "Orientals" as inferior beings, deficient in moral sense, unamenable to kindness, and only responsive to a "firm hand", inhibited any mutual feelings of sympathy between British officials and their Egyptian colleagues.' John Marlowe, Cromer in Egypt p 285

Lord Salisbury, who had taken over the Foreign Office in January 1887, wrote to Sir Henry Drummond-Wolff: 1 heartily wish we had not gone into Egypt...but the national or acquisitional feeling has been aroused; it has tasted the flesh-pots and will not let them go.' Lady Gwendolen Cecil, Life of Robert, Marquess of Salisbury Vol IV p 41.

Sir Colin Scott-Moncrieff rehabilitated the Barrage north of Cairo and master-minded a number of irrigation improvements throughout the country which resulted in a steady increase in Egypt's agricultural productivity. Even more spectacular, the Assouan Dam, completed in 1903 on the design of Sir William Willcocks, at a cost of approximately £3,500,000 enabled part of the Nile flood water to be stored for irrigation purposes, and converted at least a quarter of a million acres to perennial irrigation, yielding two and even three crops a year.

Chapter 12

War and Rebellion

The war changed the face of Europe, but in Egypt it merely shed the pretences and diplomatic niceties and recognized what had for so long been obvious—that Egypt had become part of the British dominions by simple right of conquest, and that London had no intention of slackening her grip on an area of such strategic importance.

In November 1914 the Turks, cleverly maneuvered by Germany on to her side, declared war on England, and shortly afterwards Great Britain abolished the Turkish suzerainty and declared a Protectorate over Egypt. The Khedive Abbas Hilmy was deposed, and his uncle, Hussein Kamal, was given the title of Sultan.

Within a matter of days Djemel Pasha, one of the brightest young Turks, crossed Sinai with an expeditionary force to retake Egypt from the Infidel. 'I shall return by sea from Cairo' he confidently told his friends. But British defenses along the Canal broke up the attack, and no one in the Delta showed any signs of rising up as a fifth column as the Turks had hoped. However, the desert campaign, which dragged on until 1916, focussed such attention on the Canal that Egypt, although theoretically neutral, very soon found itself firmly anchored on the side of the Allies. Within months the whole country became a vast base depot for the British Expeditionary Force, and the Egyptian people themselves, far from being influenced by Pan-Islamic propaganda, made no efforts at all to rise in support of the Turks, as they might very well have been tempted to do, since most of the ruling class were of Turkish origin.

From this, deduces Tom Little, 'the Pan-Islamic movement was not in itself the motive force of popular action in Egypt, but the vehicle of Egyptian nationalist resistance; deprived of nationalist leadership, which had been compelled to quiescence by rigorous war-time regulations, the mass of Egyptians worked faithfully behind their British rulers until at last they found Islam itself, in the shape of Shereef of Mecca, on their side.'

The British had given their word that Egyptians would not be called on for active war service, but this soon went by the board and a labor corps was raised, at first by voluntary recruiting and later by conscription. The good wages paid by the British army were probably a greater incentive than any particular conviction for the Allied cause itself, but the fact remains that over 120,000 Egyptians saw service not only in Egypt but also in the Gallipoli and Mesopotamia campaigns, and 10,000 in France. The view, sometimes heard, that Egypt did nothing in the war but grow rich is both distorted and unfair: after all, the war was no concern of Egypt's and the enormous prosperity which it brought to the country benefited the foreign business communities rather more than the Egyptians themselves.

And together with the mounting piles of gold came a flurry of civil regulations from British GHQ, most of which seemed designed to turn Egyptians into Englishmen. It was forbidden, for instance, to sacrifice sheep at Kurban Bairam, and drinks could only be served in public establishments between midday and two-thirty, and from six-thirty until ten o'clock at night. Also, as old Cairo residents still recall with something approaching awe, the Australians came.

Suddenly the place was full of sunburnt figures in large felt hats turned up on one side whose daily progress through Cairo was similar to Boat Race night. They commandeered gharries and raced each other down the main streets until the horses were exhausted, and then played football in Opera Square with policemen's tarbooshes. Authority meant nothing to them. 'They were blissfully naughty boys forever out on some gigantic spree' recalls Priscilla Napier in her delightful childhood reminiscences of Egypt. 'They raced each other up and down the Great Pyramid: within the first fortnight ten of them broke their necks falling down it. It was put out of bounds and they gave a repeat performance up the Step Pyramid at Sakkara. They sat on top of trams...disregarding the Egyptian tram conductors, shouting, smoking, laughing, singing, and constantly getting themselves electrocuted. They raced each other along the parapets of the Nile bridges for bets and fell off into the river and were drowned.' Before leaving for Gallipoli, that sad promontory from which so few of them returned, they raided all the shops and bars that they had a grudge against, and completely demolished the red-light district, pitching furniture and inmates out of the windows and setting the buildings on fire. The 'Birka', say those who knew, was never the same again.

Compared with the grim struggle which was raging in Europe, the desert war was almost a safari, and the fleshpots of Cairo became legendary among the thousands of allied servicemen who flocked gratefully there for their brief periods of leave. These were great days for Cairo, thronged as it was with newsmakers of all sorts, from Lawrence of Arabia to the inevitable *femme fatale* so obviously on the German payroll. But the bustle and glamour did not reach down to the man in the street or the fellahin working their fields, who, as the needs of the war increased, began to find their donkeys and camels commandeered, their corn requisitioned, and even themselves conscripted for service in the desert, much as in the old days of the corvée. Everything was paid for, of course, by the British authorities, but as often as not the compensation got diverted by sly folk along the line before it actually reached the owner's pocket. Inevitably a great deal of injustice occurred, and the general sense of grievance was fed by a heavy-handed censorship and security police measures which often violated the harem, in a manner which *The Times* described as 'the most incompetent, inept, and savagely ruthless in any country under British control'. The puppet government of Sultan Hussein co-operated with a shrug of the shoulders. There was little that ministers could do to prevent the abuses, and they were quite content to transfer the blame for the hardships and iniquities of wartime on the British. By the end of four long years of war the British had fallen from being feared and respected rulers to feared and hated exploiters— 'myopic policemen of a nation now thirsting for its rights', as Simone Lacouture puts it. Hatred of the occupation, of foreign meddling in their daily affairs, of being constantly pushed around by foreigners in their own land had sunk deep into the marrow of their bones, and it was not just the extremists but Egyptians of all classes who whispered:

> *Woe on us England*
> *Who has carried off the corn*
> *Carried off the cattle*
> *Carried off the camels*
> *Carried off the children*
> *Leaving us only our bare lives*
> *For the love of Allah, now leave us alone!*

In Egypt, as elsewhere, the role brings forward the man. And the man who now stepped forward into the role of spokesman for Egypt was Saad Zagloul—not so much a mere nationalist as a humanist who had no time for rancid recriminations and voiced his convictions in simple but picturesque phrases. 'Animals cannot talk but they understand', he once told a donkey-boy who was beating his beast. 'Human beings can talk, but they often do not understand.'

So long as the war lasted, Saad Zagloul kept the anger of the nationalists in check. During what seemed to them an endlessly long summer of discontent he was always restraining the firebrands who wanted to do something, anything, to let off steam against the British. But at last, two days after the Armistice, he headed a delegation which called on Sir Reginald Wingate at the Residency to ask permission to submit Egypt's case for independence to London. The time seemed appropriate: the principles of peace, embodied in the famous 'fourteen points' had just been announced by President Wilson; the Anglo-French Declaration of 1918 aimed at freeing the countries previously under Turkish dominion, and British promises to other Arab states gave the feeling that a new deal could be expected in the Near East and that Egypt's strong claims for independence would prevail.

What appeared to be appropriate timing in Cairo seemed quite the reverse in London. Whereas the British community in Egypt, and Europeans in general, were joyfully celebrating the end of the war with fireworks, jamborees, thanksgiving services and processions—the Greeks and Italians had rival victory processions which ran into each other in Kasr el Nil and refused to give way, causing a private conflict of their own—people in England had greeted the Armistice more soberly and were chiefly concerned with licking their wounds and picking up the pieces of their shattered daily lives. Practically everyone had losses to grieve over; food was still rationed, and everything needed a coat of paint if not a great deal more. Britain had emerged victorious from the war, but shabby and exhausted after four years of total unremitting effort; and was now confronted with the vast and urgent problems that peace had brought. The map of Europe had to be redrawn, Germany had to be punished and policed, and a hundred major issues resolved. A matter such as Egypt's claim for independence seemed, in the minds of harassed officials in Whitehall, to be of very small importance indeed. This was no time, they felt, for Egypt—the pivot of imperial communications and Britain's main base in the Near East, and moreover a country which had grown rich in the war—to start rocking the boat. The very idea of demanding independence when Britain had barely finished saving her from being over-run by the enemy seemed ridiculously out of place. The answer from London was a swift and uncompromising refusal.

Whitehall may have had some degree of reason on its side, but as usual it lacked understanding. The curt rejection only put more fire into the nationalists' bellies. Zagloul's first approach had been tactful. 'England is the strongest and most liberal of the Great Powers' he had said to Wingate, In the name of those principles of freedom which guide her, we ask for her friendship.' Since this failed to achieve any response, he came forward with a resounding cry of Istiklal el Tam! '(unconditional independence) and to frantic applause proclaimed the nationalists' program at a huge public meeting. The first objective was to send a delegation to London and another to the Peace Conference, and when this was again refused—although smaller countries like Hedjaz and Ethiopia were officially represented and the most insignificant states were allowed to appear— bitterness in Cairo reached bursting point. Zagloul sent notes explaining Egypt's position to President Wilson, M. Clemenceau and Signor Orlandi as well as to Lloyd George. On 8 March 1919 the British dispatched Zagloul and his delegation not to Paris, but to prison in Malta.

The next day, Egypt exploded into rebellion. From one end of the country to the other came news of strikes, riots and sabotage: rails were pulled up, trains and telegraphs wrecked, and public buildings burnt. Thousands of slogan-screaming students and schoolboys thronged the streets; pitched battles were fought in provincial towns such as Tanta, Damanhour and Mansourah, and British residents were besieged for a week at Assiout. It was a very real revolt, every bit as intense in its own way as the Hungarian uprisings in 1956, and it took the British army over a fortnight to reassert its authority with the help of armored cars and tanks, in the process of which some 100 rioters were killed and another 1,000 wounded. Yet through this paroxysm of hate there were few real atrocities, save at Deirut where the mob attacked a train and savagely murdered seven British soldiers (one of whom was hacked to pieces, and children hawked lumps of bleeding flesh round the streets shouting 'English meat for sale'), in reprisal for which, thirty Egyptians were executed. Indeed, although some British units let off steam by firing into the crowds rather than above them, the foreign communities, who had expected at any moment to be caught up in a blood bath, were astonished at the restraint they showed. 'For half of this' spluttered a French diplomat, 'For a quarter of this—for a fragment of such treatment, the French would have laid all Cairo in ashes!' They probably would have done, too.

If nothing else, the revolt shook Whitehall out of its detachment. Lloyd George, who happened to encounter General Allenby (then at the height of his fame as the conqueror of Palestine) at a party, made a snap decision to send him to Cairo as a 'Special High Commissioner' to put matters straight. Allenby's first action was to proclaim that Saad Zagloul and his colleagues would be released from Malta and free to go to Paris, whereupon in a mystifying and mercurial way which could happen only in Egypt, British troops found themselves being cheered as they marched through the streets. Even the Sultan Fouad, regarded by everyone as being in the pocket of Britain, got a clap.

On points, the Nationalists had won the first round, but the fight was still on. One side was determined to end the Protectorate, the other to maintain it. Each now maneuvered. The British government decided to gain time by sending out a fact-finding mission, headed by Lord Milner—who, as a young Fleet Street man, had been brought to Cairo in the 1880s to 'sell' the idea of British occupation. The Nationalists, realizing that violence, though effective, might run the risk of a knockout retaliation, now shifted to passive resistance. Perhaps they got the idea from Gandhi. Strikes, sabotage and go-slows brought the whole country virtually to a standstill, and when Milner and his colleagues arrived on the scene every Egyptian they met had apparently been struck deaf and dumb. The boycott of the mission was total. If its members went to a meeting, the meeting was immediately adjourned. If they spoke to a fellah, he turned the other way. After three months of such treatment the mission returned to London having learnt little about Egypt, but something about Egyptian nationalism. Lord Milner's report, when it finally appeared, was a nicely professional piece of window dressing which, while paying lip service to Egyptian aspirations, and not entirely brushing them aside, in fact proposed to continue the Protectorate, suitably veiled of course, for an indefinite period. To Cairo, itching with impatience, it was the same old mixture as before: yesterday's hash served up with a clean napkin. No self-respecting minister would accept it, or even negotiate on such a basis. He would not have had any support if he had tried. Egypt was in no mood for compromise. The cries for Istiklal el Tam grew louder, and when Saad Zagloul, now embodying the national dream, and the only man who could effectively have spoken for Egypt, was finally deported to the Seychelles with other members of the Wafd, the country once again boiled over with riots and terrorism.

At this point Lord Allenby, who had a far clearer picture of the situation than his employers at the Foreign Office, and was becoming impatient with their futilities, took matters into his own hands and came up with a plan to abolish the Protectorate and declare Egypt unconditionally an independent state. After an acrimonious exchange of telegrams (in one of which he offered his resignation) he hurried back to London and personally talked the cabinet round to his point of view. The result was a unilateral announcement of Egypt's independence on 22 February 1922, but with four 'reservations' which effectively limited her sovereignty and remained thorny questions for the next thirty years.*

One month later, on 22 March, Egypt was officially proclaimed an independent kingdom, and Ahmed Fouad could wear a crown. The Protectorate was over; independence had come. It sounded like a victory for Egypt—the first, indeed, that any people had won over nineteenth century European imperialism—but it was not, of course, a victory at all. The four 'reserved points' gave Britain justification to steer the country's policy as her interests dictated, and to maintain her influence by stationing troops wherever she fancied. King Fouad himself sat on a grace and favor throne which made him an unwilling stooge of London's policies. This, muttered the nationalists venomously, was neither independence or even interdependence: it was a cynical backhand swipe at Egypt's aspirations enabling a barely concealed occupation to continue under the guise of a constitution and their spleen showed itself in a new rash of terrorism, all the more unpleasant because it consisted chiefly of shooting quite innocent English individuals in the back.

In due course, when Zagloul was at last permitted to return, the spleen turned to zeal as the nationalist leader, now more popular than ever, took advantage of the coming elections to present himself at the head of the Wafd. The full extent to which he had the country behind him was then shown: the Wafdists were returned with ninety per cent of the votes, and Zagloul, hitherto the unofficial champion of Egypt, became the first Wafd, or nationalist, Prime Minister.

Almost concurrently, the first Labor government came to power in England, and since Ramsey Macdonald, when in opposition, had always declared himself in favor of Egyptian independence, it seemed as though this was a ready-made chance to get rid of the occupying troops. But if Zagloul reckoned that the Labor Government would meekly pull out of Egypt, he was in for a disappointment. Ramsey Macdonald simply pointed to the 1922 Declaration. This, he said firmly, gave Egypt all the independence she needed for the present.

Blocked on this issue, Zagloul shuffled his cards. The nationalist abruptly turned imperialist. He demanded the Sudan.

Notes:

Lord Allenby's reservations concerned:

1. *the security of British Imperial communications in Egypt;*

2. *the defense of Egypt against all foreign aggression or interference, direct or indirect;*

3, *the protection of foreign interests in Egypt and the protection of minorities;*

4. *The Sudan.*

Chapter 13

A Glance at the Sudan

Egyptians have always been obsessed by the Sudan. To them it is not just a neighbor to the south, friendly or otherwise, but the hazy hinterland from which the Nile comes: a perpetual, traumatic reminder that Egypt herself is the gift of the Nile, and that should ever the rich brown waters fail to appear through their spout at Wadi Haifa, the whole delta would become as uninhabitable as the desert which surrounds it. The cry 'Unity of the Nile Valley' is not merely a demagogic *spiel* dreamt up by Mustapha Kamal. It is a yearning as old as history itself.

Bilad-as-Sudan, 'the country of the Blacks', as it was known, was regarded by most Egyptians as a steamy, sullen vastness in which lurked riches as improbable as a State lottery for those hardy enough to go treasure hunting through the heat and discomfort and danger. To the nineteenth century mind the Sudan had the same magnetic appeal as the moon has to adventurous spirits today. Mohammed Ali sent expeditions there to scavenge for gold, and ivory and slaves. Said made a state visit. Ismail inherited from them a million square miles of uncharted provinces and immediately thought of annexing some more. He sent Sir Samuel Baker in charge of an Egyptian expedition to the upper reaches of the Nile, installing him—and subsequently Colonel Gordon—as governor of a dominion as vast as the various countries of the European Common Market put together, extending from Assouan to the equator, and from the Red Sea to the western limits of Darfur.

Under Ismail's patronage, Gordon had a free hand in the Sudan, which, in his moody and dedicated fashion he administered quite competently, restlessly criss-crossing the vast country on camel back. But the officialdom that had battened down on Cairo after Ismail's abdication soon started clipping his wings, and in 1879 Gordon resigned his governor-generalship in disgust. His place was taken by Raouf Pasha, a bullying Turk of the worst possible sort, whose cruelty and corruption soon became so unbearable to the Sudanese that they began flocking to the side of a strange fanatical figure on an island in the Nile, who whispered that he was the 'Messiah'. Half witch-doctor, half showman, this imposing warrior-priest with his pointed black beard had a mesmeric effect on his followers. He proclaimed the ancient austerities of Islam, and with torrents of oratory incited them to drive the hated Turk 'into the sea'.

'There was a strange splendor in his presence' says Lytton Strachey. '...the eyes, painted with antimony, flashed extraordinary fires...thousands, when he lifted up his voice in solemn worship, knew that the heavens were opened and that they had come nearer to God...the nahas—the brazen war drums—would summon...with their weird rolling, the whole host to arms. The green flag and the red flag and the black flag would rise over the multitude. The great army would move forward...'

At the identical time, and for remarkably the same reasons as Arabi and the nationalists were turning against the Turko-Egyptian regime in Egypt, the Mahdi began his revolt in the Sudan. At first it was not taken too seriously by the Pashas and their British advisors in Cairo, who had enough trouble to cope with anyway in Egypt, but when first Sennar and then El Obeid fell to the rebels it became plain that something would have to be done. This was by no means easy, with money and troops in short supply; but eventually a scratch expedition—manned chiefly by ex-Arabi followers who were dragged out of jail to take part—was sent up the Nile under the command of a British officer to suppress the uprising. Against the mystical fervor of the Mahdi's hordes, Colonel Hicks' ramshackle army was doomed from the start. When finally the news filtered through that the expedition had been slaughtered to a man, public opinion in England was thoroughly outraged. There were two schools of thought. The one was to evacuate the Sudan and leave it to stew in its own juice. The other, voiced strongly by the popular press, was to take tough action to make up for the humiliation of the Hicks' disaster.

The editor of a daily paper now remembered the former governor-general. Gordon, stated the headlines solemnly, was the man to be sent to Khartoum. With his vast experience of the Sudan, he would know how to put matters right. Interviewed in London, the General agreed. A firm line was essential.

In the face of this uproar about what should be done to save the garrison of a foreign country from a revolt by another foreign country, the cabinet hummed and hawed. Gladstone had already decided in his own mind to pull out of the Sudan. But public opinion had to be heeded; and so, against his better judgement he agreed to a compromise plan. General Gordon, who had publicly gone on record as advocating strong measures, was sent out to do just the opposite. His terms of reference were to wind up affairs in the Sudan and evacuate Egyptians and Europeans as quickly as possible.

What followed is now the legendary story of Gordon at Khartoum—a classic Greek tragedy with the ingredients for a successful western. Once back in his old haunts, Gordon did begin to put things right, as best he could. Taxes were remitted, prisoners released, and the worst excesses of Raouf's administration removed. Likewise he did follow his instructions and announce that the Sudan was to be evacuated. But then, in the truest public-school tradition, he pledged that he would not leave Khartoum until all Egyptian troops in the outlying provinces had the chance of being brought to safety. In the meantime, the Mahdi and his vast armies advanced, surrounded Orndurman, and cut the telegraph. Thus Gordon was bottled up in Khartoum with a bunch of garrison troops and some 30,000 civilian inhabitants.

Again it was public opinion in England that stirred the government, this time to rescue Gordon. The cabinet felt vaguely that if he was in danger, it was entirely his own fault. In fact they suspected, rather huffily, that he had probably engineered the whole matter to pressure the government into sending a relief expedition out. Backwards and forwards went telegrams to Cromer in Cairo. What was going on in Khartoum? If General Gordon continued to stay there, said Whitehall, it was essential he should 'state to us the cause and intentions with which he so continues'.

To which piece of bureaucracy, when it was finally smuggled through the enemy lines, and he could smuggle an answer back, the General replied 'You ask me to state cause and intention in staying in Khartoum knowing government means to abandon Sudan, and in answer I say, "I stay in Khartoum because Arabs have shut us up and will not let us out".'

For some time longer the cabinet continued to shelve the matter, until in the end Queen Victoria made her own and the country's views quite plain to the Foreign Office. 'General Gordon is in danger' she told Lord Hartington, 'You are bound to save him.' Gladstone, who felt that it was really too bad of Gordon to have managed to blackmail the Government in this way, at last took action. He appointed Lord Wolseley, the victor of Tel el Kebir, to command an expedition to rescue the General.

With a classic inevitability, the last act of the tragedy now slowly unfolded. Upon the roof of the Governor's palace at Khartoum, Gordon continually scanned the horizon through his telescope for the first sign of the approaching relief, and somehow managed to keep the daily life of the place going, although food supplies were acute and every living animal—including donkeys, cats, dogs, rats, and even monkeys—had already been eaten. On the opposite bank of the Nile, in Ormdurman, the Mahdi and his army waited with predatory anticipation for the starving city to give in. The Mahdi himself (if his European captives can be believed) was in no tearing hurry for this to happen, for, in contrast to the drastic austerity which in the name of Islam he so ferociously imposed on his followers—who were liable to be flogged to death with a rhinoceros whip for the mere act of drinking or smoking or swearing, his own private life was not subject to such inconveniences, and he spent his days reclining on gold brocade cushions attended by some thirty young ladies who fanned him with ostrich feathers and massaged his limbs to maintain a delicious nirvana, only occasionally interrupted by the necessity of appearing at prayers or war councils. Meanwhile slowly, ever so slowly, the rescue force made its way up the Nile. Lord Wolseley reached Cairo on 9 September, and after three weeks at Shepheard's Hotel set off for Wadi Haifa, with a pause at Assouan to dig for antiquities. By the end of December the expedition had reached Korti and by mid-January was almost within sight of Khartoum. On 17 January there was a skirmish with the Sudanese, and precious days were lost overhauling the boats and attending to supply problems. So far as he could see, said Lord Wolseley, still just out of range of Gordon's telescope, a few days more or less would make no difference one way or the other: Gordon had been in Khartoum for nearly a year: he could surely hold out a bit longer.

The Mahdi might have continued his nirvana, and Gordon held out, had news of the British relief force not reached the Sudanese precisely at the time that the Nile waters were at their lowest point and mudbanks facilitated a crossing of the river. At dawn on 26 January the Mahdi pounced. A howling horde of dervishes swept through the defenses into Khartoum, and when the relief force finally steamed up the Nile the following day, all they found was smoking ruins. Whether General Gordon ever caught a glimpse of them through his telescope will never be known. The only certain thing is that when the expedition reached Khartoum, Gordon's still bleeding head was on a spear outside the Mahdi's tent. Wolseley had missed the bus.

Short of mounting a campaign to clear the whole country, there was nothing to be done but turn tail and draw a curtain over the Sudan. So for the next fifteen years, 'the land of the Blacks' was left to its own devices—which, from the sparse news which filtered through to the outside world, can hardly have been pleasant for the Sudanese.

The Mahdi himself did not enjoy his triumph for long. Five months after the fall of Khartoum, he was either poisoned in his hareem or simply died as a result of his debauches. He was succeeded by his lieutenant, the Khalifa, who, while playing up the Mahdi's memory, immediately initiated a reign of terror far worse than anything that had been seen in the past. This barbarism might have run unchecked into the twentieth century but for the colonizing fever of the nineties which set the European powers at each other's throats in a world-wide grab for land. The Germans were moving in East Africa, the Italians in Abyssinia, and if the British did not act in the Sudan it was pretty certain that the French would.*
In 1895 Gladstone's Liberals were replaced by a strong Conservative government which was quite prepared to avenge Gordon's death and the failures of Hicks and Wolseley, particularly as it was believed that the Khalifa had plans to invade upper Egypt.

Nothing illustrates better the extraordinary tangle of Anglo-Egyptian affairs than the reconquest of the Sudan in 1898. On the pretext that it was high time to remove the danger on Egypt's southern frontier, General Kitchener, as Sirdar of the Egyptian army, in the name of the Sultan of Turkey, but acting on orders from London and financed by the Egyptian treasury, advanced up the Nile with an Anglo-Egyptian army to ensure that the Sudan became British and not French. Kitchener's expedition took nearly two years to reach Khartoum, laying a desert railway line on the way as far as Berber, and only five hours to crush the Khalifa on the barren desert plain outside Omdurman. The battle was remarkable for the fact that four well-officered Anglo-Egyptian brigades routed fully 40,000 dervishes, leaving some 10,000 dead at a cost of 175 British and 273 Egyptian casualties, killed and wounded.* Also that the 21st Lancers, which included Lieutenant W. S. Churchill, made a spectacular (but probably unnecessary) cavalry charge. And finally that Kitchener, riding into Khartoum on a white charger, took a particularly macabre revenge for his predecessor Gordon. He had the Mahdi's body dug up out of its grave and flung into the Nile, but not before the head had been cut off and appropriated by himself to be made into an inkstand. Queen Victoria was greatly shocked when she heard about this—it 'savored too much of the middle ages' she thought—and Cromer, realizing the monstrosity of Kitchener's act, managed in due course to secrete the skull away from him and have it buried quietly in Wadi Haifa.

British and Egyptian flags now fluttered side by side over Khartoum, but it was obvious from the start that England intended to have a free hand in the Sudan. Just as the British administration in Egypt had been artfully camouflaged as a financial 'condominium', so the annexation of the Sudan to the British Empire was now announced as a political condominium; a juridical piece of juggling signed in Cairo on 19 January 1899 which blandly 'desired to give effect to the claims which have accrued to Her Britannic Majesty's government by right of conquest,' and in fact set Egypt and England on a collision course over their respective rights. The Khalifa's rule had not only laid waste the whole country it had also swept away all traces of the old Egyptian government. A special British 'Sudan Civil Service' was now created, and the administration became progressively more British, until in the end the Egyptian participation was about as effective as the Turkish sovereignty over Egypt itself.

Of the efficiency of this new administration there can be no doubt, and from a dreary wasted land (with in 1898 a revenue of barely £35,000 against an expenditure of £235,000) the Sudan grew into an economically viable unit quite separate from Egypt. But the feeling of being elbowed out after contributing most of the men and the money for the reconquest of the Sudan, to provide yet another link in the Imperial march from Cairo to the Cape, was increasingly abrasive to Egyptian national pride. Even if, personally speaking, Egyptians might prefer to give the whole sultry Sudan a wide berth, it was still the land from which the life-blood of the Nile flowed, and from the moment that Mustapha Kamal raised the cry for 'Unity of the Nile Valley', the desire for full sovereignty over the Sudan became as much a part of the nationalists' aspirations as evacuation by the British from Egypt itself. So when Zagloul, frustrated by the way Egypt had been maneuvered by the 1922 Declaration from hopeful dependence into a blatantly artificial independence, began to press for what London reluctantly recognized as 'the natural historic rights of Egypt on the Nile'—though in fact Zagloul meant full sovereignty over the Sudan—the struggle focused a most embarrassing attention on one man: Sir Lee Stack. As Sirdar of the Sudan and at the same time Commander-in-Chief of the Egyptian army he personified in his job not so much a tenuous gesture towards Egypt's rights, as intended, but a blatant symbol of Egypt's subservience to the British Raj. When Zagloul complained that a foreign Commander-in-Chief of the Egyptian army was 'inconsistent with the dignity of independent Egypt' the Foreign Office replied frostily that this placed the Sirdar in a 'difficult position'; but when Zagloul shifted his diplomatic attacks to the Sudan and encountered the same unfortunate person, Sir Lee Stack's position became not only difficult but acutely dangerous, particularly when both Houses of Parliament heard the statement that Great Britain was 'not going to abandon the Sudan in any sense whatsoever'. It was an open invitation to the finger on the trigger. On 19 November 1924, as Sir Lee Stack was driving from the Ministry of War to his house on Gezira island, he received a volley of shots from seven men dressed as students. Within an hour after the shooting, a distraught Zagloul hurried to the British Residency to express his sorrow and dismay. It was no use.

Lord Allenby, described by Wavell as 'an explosive general' drove in full military state to the Council and delivered a thunderous ultimatum. He demanded an official apology and a thorough enquiry into the assassination, the prohibition of all political demonstrations, an indemnity of £500,000, the immediate withdrawal of all Egyptian troops from the Sudan, a diversion of Nile waters for irrigation projects in the Sudan, and a tightening of British control in the ministries of Justice, Finance, and Interior. When the Council jibbed at the last three items (which had little relation to the tragedy anyway) British troops occupied the customs at Alexandria, and enforced the instructions in the Sudan itself.

It was touch and go whether Egypt would not lose her own shadowy independence along with the Sudan. Zagloul took the only possible step, which was to resign. The King dissolved the Wafdist parliament, a puppet ministry was formed under a palace nominee—the immensely fat Ziwar Pasha—a number of prominent nationalists were executed, and when all concerned had regained their senses, it was clear that a watershed had been passed. The revolutionary period, which began in 1919, had ended.

It had achieved a token form of independence, in the sense that Ahmed Fouad was outwardly king of a sovereign state. But Zagloul, bearing with him the hopes and yearnings of nearly all Egyptians, was out on a limb under the suspicion of being responsible for the terrorist campaign as a whole, if not the actual murder of the Sirdar; and Britain, henceforth represented by Lord Lloyd, was still very much in command. For the next twenty, seven years the political scene was to be dominated by the triangular struggle between Residency, Palace and Wafd.

Raymond Flower

Notes:

A further important reason for the decision to reconquer the Sudan was the effect of the Italian defeat at Adowa.

In the light of superior British fire-power, the size of the respective casualties is not surprising and Captain Blood can perhaps be quoted as a verdict on Omdurman:

> *He stood upon a little mound*
> *And cast his lethargic eyes around*
> *And said beneath his breath*
> *'Whatever happens we have got*
> *The Maxim gun, and they have not.'*
> *(Hilaire Belloc, A Modern Traveler.)*

Chapter 14

The Triangles of Power

Wafd means 'delegation'. As a political party it was a curiously amorphous affair, as typically Egyptian as *molochia,* the spicy and indigestible national dish of glutinous green soup into which everything is poured: mountains of rice, chicken, mutton, onions, raisins, vinegar—everything, in fact, that the cook finds around. The Wafd was an amalgam of all political groups, the heterogeneous mouthpiece of a whole people. It contained, in the words of Lacoutures: 'all the generosity, intellectual muddle, good nature, contradictions and mythomania of its millions of supporters'. It was a follow-up of Zagloulism: Saad Zagloul was its high priest; it sprang from its conflict with the Residency, having no real policy beyond that of getting rid of the British. The Wafd had no political color either: it was neither liberal nor socialist, nor indeed anything definable. The Wafd was all things to all men. Its democratic pluralism attracted people from all classes, the greatest landlords and the poorest fellahin, the noisiest rabble-rousers and the coolest intellectuals, each drawn by his own particular conviction of what the national cause should be—and what could be fished out of the pond.

For thirty years it was a sort of emotional safety valve, a comfortably safe hunting ground for the Pashas, because it had no left wing bias, and a noisily protesting platform with which the humblest fellah could identify something of his muddled hopes and resentments. Even the leftist-inclined youth and intellectuals found themselves wooed by the uncomplicated demagogy of Saad Zagloul and Mustapha Nahas, both of whom had fellah backgrounds and could play most skillfully on the country's moods. But because of its lack of doctrine or program the Wafd was always most heady and effective when in opposition. Once in power—and every time there was a free vote the Wafd was returned with an overwhelming majority—it floundered uneasily and the seamy side appeared, its leaders so blatantly concerned with feathering their nests. The corruption of the Wafd was a music-hall joke, and the antics of the Nahas Pasha's wife and her family in the 1930's and 1940's were followed with rueful glee in the cafés and bazaars; nor was the Wafdist image much improved by the constant quarrels of its leaders and the splinter parties it threw off. But fully three-quarters of the time the Wafd was simply in opposition, cunningly maneuvered out of power by the Palace on the one hand or the British on the other, and only tolerated in office when it was necessary—as in 1936 for the signing of the Anglo-Egyptian Treaty, and at the most dangerous period in the Second World War—to have the weight of popular support behind the government.

That such maneuvering against a party representing the bulk of popular opinion was possible at all is explained by the fact that the 1922 Declaration making Fouad King of Egypt had the effect of returning the reins of power to the Mohammed Ali dynasty. Under the constitution, the king was empowered to appoint ministers and suspend parliament. Like most monarchs who govern without the consent of their peoples, he viewed the Wafd and its popularity with suspicion, knowing only too well that it was fundamentally republican in inclination and emotionally opposed to the Palace or Pasha elite who were the 'king's men'. The influence of the Palace and the pashas was maintained by the presence of British garrisons, and the Egyptian army commanded by British senior officers. It was wholly to the interest of the Palace to have a solid and long-term agreement with England.

Throughout the meaningless shuffle of Egyptian politics during the 20's and 30's—and in fact right up to the revolution in 1952—the pattern was always the same: the Palace trying to rule without the support of the masses; the Wafd wanting to get rid of the British and the reactionary Pasha elite as well; and the British (who remained in Egypt for imperial and strategic reasons) with the real power in the background. It was a political triangle in which two sides kept the third in place. Every time free elections were held, the Wafd was returned with an overwhelming majority. As soon as their agitation for the removal of the British became too embarrassing, the king would dissolve parliament and rule by decree. Fouad, who had been educated in Italy, had no love for the British whose pro-consuls were only too apt to stamp painfully on the royal toes. But king and Pashas alike needed the British presence as a sort of insurance policy for their continual existence, although politically they had to pay lip service to the popular clamor for evacuation.

So whereas the Wafd screamed noisily for the British to go, and were pushed out of office by constitutional means if they overstepped the limit, the palace went through the motions of demanding evacuation, while privately assuring the Residency that this was only for public consumption, and that in reality they wanted the British to stay.

Whatever the other two sides of the triangle might say or do the British were the dominant power and intended to remain so as long as it suited them, and this was made abundantly clear by the High Commissioner, Lord Lloyd, an ex-governor of Bombay, whose remedy for all situations was to send for a battleship—until even Whitehall grew exasperated, and replaced him with the more diplomatic Sir Percy Lorraine.

A racehorse owner and a *seigneur* in his own right, Sir Percy was adept at smoothing ruffled feathers, and his courteous ways and personal popularity were largely instrumental in preparing the ground for the 1936 Anglo-Egyptian Treaty. The main reason for this Treaty was the deteriorating world situation. The Italian invasions of Tripolitania and Abyssinia, and the belligerent noises emanating from the Palazzo Venezia in Rome could not be ignored, and although for considerations of world strategy the British were in no circumstances prepared to allow any erosion of their dominant position in the eastern Mediterranean, it was evident that a solution to the Egyptian situation—which could at any moment become explosive—must be found. Tactful maneuvering brought all three sides of the triangle to agreement. In May 1936 elections were held, which, as usual, brought the Wafd into power, and Nahas Pasha, heading a delegation of Wafdists and leading politicians from other parties, reached a sensible agreement with London at long last. The 1936 Treaty was a realistic document under the circumstances then prevailing. It declared that the British military occupation of Egypt was ended, but that Britain retained the right to station troops along the Suez Canal for the period of the alliance, which expired in 1956 if not extended by mutual agreement. The capitulations system was abolished, and Britain agreed to sponsor Egypt's membership, as an independent state, in the League of Nations. The question of the sovereignty over the Sudan was carefully by-passed, but restrictions on Egyptian participation in the condominium, enforced since the murder of Sir Lee Stack, were lifted.

The agreement carried an impressive list of signatures, including just about everyone of influence in Egyptian politics at the time. It satisfied moderate and nationalist aspirations, and gave Britain the foothold on the Canal she required. It was a genuine step forward for Egypt, and gave every hope that friendly relations between the two countries could now be consolidated. But certain factors eluded the crystal-ball gazers of 1936. The gathering war clouds were to bring more, not less, British interference in Egypt. Sir Miles Lampson, who signed the Treaty on behalf of England, was to develop into a paunchy caricature of British officialdom. And the astute King Fouad, who died on the eve of the Treaty, was to be succeeded by his schoolboy son; a slim and popular boy called Farouk.

Apart from the revolutionary outbursts of 1919 which brought politics into the streets, the triangular power struggle of the 20's and the 30's ebbed and swirled behind the italianate facades of the royal palaces, the studded neo-Venetian doors of Princess Chivekiar's palazzo (which housed the Council of Ministers) and in the pillared drawing rooms of the British Residency. Discounting certain turbaned groups who met in the recesses of Fashawi's cafe in the Khan el Khalil, and periodic shoutings of sloganeering students who let off steam by burning a tram or two until chased home by the police, the average foreigner (unconsciously protected by the British garrisons) went about his business with sublime unconcern, particularly if he lived in Alexandria, where the goings-on in Cairo were greeted with a mere shrug of the shoulder, and a wry, dismissive smile.

For Alexandria, although the commercial center of Egypt, hardly considered itself Egyptian at all. In its curious, island-like location, almost guillotined from the mainland by the tepid salt lakes of Mariut, Alexandria might send its trading tentacles deep into the brown heart of the country and even far beyond into Africa, but its whole mould and ambiance was European, not Egyptian, just as Alexander's great capital had been two millenniums before. And if it could no longer boast, as in Graeco-Roman times, of being the Queen city of the Mediterranean, it was statistically the largest port (just ahead of Marseilles) and its cosmopolitan business people were linked with the capitals of Europe not only by Bentley's Number Two code,* but by their passports as well. Like the Macedonian Ptolomys, they were a European implant, unconnected by culture or tastes or way of living with the teeming delta behind them.

Yet even though Mohammed Ali's nineteenth century creation bore little resemblance to the glittering marble-lined city which Amr, the Arab conqueror, described as having '4,000 palaces, 4,000 baths, 400 theatres, 12,000 greengrocers and 40,000 Jews', in a strange way the booming modern Alexandria of the cotton-brokers and onion merchants had managed to recreate, in the tenor of its daily life, something of the flavor and the easy, malicious elegance of Hellenic days.

Perhaps a great deal of this shimmering ambience was simply the Mediterranean style of life. For it was more than just an illusory quality. Day to day business may have been conducted in a miasma of chicanery, always hovering on the edge of sharp practice, but the social scene was infinitely cosmopolitan with a seductive blend of leisure and lushness which echoed but assuaged the international radiance of Rome, the scruffy patricianship of Athens, and the parochial *dolce-vita* of Palermo or Algiers. It was normal to dine out four or five nights a week, and the least to be expected was sixteen at table with a succession of out of season dishes as often as not brought over from France or Italy. Needless to say, no woman in society would dream of wearing the same dress twice, nor even the same hat. (There were some useful little boutiques which would hire them out for the evening; but for great occasions it was *de rigeur* to have one's wardrobe and hairdresser shipped out from Paris to arrive on the morning of the event, and to suffer palpitations of anxiety lest they should fail to arrive in time, though they always did.) Fads were considered amusing, and a hostess, if she were slimming, would preside at the head of the table through a twelve-course dinner with simply a soup plate of hot water in front of her. From time to time the telephone would be brought in by the suffragi and the *mutresse de céans* would carry on an animated conversation, full of the latest *potins*, or the host would negotiate some enigmatic deal. Business flowed unhesitatingly out of the office, to be conducted around the tea tables of the Sporting Club or in the private boxes at the cinema, where interesting speculations in such commodities as shipments of lavatory paper or canned beer were transacted. No one was ever young in Alexandria, at least in his behavior, but the everyday program for sophisticates of all ages was full of pleasant diversions—iced coffee at 'Wenki's' in the morning followed by an aperitif at Baudrot; luncheon at the Union Bar (in its heyday perhaps the best restaurant in Africa); golf and tennis or polo in the afternoon at the Sporting Club. Behind the brass-framed windows of the Royal Yacht Club, faded old ladies with blue-tinted hair and diamonds, who prided themselves on being the 'beau monde', stared through their lorgnettes at groups of young people being helped into spanking white cutters for an afternoon's sail in the harbor, complete with portable gramophones and parcels of cream cakes. Inside the clubroom, yachting dress was not permitted, and on one occasion in 1943 a party comprising the King of Greece, Noel Coward and Lord Keyes was asked to leave by the English secretary because they were wearing white naval shorts.

Once or twice during the winter season there were balls at the various hotels, and the San Stefano casino specialized in topical decors which were executed with much ingenuity by the Russian designer Rankovitch—for instance, when the coal strike was on in Europe, the ballroom was done up as a coal-mine. *Thé-dansants* were popular, but *thé-prolonges* in a private house rarely started before seven-thirty, and involved, in fact, an enormous cold buffet. All this meant that evening dress was worn most nights by women of fashion—though rather less so by the men after the head of the Greek community had the misfortune to be taken for a waiter.

The beauty and sophistication of Alexandrian women, and the attentiveness of the men were legendary: indeed, over everything there hovered the light play of sex, often bizarre and narcissistic, which together with the love of money, constituted the only real passion of Alexandrians, and was the touchstone not only for their wit, metallic and malicious, but also for the warm crinkly friendships which were so eager and tantalizing. Culture, in this city of Plotinus, Euclid and Anastasius, tended barely to ruffle the surface of the lives dedicated to ease and luxury. So many of the elegant figures being driven in their limousines to a concert at the Alhambra or a conference at *L'Atelier* could speak half a dozen languages, but were proficient in none. But for all their shortcomings, there was a fatal, brilliant fascination about Mediterranean Alexandria, now as dead and departed as the Greek city of the Ptolomys, which inspired E. M. Forster to produce the best guide book that has been written about any place, and Laurence Durrell to chart its many-splendored decadence, but above all moved Cavafy to become the poet of the city. Can he have realized that his Alexandria was doomed? Perhaps so, because even as he harked back two thousand years to the dying Anthony, he seemed in a curious way to be writing the epitaph of his own chimerical city, then so prosperous and self-assured, and yet so suddenly to disintegrate into an insubstantial, jasmine-scented memory. Today only the streets and buildings and the balmy north breezes remain of the city he loved so well, and to which he wrote a prophetic farewell:

Raymond Flower

When, at the hour of midnight
An invisible choir is suddenly heard passing
With exquisite music, with voices—
Do not lament your fortune that at last subsides
Your life's work that has failed, your schemes that have
proved illusions.
But, like a man prepared, like a brave man,
Bid farewell to her, to Alexandria who is departing.
Above all, do not delude yourself, do not say it is a dream,
That your ear was mistaken.
Do not condescend to such empty hopes.
Like a man for long prepared, like a brave man
Like a man who was worthy of such a city,
Go to the window firmly
And listen with emotion
But not with the prayers and complaints of the Coward
(Ah, supreme rapture!)
Listen to the notes, to the exquisite instruments of the
mystic choir
And bid farewell to her, to Alexandria whom you are
losing.

Note:

It was customary for business firms to send their cables in code, usually Bentleys Number Two.

Chapter 15

Seeds of Revolution

Midway through the thirties, a British official wrote jokingly that, whereas Egypt was ruled by a monarch advised by a parliament, this method was so cumbersome that it had adopted schoolboy and blue-shirt rule: the schoolboys enforcing their arguments with stones and broken bottles, and the blue-shirts employing daggers and life-preservers. 'Those two far-seeing and sapient political parties have now combined together' he explained for the benefit of the readers of *Oriental Spotlight* 'and call themselves the United Front. It is a moderately cheap form of government as no salaries or emoluments are paid to the rulers, and all the country has to do is to reimburse tramway companies for burnt trams, replace all the street lamps once a week and compensate police for broken skulls.'

Perhaps the readers of *Oriental Spotlight* saw it that way. But as it happens, one of the noisiest figures of what Major G S Jarvis called the schoolboy government was a tall, olive-skinned student of seventeen who, in eleven years of schooling, had only managed to pass one secondary and three primary grades. During the period of Ramadan in 1935 the British Foreign Secretary made what had now become a routine pronouncement pouring cold water on Egypt's proposal to rid the country of British troops. Nahas Pasha, as leader of the Wafd, retaliated with a routine vituperation in Garden City; Egyptians, he shouted, would fight and die so long as a single Englishman remained on Egyptian soil. The crowd responded, as it always did, and a series of disorganized demonstrations, led by the students, swarmed through the streets. There was a clash with the police. The olive-skinned schoolboy had his forehead cracked wide open. The following morning a newspaper, describing the fracas, listed among the casualties the Minister of War with a fractured skull, and Gamal Abdel Nasser, student. A month later, under the pressure of a wave of demonstrations, Britain agreed to negotiations which culminated in the 1936 Treaty.

Gamal Abdel Nasser had been born on 15 January 1918 in the teeming bazaar-filled district of Bacos, in Alexandria, where his father was in charge of the post office. Later, when his father was transferred to the tiny village of Khatatba on the edge of the western desert, the boy was sent to school in Cairo. There he lived with his uncle in a tiny ramshackle flat in the heart of the Musky. His uncle was a revolutionary who had recently been to prison for several years for organizing anti-British demonstrations. From him, the young Gamal began to develop a passion for secrets and intrigue. A stubborn and fiercely independent little boy, he spent his days in the narrow, crowded alleys of the El Azhar district, a typical street urchin, intolerant of authority in any shape or form. He was nine when his mother died, and from then onwards family life ceased to have any meaning for him. He drew more and more into his shell, cloaking the most humdrum events with mystery, delighting in plots and counter-plots, and gradually acquiring from his uncle a taste for revolutionary dreams.

At his secondary school, he was soon involved in the demonstrations fostered by the opposition parties. He joined Misr el Fatat, the young Egypt party, and before long his schooldays were spent defying his teachers and causing disturbances in the grounds of Cairo University, or fetching and carrying for the party. It was so much more exciting than sitting drearily in a classroom. Looking back on those days he remembered that one of the set books for his English class was *The Scarlet Pimpernel* by Baroness Orczy. This he enjoyed. 'Here is a man who seemed to be good for nothing,' he noted, 'yet he turned out to be a leader.' Another of his boyhood heroes was Nelson. And so the schoolboy rebel weaved his private fancies. He began to see himself as a hero in search of a role. Much later, in his *Philosophy of the Revolution* he came back to the same theme.

Meanwhile, along with the bump on his head, he had acquired a police record and the headmaster of the school, who was fed up with such a troublesome boy, used this as a pretext for expelling him. The immediate result was that the other boys presented a petition for his reinstatement, and when this was refused, they went on strike and threatened to burn the school down. In the end the headmaster was forced to fetch Gamal back in his own car. It was a personal triumph for Nasser, his first.

A few months later, Britain and Egypt signed the 1936 Treaty, recognizing the equal status of the two countries, and confining British troops to the narrow area of the Canal Zone until Egypt herself was able to guarantee the safety of navigation through the waterway. The agreement was hailed as a great victory for Egypt, but with the keen eyes of youth, Gamal Abdel Nasser was not convinced. The English were still on Egyptian soil. However, the days of demonstrations were now over, and he had to think of a career. He applied for admission to the military academy, but, having no family influence, his application was rejected. For a while he joined the law school at Cairo University. This meant living at home almost indefinitely, and he was on bad terms with both his father and his stepmother. So he tried again for the army, bearding the secretary for War in his own office. His initiative, and the intensity with which he presented his case, impressed the general, who put him up for a selection board. Hitherto, commissions in the army had been reserved for the sons of the well to do. To become an officer the candidate had in most cases to satisfy the authorities (unofficially, of course) that his family had an income of not less than £2,000 a year—to ensure, presumably, that they were part of the 'establishment'. But after Egypt gained its independence in 1936 the military academy was open to boys of all classes of society; a vital step, as it turned out, since the leaders of the 1952 revolution were nearly all members of this first intake of cadets drawn solely on merit. Even so, only about ten per cent of the applicants were accepted, and among them, to his great surprise, was Gamal Abdel Nasser. Sixteen months later he was a second lieutenant.

The first posting was to Assiut, only a few kilometers from the dust-ridden earth-brown village of Beni Mor, where his family had its roots. Here young Gamal, himself only a generation removed from the fellahin in the fields of Upper Egypt, found his regiment working alongside and in collaboration with British officers. Officially, that is, and unwillingly: the patronizing way they dealt with their Egyptian opposite numbers was only too marked, and his blood boiled at their careless reference to 'gyppies' and 'wogs'. His private Anglophobia and hatred of those in authority grew. The senior Egyptian officers struck him as being a disgrace to their uniform. They were lazy, corrupt, and fat, and he was almost inclined to agree with the Englishman who said that their seniority went entirely by weight. He was infuriated, moreover, by the way they paid court to the British military mission. Almost instinctively he began to rebel. Some of his brother officers shared his feelings: one was called Anwar el Sadat, another Zacharia Mohieddin. Sitting in front of their tents in the evening, they endlessly discussed their grievances. The country was in a hopeless mess, they told each other, run by foreigners solely for the benefit of foreigners who not only exploited the Egyptians but despised them into the bargain. Despite, or perhaps because of, the 1936 Treaty the British dominated the land, and Egypt was trapped in a network of political and military obligations which were against her real interests and from which she could not free herself.

'When was it that I discovered the seeds of revolution implanted in my inmost soul?' Gamal asked rhetorically in his *Philosophy of Revolution'*. Seeds he discovered '...in the depths of the souls of many others...inborn seeds—a suppressed aspiration left as a legacy to us by a former generation.' In plain speech he was becoming an 'angry young man.' Many young Egyptians were doing just the same in the twilight of 1939.

On the outbreak of war his unit was dispersed and Lieutenant Abdel Nasser found himself posted to an isolated garrison deep in the Sudan. The only other officer with him was a lieutenant of the same age called Abdel Hakim Amer. Even as Hitler's armies swept through Belgium, Holland and France, and the Italian troops invaded Egypt, advancing as far as Sidi Barrani, the two young Egyptians talked ceaselessly of the future. 'The British are going to lose the war' they told each other gleefully. Maybe this would be the chance to cut free from the British yoke, once and for all.

Britain's own attitude towards Egypt at this period was quite simple. She sympathized to a large extent with the aspirations of the Egyptians. She had made, in the 1936 Treaty, as many concessions as she possibly could to Egypt's desire for absolute sovereignty. But the Egyptian question had to be viewed against the world background. Britain was engaged, almost alone, in a death struggle with the dictatorships of Nazi Germany and Fascist Italy. This was no time to start worrying about Egyptian susceptibilities. For good or for ill Egypt was a vital theatre of war and had to be denied to the enemy.

It was no secret that many Egyptians had pro-axis sympathies, not simply because, as the Arabs say, 'the enemy of my enemy is my friend', or because it looked as though the Nazis were going to be victorious, but also because the peculiar creed of national socialism put out by Dr Goebbels was meat and drink to anyone with a chip on his shoulder. Moreover the military might of the totalitarians fascinated young officers like Nasser and his friends who could not believe it held any menace for Egypt. Thus, suspicious of its loyalties, the British were inclined to treat the Egyptian army as a necessary nuisance which had to be kept well neutralized—a feeling which appeared to be justified when the Egyptian chief of staff, sacked at the request of British GHQ, attempted to join the Germans in Farouk's private plane.

Certainly in the early days of 1942 things looked black for the Allies. In the previous few months there had been numerous air raids on Alexandria; Greece had been lost; a pro-axis coup d'etat had taken place in Iraq: the Americans were still stunned by Pearl harbor, and Rommel was advancing in Libya. Hussein Sirry Pasha's ministry did its best to string along with the British, but shortages, particularly of food, and rocketing prices were beginning to cause serious unrest among the ordinary people in Egypt who felt they had been elbowed into a war which was no concern of theirs, and on the wrong side, too. Students paraded the streets shouting: 'We are Rommel's soldiers'. The Palace, traditionally pro-Italian, wanted to re-insure against an axis victory which now seemed likely, by naming a government favorable to Germany and Italy. The British, on the other hand, were desperately anxious to keep the country quiet, which only Nahas and a Wafd ministry could achieve.

At the beginning of February 1942 Sirry resigned, after being forced by the British to break off relations with Vichy France, and King Farouk appeared to be arranging for Maher Ali Pasha, whose pro-axis inclinations were notorious, to be called back to power. Upon which the British Ambassador, Sir Miles Lampson (by now Lord Killearn) paid a visit to the Palace. Without beating about the bush he told the King that the only man who could control the internal situation to the satisfaction of the British Government at a time when the strategic outlook was far from good was Nahas Pasha, the leader of the Wafd, and went on to deliver the warning that 'unless I hear by six o'clock tomorrow that Nahas Pasha has been asked to form a cabinet, your Majesty must expect the consequences'. Farouk rejected the ultimatum, but as soon as the Ambassador had left, he telephoned the heads of the various political parties to get together and form a coalition government under Nahas. All agreed save Nahas himself, who refused to preside over a coalition and insisted on a cabinet of his own choosing—that is to say, composed entirely of Wafdists. Between the old Britain-baiter and the Embassy, a deal had obviously been done.

A few minutes after nine o'clock the following evening, 4 February, British infantry moved into Abdin Square. Then a squadron of Stuart Mark 3 tanks lumbered into position and trained their guns on the Palace. Finally Lord Killearn's yellow Phantom III, preceded by an armored car, drove up to the Palace. The gates were shut but the armored car burst straight through. The Royal Guard was disarmed, and accompanied by General Stone, the new GOC British Troops in Egypt and eight officers with drawn revolvers, the Ambassador made his way up to Farouk's study. The twenty-two year-old King, who had been watching the proceedings from his window, reached furiously for his own gun, but was dissuaded by his chamberlain. A single false move and the throne would be toppled. When Lord Killearn and his party entered the office, Farouk was seated at his desk. 'I have come for your Majesty's answer' said the Ambassador curtly. 'We have already instructed Nahas Pasha to form the government of his choice' replied Farouk, with as much dignity as he could muster.

Probably the most embarrassed man in the room was General Stone, who until three weeks before had been a personal aide to Farouk. 'It was terrible to have to meet him again with an ultimatum like that' he confided later. Yet to a certain extent the ends justified the means. The Wafd faithfully repaid its debt to the British Ambassador and for the next two years Nahas kept the country firmly behind the Allies.

But for many Egyptians, the shock of 4 February was corrosive. By his high-handed action, Killearn left a wound which never really healed. Moreover, in shattering the triangle of power which had kept Egypt going for so long, he discredited the Palace and made an enemy of the King, and at the same time showed up Nahas as being a puppet of the British—of 'neglecting the nation's interest for the benefit of the British' as Makram Ebeid put it. The Wafd, so long identified as leaders in the struggle against the British, never recovered from the stigma of having been brought to power by British bayonets. 'I flame with anger' wrote Nasser to a friend. 'This is the cut of the knife which...has put souls into some bodies. They have learnt there is something known as dignity.' Angry voices were raised at the officers' club. The head of the Egyptian state had been spat upon, they cried. The King had become no more than an empty cipher, imprisoned in his own Palace. His army, his whole nation, had been humiliated. Egypt was no better than an occupied country, subdued by a single squadron of tanks. A staff officer, Colonel Mohammed Naguib, sent in his resignation. Three young lieutenants, Abdel Latif Boghdadi, Saleh Salem and Anwar Sadat, offered themselves as a suicide squad to perform any anti-British action that might be suggested.

Napoleon To Nasser

But Gamal Abdel Nasser, on 4 February 1942, began systematically planning revolution.

Tobruk fell. The Afrika Korps entered Egypt. Mersa Matruh fell. Rommel was at El Alamein. A troop of German tanks reached Burg el Arab, only a few miles west of Alexandria. A column of smoke in Garden City showed that GHQ were burning their secret papers. British families were evacuated from Egypt— On 3 July, as hourly the news became more desperate, the AOC'S secretary announced that she was marrying a Rhodesian tank officer immediately, that morning. The manager of Shepheard's produced his finest champagne for the luncheon. 'We'd better drink it now while we still can' he said wryly. Toasting the bride and groom, a British general declared melodramatically: 'Ladies and Gentlemen, we are witnessing the downfall of an Empire...'*

Outside, in the street, the crowd was chanting 'Rommel, Rommel'. At the Royal Automobile Club, whose chairman, Prince Abbas Halim had been in the Richthofen squadron in the First World War, plans for a welcome for the Germans were discussed. Some Egyptian officers, among them Anwar Sadat, whispered that the time had come to carry out a military coup in Cairo, overthrow Nahas, reinstate Ali Maher, harry the British troops and join up with the Axis. The supreme Guide of a fanatical religious organization called the Moslem Brotherhood, Sheikh Hassan El Banna, declaimed mystically about Egypt in arms, delivering herself from her bondage. But it was still only words, not deeds. Nahas Pasha remained unshakably behind the British, keeping a tight hold on security, closing down the Automobile Club, arresting fifth columnists, and reassuring the civil population. The moment of razor-edged anxiety passed. Rommel was held at El Alamein. Three months later he was being hounded back through Lybia, and the war had receded from Egypt. Soon the Germans were swept out of the whole of North Africa. The Italian campaign began. The Second Front was launched in Normandy.

In Cairo, Captain Gamal Abdel Nasser was appointed as an instructor at the Military Academy, about the same time as his friend Abdel Hakim Amer was sent to the staff college. For an embryonic revolutionary, it was an ideal point of contact. Hundreds of young officers passed through his hands. Slowly and methodically he began to vet each one in turn, listening to what they had to say, gauging the fire in their bellies, seldom talking much himself but all the time filing away in his mind the potential of each individual in the revolution he was already beginning to plan. Gradually the secret society of Free Officers was formed. Nothing was ever put on paper: it would have been far too dangerous. Who the Free Officers were, and the specific tasks assigned to each one, was known only to Gamal Abdel Nasser and Abdel Hakim Amer. There was never anything like a membership list; but the organization grew. Various sections were formed: finance, personnel, security, propaganda, and civilian terrorists. Each

137

section comprised some twenty cells of between five and ten members. No Free Officer knew any but the members of his own cell. The most carefully kept secret of all was the identity of the leader, which was so successfully concealed, that, although the existence of some sort of officers' movement was known to the authorities in Cairo, no one outside the conspiracy guessed the source of inspiration, or knew, even after the revolution had taken place, who the real leader was. Even the hard core of Free Officers were kept in the dark about their colleagues, and Nasser's habit of conferring with only one member at a time, and then listening rather than talking, gave each of them the feeling that it had been 'himself and Nasser'. Khaled Mohieddin was later to illustrate the technique in a newspaper article.

'Towards the end of 1944', he wrote over a decade later, 'I was walking along Ramses Street with a friend of mine. We were both members of a secret organization founded within the army in 1942. Suddenly my friend said: "Listen, Khaled, I've got a date with another officer. He's a good chap. You'll like him. Come and meet him." We turned into El Galali Street and climbed up to the third floor of a block of flats. A tall young man opened the door, and my friend introduced me. "Captain Gamal Abdel Nasser" he said, "instructor at the Military Academy". Gamal took us into the dining room. We sat on opposite sides of the table which was covered with books. He smiled at us and said he was preparing for his examinations for the staff college...the conversation turned to the secret political organization of which we were all members. He seemed to know all about it...As I left, he said: "I'd like to see you again soon—there are a lot of things to talk about."'

So circumspect were Nasser's methods that Khaled was unaware that he was dealing with the leader of the Free Officers, or that his own cousin Zacharia Mohieddin had been the original member to be signed up. This sense of caution characterized all the activities of the secret organization. Some of the officers were impatient for immediate action. Anwar el Sadat, who had been imprisoned by the British authorities for collaborating with two German spies who operated from a houseboat on the Nile, proposed to blow up the British Embassy—but Nasser absolutely vetoed the plan, reminding him of the reprisals which had followed the murder of Sir Lee Stack in 1924. Instead Anwar began to plan political assassinations. After a daylight attempt on Nahas Pasha—the leader of the Wafd who had shown himself so staunch a friend of the British—had failed, Sadat's terrorist group concentrated on the next politician on their list, Amin Osman Pasha, Finance Minister in the wartime Wafd government, whose steadfast efforts at improving Anglo-Egyptian relations had earned him a KBE from London and his death warrant at the hands of the Free Officers. As he entered the Old Victorian Club at lunchtime one day he was shot at point blank range. But the murderers were caught, and Anwar el Sadat, implicated in their confession, received a long prison sentence. After this, Nasser clamped down on such actions, which could have jeopardized the whole secret organization, and concentrated solely on weaving the tapestry of revolution in quiet, out of the way places, moving from one colleague's house to another, perpetually on the lookout for that fanatical glint in a young officer's eyes which foretold a potential new candidate; educating himself in the techniques of revolution; and laying down the groundlines for the coup that one day he promised himself he would make.

Raymond Flower

Note:

This luncheon for my cousin's wedding (I happened to be the best man) turned out to have some historical interest. During it, news that the German thrust had been checked short of Alexandria was brought to the Chief Engineer, British troops in Egypt, who was thus able to countermand the order, already given, to open the dykes of Lake Mariut and flood Alexandria.

Chapter 16

Twilight of the *Ancien Règime*

Not all the revolutionary factions of this period were so circumspect. The Moslem Brotherhood, originally formed in 1928 by Sheikh Hassan el-Banna as a religious movement to revivify Islam, had now openly become a fanatical organization propounding a heady sort of mysticism and the more extreme forms of Koranic doctrines. Clothed in a red cloak which covered most of his face, the 'Supreme Guide' traveled around the country preaching against the presence and privileges of the Infidel and the corruption of the political parties. Some people thought him a saint, others an eccentric. But el-Banna's personal magnetism was such that thousands of people, particularly the disappointed extremists from the Wafd, spoke of him in rather the same voice as the Sudanese dervishes had spoken of the Mahdi.

Basically the Brotherhood's message was one of revenge and hope: a palliative for action rather than a revolutionary force, and significantly enough the Brotherhood was prepared to play ball with both the Palace and the British, while outwardly reviling both.

Early on the Free Officers had tentatively put out feelers for a working agreement with the 'Supreme Guide', but had come to the conclusion that for all its grandiloquent appeal to the hate-ridden extremes of the population, the Moslem Brotherhood was in reality a relatively harmless safety valve for the burgeoning discontent which was once more sweeping through the nation. It was for this very reason that the authorities took no action against it until a wave of assassinations was traced to the Brotherhood in the post-war period.

The end of the Second World War found Egypt in as explosive a state as it had been after the 1914-18 war. The British army, which according to the terms of the 1936 Treaty should have long since disappeared off into the Canal Zone, was still more in evidence than ever. That the troops remained by virtue of clause 7 of that same Treaty safeguarding the territorial integrity of Egypt was little consolation to those Egyptians who felt, with some justification, that Britain and the Allies had been fighting a war for their own survival and not Egypt's.

To be subject everywhere to the often heavy-handed regulations of martial law enforced by British military police was exasperating, to say the least, a full four years after the Axis threat to Egypt had dissolved. But there were other reasons for discontent as well. High war profits had once again made the rich richer, and inflation was hitting the masses hard. The gap between the social classes had grown. Wartime planning had centralized control of the economy and of all business affairs in Cairo, and almost doubled the population of the capital in less than five years, while the resumption of imports was closing down many small 'war-boom' factories and swelling the number of unemployed. But perhaps the greatest source of discontent was the bland futility of the government. Political leadership, still in the hands of the Palace and Pashas, was progressively growing worse.

During and after the war, the great landowners continued to run their estates as feudal fiefs, drawing huge incomes from the fertile delta land which could give up to three crops a year and yielded a minimum return of £50 per acre. But the nearest that most of them ever got to their domains was a routine half-hour at the Daira (estate office) in Cairo—usually to collect some petty cash, telephone friends at the ministry, lay bets on the afternoon's racing, and study the specifications of a new car or the itinerary for a forthcoming trip to Europe—before being driven to the Mohammed Ali Club for an hour's chat about politics before luncheon. The actual running of their estates was left to the wakil (factor) who, while cheating them on every side, could always be relied on to see that the electors in the neighborhood, most of whom worked on the estate, put their crosses against the Pasha's name at election time.

With certain conspicuous exceptions, such as Talaat Harb Pasha, who founded the Misr group of Companies, and Ahmed Abboud, whose industrial complex made him one of the richest men in the world, few of the Egyptian notables ventured into commerce. They were content to leave business in the hands of the foreigners, and to decorate occasional board meetings quite unashamedly as 'names'. Perhaps it was because they felt at a disadvantage against the sharper business intellects of the European and the Jew, perhaps because they sensed the uselessness of setting up new projects in a tightly held market. Probably they did not seriously care one way or the other. Land and politics were sufficient with the enervating roundabout of the Cairo 'season' and long summers spent in Europe.

Rich foreigners who owned factories, the great Jewish families with department stores, Syrian importers and diplomatic attaches likewise moved through the glittering circles of society. Polo, golf or tennis in the afternoons, followed by enormous parties: 'Remember the period between 1941 and 1951? How fantastic it was!' an Egyptian of the *ancien regime* recollected with more than a touch of nostalgia recently, 'Three cocktail parties every evening...dinners at the *auberge*...gambling at the Automobile club. I remember Farouk playing *chemin-de-fer* with a group, Mohammed Sultan, Barouk, Nabil Ismail, Emile Ades and so forth. At each throw there was £100,000 on the table. Toto Ades lost £30,000 that night. Not much compared to Monte Carlo, perhaps, but quite good for Cairo...'

It was hardly surprising that with such stakes an unwritten rule for membership of the Royal Automobile Club was that the candidate should prove he was a millionaire, or that members should address each other as 'Your

Excellency'. The New Year's Eve dinners at the club were prestigious affairs with thirty or forty courses on the menu, champagne bars in every room and a running buffet for anyone who still felt pangs of hunger. Nor was this out of the ordinary: when Abdel Hamid Chawarby's daughter was married, the whole immense garden of the pasha's villa was covered with persian carpets, and the buffet included a special 20 metre long table serving caviar alone, ladled out like porridge to the thousand-odd guests who danced to a choice of three orchestras. The same lavish *train de vie* spilled over into the fashionable resorts of Europe each summer. Not without cause could Andrea Badrutt complain at the Palace Hotel, St Moritz, that the 1952 revolution completely ruined his summer seasons.

Leading this gorgeous but gangrenous set-up was the gross figure of the King. Farouk had come to the throne in a burst of popularity. Everyone's heart had gone out to the slim, handsome prince, still in his teens, who had been summoned back from England by his father's unexpected death in 1936. His marriage to the lovely young Farida had enhanced his prestige. Literally thousands of babies born at this period were named after him. Even the most anti-royalist of politicians had been won over for a time. But his education, so abruptly cut short at barely seventeen, was not proof against the softly oozing malice of the italianate clique at the Palace, and the war brought a schizophrenic rupture to his loyalties. Perhaps he might have ridden the shock had his wisest councilor, Hassanein Pasha, not been killed by a skidding British lorry, and Lord Killearn not so traumatically confronted him, on 4 February 1942, with the clear-cut choice of abdicating or obeying. There were other members of the royal family—Prince Mohammed Ali and Prince Abdel Moneim especially—who would have been only too ready to take his place, and Prince Abbas Halim enjoyed recounting, at the bar of the Automobile Club, how a few days before his *coup de main* Killearn had taken him to one side. 'The boy is misbehaving' the ambassador had said to him. If we decided to make a change, would you be prepared to take over the Crown?' Abbas lit a Partagas before replying. 'And if I misbehaved, would you replace me by Mohammed Ali or Abdel Moneim?'

'I suppose we would' answered Killearn frankly.

Abbas puffed a cloud of smoke. 'It sounds like a joke,' he said wryly. But the ambassador was in no joking mood these days, as Abbas Halim himself discovered a few weeks later, when he was jailed for two years on Killearn's orders for having given a champagne party at the Automobile Club the night that Tobruk fell to the Germans. In fact, he did give a party that night—but it was a party for Bobby Khayatt, a well-known Copt, whose birthday happened to be on that date, and it had been arranged long before the news from Tobruk had come through. Abbas Halim relates that when he was finally released, the first person he met in the Mohammed Ali Club was Killearn, who patted him on the back and said benignly: 'My dear chap! It's been ages since I saw you. Where on earth have you been?'

Farouk would have fared no better than his cousin had he not capitulated to the British ultimatum that February evening, and the event turned out to be a watershed in Egyptian history. Not only was it the acknowledged spark-point for the Free Officer's movement; it was also the moment at which Farouk abdicated in spirit. From then onwards, observers agree that he ceased to care any more for the affairs of state, and turned to the consolations of personal pleasure, cynically playing the game of royalty, and keeping the dinner tables of the capital in a constant state of titter at his *boutades*. It was amusing, of course, to be able to describe how Farouk had been driving his black 'gangster' Citroen round and round Opera Square on the pavements, blowing the horn designed to sound like the screams of a dog being run over, or to visualize the scene at the Wadi Natrun rest-house when a royal party had arrived in the middle of the night and shot the place up. It was diverting to list the number of prominent businessmen who had gone into hiding because Farouk was making after their wives. It made a good story that the uniformed King, who had just grown a beard, should have had his face slapped by an ENSA girl who mistook him for a naval officer when he pinched her behind. But it hardly improved the image of the Crown.

A Falstaffian sense of humor, which developed with his girth, gave him an occasional laugh at the expense of the British. Once, at the Royal Shooting and Fishing Club, to which the Allied services were admitted on temporary membership but which the APM had decreed should be 'officers only', the British C-in-C arrived with a party of senior officers, all resplendent with red tabs and scrambled egg hats save the most junior, a single lieutenant-Colonel. From his table on the other side of the room, Farouk eyed the top military brass with distaste until suddenly the doors opened and a couple of New Zealand privates walked in, sat down and ordered a beer, apparently oblivious of the outraged looks from the C-in-C table. After a short while, at a nod from the general, the half-colonel got up and went over to the private soldiers. 'You are out of bounds,' he said, taking their names and numbers, 'You will leave immediately!' But before the two New Zealanders had time to move, the maitre d'hotel swept up bearing a magnum of *Veuve' Clicquot* which, with a ceremonious bow, he presented to the privates. 'With the compliments of His Majesty' he explained, pouring out the champagne. A royal smirk met the angry glares from the C-in-C table.

Sometimes the pinpricks were blunter—for instance, when the King was reported to have remarked at the Syrian Club, quite unfairly, that it would be better for Lord Killearn not to gamble at all if he did not intend to pay his debts. Or the party at a Zamaiek flat when Farouk spent the evening throwing British officers' hats off the verandah and snap-shooting at them with his revolver as they spun to the ground.

Against a background of pomp which required that all traffic should be kept off the streets an hour or more before Farouk sped by in his scarlet Rolls Royce, the royal buffoonery continued. Members of the Royal Automobile Club became accustomed to finding, as they nonchalantly handed in their hats and tarbouches, that the porter's desk was occupied by the King behind a plate of oysters. With Farouk, anything was possible. On an official occasion in the middle of summer, a number of dignitaries were lined up to be presented to the King. Among them was the young and attractive wife of a prominent surgeon. When her turn came, she made a deep curtsy only to find that Farouk had placed his hand on her shoulder and prevented her from rising.

It is such a hot day;' he said sympathetically, let me give you something to cool you down.' And taking a piece of ice from a bucket on the table behind him, he slipped it down her bosom.

A joke of Farouk's which had the business community of Cairo chuckling happened one evening on the roof-garden terrace of the Semiramis Hotel when, by coincidence, a party to celebrate the visit of the President of Coca-Cola coincided with another reception for the head of Pepsi-Cola. Such a situation was too good to be missed: within minutes the hotel staff was mobilized, and to the President of Coca-Cola was delivered a case of Pepsi, while to the Pepsi-Cola executives went a case of Coca-Cola, with the 'compliments of His Majesty', who was there to acknowledge the toast they reluctantly had to drink with their competitor's product.

Another of Farouk's passions was gambling. He frequently spent all night at the tables, which meant, of course, that none of the other players could leave; and if partners were lacking he would go to people's houses and blow the horn of his car until he had dragged them out of bed. He gambled with some flair, bluffing continuously, but he nearly always lost. A notebook found at Abdin after the revolution showed that in a single year he was down £850,000. Since he hated losing, he was not above manipulating the cards in his favor, and certain business men who were dependent on his favor literally had to go into hiding when the going became too expensive. On one famous occasion at the Automobile Club, for instance, he drew a hand of three kings and tossed £10,000 into the pot. The betting mounted quickly, and finally he was called. His opponent laid down a full house. Producing his three kings with one hand, Farouk raked in the chips with the other. His opponent objected tactfully, but Farouk waved the protest aside. 'Your Majesty,' insisted the other player, 'my hand beats yours. You have only three kings.

'I am the fourth king,' replied Farouk regally, and pocketed the chips.

But his greatest passion, undoubtedly, was women. Almost from the wedding day, his marriage to the lovely and long-suffering Farida went on the rocks, and an endless succession of names were linked with his, so that before long the royal favor ceased to rate more than a coarse snigger. A recent biographer estimates that in his relatively short life (he died at forty-five) Farouk had sexual relations with over 5,000 women. It was no secret in Cairo that his performances in this sphere were inadequate, to say the least, which led some people to suppose that despite everything he was impotent. This was not so, in fact: the trouble was that he was underdeveloped—which no doubt accounts for much of the oddity of his behavior.

In the capital, every night club had a special ring-side table reserved for the King, which at regular intervals Farouk would 'deign to honor with His Presence' as the newspapers always reported it, accompanied by a couple of aides who would be sent with a royal invitation to any young woman who caught his fancy—frequently with embarrassing results, for woe betide any stranger who objected to such advances.

On one occasion he picked up a cabaret singer and within minutes was speeding with her in his Cadillac convertible along the main road to Heliopolis—where he pulled the car into a suitably shady lay-by and began a front-seat seduction routine worthy of any college student. As it happened, the vice-squad was patrolling that night and the not-so-touching scene was suddenly picked out by the police spotlights. Farouk jerked a gun from his holster and fired wildly in their direction, at the same time accelerating violently away, with the police car in hot pursuit. When he was finally cornered, and the officer strode grimly over to make an arrest, he was unnerved to be confronted by the fat bulk of his monarch, who slapped his face, seized his revolver, fired a volley of shots over the patrol car, and then laughing boisterously, got back behind the wheel of his Cadillac and sped off into the night.

On another similar occasion, he and his partner were waylaid by a band of thugs on a country lane near Helouan, who—failing to recognize Farouk—stripped both of them of their valuables and were about to cut his throat when the leader shouted disdainfully: 'All right, leave the fat pig. He's not worth the trouble of killing.' The following morning, the whole police force of Cairo was mobilized and in due course the bandits were caught. On Farouk's orders, they were executed on the spot—save the leader, who was given 100 lashes for referring to his monarch as a 'fat pig', and £1,000 for having spared his life.

Often there was a sinister aspect to his escapades. A young army captain with an attractive wife, for instance, found himself suddenly posted to the Sudan. Some weeks later he was able to snatch a few days' leave and was astonished, when he opened the door of his flat, to find a notorious General, the king's chief ADC, sitting inside the living room. After an interval of polite conversation, he moved towards the door of his bedroom, at which the ADC said sharply: 'Don't go in there!' The young man's chin went up. 'I warn you' repeated the general, drawing his revolver, 'don't open that door!' And as the young officer, suddenly wild-eyed, made an impulsive move towards it, the general lifted his revolver and shot him dead on the spot. As cold-bloodedly as that, said the whispers. After all, it was the King who was in bed with his wife.

Still bolstered up by the loyalty of the army (and the reassuring presence of British troops in the Canal Zone) and surrounded by an increasingly seedy clique in the Palace, the gargantuan monarch seemed to thrive on openly shedding any dignity the throne might still have had. Of the outcome, he apparently had no illusions. Soon, he was fond of saying, there would only be five monarchs left in the world: the king of England, and the kings of hearts, spades, diamonds and clubs. As time wore on, he took to governing less through his ministers than through his personal 'privy council', consisting of his valet, his barber, his chauffeur, and a few others, who manipulated ministries and made promotions as blandly as they arranged his private assignations. These were the men of power in the final stages of Farouk's reign.

In the spring of 1949, when Cairo was seething with frustration at the fiasco in Palestine, they persuaded the king that it was time for him to get married again. His divorce, at the height of the Palestine War in 1948, had upset public opinion; it was essential for his prestige to have an heir to the throne. Farouk shrugged his shoulders. He was not particularly interested in marrying again, he said, but if they insisted—well, they knew his tastes; they had better find him a wife.

A few days later, a young couple walked into the king's favorite jeweler's shop in Soliman Pasha Street to select an engagement ring. The girl had a pudgy face, a pert, well-rounded figure, and the creamy white skin of a Circassian. As he showed them his trays of rings, the jeweler had a sudden thought. From his inside office, he dialed the king's private number. "Your Majesty,' he said, I think I have found just the person you want.' The king told him that he would come round immediately: meanwhile to keep the girl there in the shop. By this time the couple had already made their choice, with the finesse of his calling the jeweler insisted on showing them everything he had. Half an hour later he spotted the king looking appraisingly at the girl through the window. After a moment Farouk caught his eye and made an affirmative sign with the tips of his fingers and his thumb in the shape of a circle. The jeweler took his cue. From the back of the safe he brought out a magnificent diamond ring and to the dismay of the young man he gently substituted it for the modest jewel which the astonished girl already had on her finger. 'By command of His Majesty,' he murmured.

Such were the circumstances it is said in which Narriman, a girl from Heliopolis, became the last Queen of Egypt.

Three years previously, in the spring of 1946, a series of ugly riots against the continued presence of the British army in Cairo had finally convinced GHQ, very much against their will, that it was time to say goodbye to the amenities of Shepheard's and Gezira Sporting Club, and on July 4th (a significant day, as Americans know) a full ten years later than intended by the 1936 Treaty, the British GOC handed the Egyptian Chief of Staff a silver key to the Citadel, and left after lunch for his new headquarters in the desert wastes of Fayid in the

Canal Zone. The departure of the British troops, and subsequent negotiations in which Mr. Attlee's Government gave the impression they might evacuate the Canal Zone as well, removed much of the sense of resentment from the minds of the Free Officers.* Some of them felt they could now relax. But Gamel Abdel Nasser objected strongly to such talk, and argued that their aims would not have been achieved until the last foreign soldier had left the soil of Egypt. In reality, his objectives were now a great deal more far-reaching than just this. The idea of revolution was becoming a part and parcel of his very being. With the utmost patience and circumspection he continued to spin his plans, surreptitiously sounding out all possible contacts, 'a veritable dynamo' as Sarwat Okasha recalls, 'always working or reading or discussing', in anticipation of the moment he would launch his desperate coup against everything that in his eyes was throttling the very soul of the country.

But in 1948 the band of Free Officers found themselves suddenly projected into an adventure of quite a different sort. The United Nations voted for the partition of Palestine. On 15 May, the British mandate ended; the Jews declared an independent state of Israel; and the Arabs ordered their troops into Palestine.

For most of the Free Officers, the Palestine War was a searing experience. Many of them were killed or wounded. Some who had gone to the front full of patriotic zeal returned disillusioned but matured. Others, like Brigadier Mohammed Naguib, who was wounded for the third time, and Major Gamal Abdel Nasser, who was also wounded, made reputations for themselves. But the campaign itself was a grotesque flop. For all Cairo radio's stirring reports of how Egyptian troops had stormed enemy kibbutzes shouting 'Long live King Farouk, the glorious supreme commander of the army! ', the plain fact was that most of them were on the run. Inadequately armed and meaninglessly commanded by senior officers who barely left Cairo, their logistics in hopeless disorder, the Egyptians were routed by a small army of Israelis whom they out-numbered by fifty to one. Only a tiny pocket hung on near Gaza and saved the Egyptian army from utter humiliation. It was in this holding operation at Faluja, where many of the Free Officers found themselves besieged—Nasser, Amer, Zacharia Mohieddin, Salah Salem and Okasha among them—that Major Abdel Nasser made his military reputation through a dashing counter attack which prevented the Israelis from overrunning the Egyptian positions. To him, Faluja became a symbol. 'Is not our country another Faluja, a much greater Faluja, besieged by the enemy, a prey to the climbers and traitors and greedy?' he was later to write in his *Philosophy of the Revolution.* And always in his mind were the dying words of his friend Ahmed Abdel Aziz, a Free Officer killed in action: 'Remember, the real battle is in Egypt!'

Gamal Abdel Nasser returned from the front with a deep distaste for war, vowing that if ever the matters were in his hands, he would 'think a thousand times before committing his countrymen to war...only if there was no alternative, and the honor and integrity of the nation were threatened and nothing else could save them but a battle' would he, in this mood, consider resorting to arms. But above all he and his fellow-officers came back in a burning rage against the whole corrupt 'establishment' in Cairo which had not only involved Egypt in such an ignominious situation but had openly been making money out of it. It was no secret that the Palace itself was mixed up in shady arms deals through which defective equipment had been supplied to the forces. The whole army felt that it had been treacherously let down by its leaders, and in the sullen atmosphere of defeat, which no amount of propaganda and victory parades could camouflage, the last shreds of faith in the *ancien régime* disappeared.

Before long the Moslem Brotherhood were making capital out of the general unrest, and probably would have staged a coup themselves had the Prime Minister not ordered their suppression. A month later, Nokrashi Pasha was assassinated in the Ministry of Interior while surrounded by his security officers. His successor, Abdel Hadi Pasha, took firm measures against the extremists, imprisoning all known communists and crowding thousands of Brotherhood members into detention camps. The assassination of Sheikh Hassan el Banna was a part of this cleaning-up action. Even the Free Officers organization came close to being unmasked. Nasser himself was interrogated by the Prime Minister who suspected a conspiracy between the army and the brotherhood. But somehow he talked himself out of trouble, reminding his interrogators in a burst of righteous anger that he had only just returned from fighting for his country. He was allowed to go free, but for a long time remained a marked man, and only extreme care and a good deal of luck prevented the army rebels from being exposed.

Once Ibrahim Abdel Hadi and his secret police had rounded up the most dangerous terrorist elements, the Palace tried to soften public unrest by bringing the Wafd back into power. Nahas Pasha immediately instituted a number of social reforms, which included the distribution of government and royal lands and special funds to the needy, but it soon became apparent that the Wafd were up to their old tricks, and that most of the beneficiaries were relatives of Madame Nahas and other ministers. A further serious scandal which could not be hushed up was the rigging of the Alexandria cotton market in the wake of the Korean war boom. To take people's minds off the corruption of the Wafdists, a smoke screen was urgently needed. Nahas, an old hand at the game, knew just what to do. Beating the anti-British drum was always a sure way of distracting public opinion from troubles nearer home. On 8 October 1951 Nahas unilaterally abrogated the 1936 Treaty—which he himself had signed—and proclaimed Farouk as King of the Sudan as well as Egypt.

Dangerous as the move was, it suited the government's purpose as a safety valve for overheated emotions. Nahas had no intention of declaring war on England, which would have been folly considering the strength of the great Canal Zone base, but it gave scope to harness extremist discontent into guerrilla operations against the British and make some political capital into the bargain. Predictably, the mobs who had been shouting against the crimes of the Wafd now surged through the streets crying: 'Down with the British! Long live Nahas! '

What the Cairo newspapers grandly called 'The battle of the Canal' was little more than a series of hit and run tactics by the terrorist elements—Moslem Brothers, Communists, and Ahmed Hussein's green shirts—who in Nahas' view, were better employed throwing hand grenades at British sentries or kidnapping military lorries than stirring up trouble in the capital. The Egyptian army itself took no part in the affair, though the Free Officers secretly did what they could to help the partisans.

On the insistence of the British Embassy, the garrison troops at first countered these activities (which were more of an annoyance than a threat) with little other than a defensive routine. It was obvious to the ambassador that nothing would be gained by losing one's temper; to crush the partisans would mean moving out of the Treaty area, which would be diplomatically compromising, and once started a campaign might escalate into complete military occupation of the country, which was simply not practical under the circumstances (a fact which was apparently overlooked in 1956).

There was a limit to the patience of the GOC, General Erskine, who was a soldier, not a politician. When, following an attack on the munitions depot at Tel el Kebir, it was discovered that the Egyptian auxiliary police (the Buluq Nizam) were working behind the scenes with the guerrillas, he decided to give them a lesson they would not forget. At seven o'clock one morning the police headquarters at Ismalia was surrounded by tanks, and an ultimatum, was given to the Buluq Nizam to hand in their arms and surrender. News of this development reached Fouad Serag el Din, the Minister of the Interior, in his bath. Loftily, he snapped back orders to fight 'to the last man and the last bullet'.

On 25 January, with pathetically inadequate arms, the Buluq Nizam resisted bravely until their ammunition gave out. By eleven o'clock the police station was a heap of rubble; forty-six auxiliaries had been killed and a further 100 wounded.

Solicitous Egyptian friends warning that the situation was dangerous for foreigners. A heavy, crackling sense of doom as the day dawned. Thousands of sullen yet apparently disciplined demonstrators forming up near the university. A string of Rolls Royce and Bentley cars, gleaming in the bright winter sunshine, being driven from down-town showrooms to a less vulnerable location. Hostile, knowing sneers on the usually smiling faces of the black-uniformed police. An apprehensive hush in usually bustling offices. Towards three o'clock in the afternoon, a huge growing gray-black cloud of smoke over the city, drifting gradually towards the pyramids. A hysterical voice sobbing down the telephone: 'Everything is burning...they're burning everything...the whole of Cairo is on fire...everything is destroyed!' Wild rumors of foreigners being massacred.

Through the shocked, dumbfounded twilight, the harsh tones of Nahas Pasha declaring martial law. In the aftermath, a stupefied drive through the litter-filled streets of a ghostly, smoking city, with nothing but rubble and fire-twisted ruins where familiar landmarks had been. Hushed, black-looking crowds with a detectably malicious gleam of triumph in their eyes: Black Saturday, 26 January 1952, the day in which a volcano of passion, smoldering for decades, exploded in a holocaust of revenge, and the whole frame-work of the *ancien régime* went up in smoke.

Raymond Flower

Notes:

On 7 May 1946, the Prime Minister, Mr. Attlee offered 'the withdrawal of all British...Forces from Egyptian territory and to settle in negotiation the stages and date of completion of this withdrawal, and the arrangement to be made by the Egyptian Government to make possible mutual assistance in time of war or imminent threat of war in accordance with the alliance.' (H. C. Deb 5th series Vol 423 cols 774-5). Unhappily the negotiations broke down through political opposition and mistrust both in England and Egypt. Lord Stansgate later asserted that 'had we been able to announce that in future British troops would only be in Egypt by Egyptian consent, we would have had a treaty in a month.' (RIIA Information Papers No 19 p 88)

Chapter 17

The "Free Officers" Act

Who exactly it was that master-minded the burning of Cairo may never be known, just as the full facts regarding the assassination of President Kennedy may never quite clearly be settled. Some people believed it was engineered by the King, to discredit the Wafd. Others believed that it was the Wafd, to discredit the king, or the communists, in the hope of seizing power in the disorder. Some even suggested, so instinctive was the reflex to see the hand of the British everywhere, that the British Embassy was behind it. The most likely answer is that it was the self-combustive outcome of a tacit but irresponsible conspiracy between authorities and extremists of all complexions to stage a monster demonstration which got completely and disastrously out of hand. That it could have been avoided is shown by the parallel situation in Alexandria, where firm measures by the Governor, Mortada el Magraghi, prevented any serious disorder.

Overnight, the news of the slaughter of the Buluq Nizam had brought tempers to boiling point. From early morning mobs began to flock into the great square in front of Cairo university, a pulsing throng representing every fracture of discontent—Moslem Brothers, communists, green-shirted socialists and ordinary people in galabiyas—all roaring for blood. They could not know that the Council of Ministers had decided in a midnight session to break off diplomatic relations with Great Britain and to seize eighty prominent English residents as hostages. But they soon perceived that the police, instead of beating them over the heads as usual, were actually demonstrating at their side, and that no holds were barred as the Minister of Social Affairs shouted from a balcony: 'This is your day...you will be avenged!'

For most of the morning the mobs did nothing more serious than scream slogans. But just before midday there occurred an incident that sparked the holocaust. On the terrace of the Badia cabaret in Opera Square a police officer was drinking whisky with one of the establishment's hostesses. Someone rebuked him for enjoying himself in such a manner while his comrades were being butchered in Ismalia. A fight started; the mob swarmed into the cabaret, drenched the furniture with paraffin, and within moments the whole place was ablaze. But almost simultaneously in other parts of the city jeep-loads of men with paraffin and flaming torches were beginning methodically to set fire to one building after another. Mainly they seem to have been concentrating on firms and institutions which were known to be either British or Jewish. No one knew who they were, although the sinister figure of a professional incendiary, said to be from the Polish Embassy, was always in the center of any trouble.

At the British Turf Club, a number of habitués were having their customary drinks before luncheon. Among them were the Canadian Chargé d'Affaires and the arabist, James Craig. No one was taking the riots very seriously; they had seen this sort of thing before.

'Suddenly my driver appeared in the bar and insisted I should leave immediately' recalls the Ford agent, Dennis Birch, 'He literally pulled me by the arm out into my car. A couple of minutes more and I would have had it.' For by then the mob had burst into the clubhouse, drenched everything in petrol, and tossed in a match. Seven members who tried to escape, their clothes on fire, were forced back into the building and perished in the flames.

By this time buildings were now ablaze throughout the center of the city and Europeans were having hair-raising escapes. The manager of the J. Arthur Rank owned 'Rivoli' cinema was chased through the corridors by a gang of men with knives and only escaped by leaping from a second floor window. At the showrooms of the Cairo Motor Company incendiaries cut through the heavy iron grilles and burned cars in the street before setting fire to the offices. 'When the fire engine came they used it to spray petrol over the building' the watchman reported, In a few seconds everything was ablaze.' So drastic were their methods that two rioters were themselves trapped inside and burnt to death. Similar scenes were unfolding all over the city.

Most dramatic perhaps were the happenings at Shepheard's hotel, for so long the mecca of travelers. During the morning a lorry-load of men had presented themselves to the management saying they were a municipal DDT squad, and had sprayed powder into most of the rooms, but in fact what they used was a highly inflammable substance. When towards three o'clock in the afternoon the incendiaries arrived, it only took a matter of minutes for the whole great sprawling edifice to catch ablaze. How many visitors were trapped in their rooms will never be known, since the registers were destroyed along with the hotel.

For most of the day, pandemonium raged without any restraint whatsoever. At the height of the riots, the Prime Minister, Nahas Pasha, was having a pedicure, and his only known action during these vital hours was to send an armored car to fetch his wife from her hairdresser's in Kasr el Nil. Fouad Serag el Din, the Minister of the Interior, was closeted in his office negotiating a real estate deal. When this was concluded he telephoned the Commander in Chief at Abdin Palace, but was unable to get through. The King was holding a luncheon party for 400 army officers to celebrate the birth of his son Prince Ahmed, and nobody at the function could be disturbed. Not before dusk did the first detachments of soldiers make a belated attempt to restore order, by which time the riff raff of Cairo was scrabbling around in the ruins for whatever pickings were to be had. The looting continued far into the night. By the time sheer physical exhaustion had brought the rioting to an end, practically every bar, cinema and cabaret in the city had been destroyed, and over 400 buildings had been burnt down or gutted. The center of the city looked as though it had been through a bombardment. In fact, what had happened was the bloody prelude to a bloodless revolution.

Egypt was split wide open, like a great watermelon, for everyone to see that revolt was oozing in every seed. If the King had discredited the Wafd once again by holding Nahas responsible for the events of Black Saturday, he had also lit a time bomb under the Crown itself. No divinity could hedge him any longer.

The Free Officers had originally set the target date for their coup as late as 1955. Gamal Abdel Nasser did not plan to strike until he was absolutely certain of success. 'As a matter of principle' he explained to the others, 'I never act—I only react.' Events were now playing into their hands. But they realized that even if they were to be successful in seizing power, a group of unknown officers might very well fail to win over public opinion and general acceptance either in Egypt or abroad. The British army, after all, was only just down the road. It was known that British detachments had been alerted to move into Cairo at a moment's notice had the riots escalated. The British army had always been a last ditch insurance policy for the Palace. In desperation the King might call them in if the throne was in danger. On the other hand, the conspirators argued, the British themselves were known to be sick to death with Farouk and his clique, and would very likely welcome an army dictatorship, provided it seemed respectable. (This assessment was absolutely true: GHQ always regarded the army as the most reliable factor in the country, perhaps because they felt it was largely British-trained). What the Free Officers obviously needed most of all was someone with prestige as a figurehead—an army man who would command widespread respect.

The first name to be considered for the job was their former patron, the foxy old Aziz el Masri, who had tried to help Rommel during the war. But they had to admit that he was too elderly and had been in retirement much too long. The next on the list was General Fouad Sadek, who had made his mark in Palestine. But hardly had they decided to approach him than the news came through that Farouk had appointed him to be chief of staff. Upon which Abdel Hakim Amer suggested his own boss, General Mohammed Naguib, and Nasser agreed immediately that this was an excellent choice. The good natured, pipe-smoking Commander of the Frontier Corps was something of a hero in the army. He had been wounded three times so seriously in Palestine that he had been left for dead, and he was the only man in the army to wear three wound stripes on his breast. Moreover he was already in touch with the Free Officers' movement through Amer, his ADC. Nasser's one misgiving was whether this ranking general would submit to being merely a figurehead; but Amer reassured him on this point.

The Free Officers were beginning to come more and more into the open; since late 1951, indeed, the movement was clandestine only in the sense that its leaders were unknown. Some of the participants, more organization-minded perhaps than Nasser, wanted to establish themselves as a formal body, with committees, plans and programs, but this Nasser absolutely rejected. As a concession, he agreed to become the head of an executive committee which, although its members changed from time to time, was usually known as 'The Nine'. However there was never anything formal about this, and indeed the only committee members who knew the names of all the Free Officers were Nasser and Amer. The tracks were covered so stealthily that neither the King's secret police nor the Ministry of the Interior had the slightest suspicion until the very day of the revolution that Nasser himself had any part in the movement.

Since it was impossible to hold mass meetings or operate at all in the open, they began to circulate pamphlets attacking the excesses of the King and the government. These were painstakingly tapped out with two fingers on Zacharia Mohieddin's portable typewriter, mimeographed, and carried into army messes under the seats of officers' cars. After a while they were boldly distributed through the open mail—though always dispatched from different post-boxes. Copies were even sent to the Palace and the Ministry of the Interior, whose job it was to stamp out the conspiracy.

Such activities were all very well, but Nasser knew that something more substantial was necessary to test the real stature of the Free Officers. There were perhaps a thousand of them in all, but the army as a whole had to be sounded to gauge what overall support a mutiny would have. And so Naguib was put up as a candidate for the politically sensitive position of President of the Officers' Club in Zamaiek, and the word went round to vote for the man with the 3 on his chest. The King's nominee was General Hussein Sirry Amer, who was much detested because of his part in some scurrilous arms deals. The election proceedings opened unexpectedly with a request for three minutes silence in tribute to one of the Free Officers who had been killed by the secret police. Then the vote was taken. Naguib was elected by over eighty per cent of the ballot.

It was a bitter rebuff for the King, who promptly cancelled the election, but it showed quite clearly how the wind was blowing. Farouk could no longer count on the loyalty of the army. This was even more strongly emphasized by an assassination attempt on General Sirry Amer, and the appearance of a dagger with a note pinned to his own desk at Abdin Palace (soon, said the note, the target will be yourself—and not in the back either). But equally it was impossible for Nasser to delay action much longer if he were to escape the dragnet which was being prepared by the Palace secret police. Indeed Mortagha el Maraghi, now the strong man at the Ministry of Interior, seemed to be on the verge of sniffing out the real hard core of the Free Officers' movement, and the King was maneuvering to appoint his brother in law, Ismail Cherine, as Minister of War. All of which pointed to disaster. As it was, a number of the inside ring of Free Officers had been transferred to units away from Cairo. The screw was tightening. It was now becoming a matter of days. At any moment, the blow might fall.

Early in July the King and his entourage moved off for the summer recess to the cool breezes of Alexandria, followed by the ministers and the diplomatic corps. By long tradition this meant a period of inertia, with government business reduced to a minimum. But this year incessant ministerial changes kept everyone on edge. In Cairo, the steaming summer atmosphere seemed charged with menace.

'On 10 July Gamal and Khaled (Mohieddin) came to my house' recalls Sarwat Okasha, a member of the inner ring of Free Officers. 'They asked me, as they often did, to play Rimsky-Korsakov's *Scheherezade*. Gamal listened dreamily. When it was over he got up and lifted the needle off the record. Then he said suddenly "We will strike at the beginning of next month".'

5 August was the date he chose, mainly to allow them all to collect their pay at the end of July. Yet barely had the decision been taken than Nasser was plagued with misgivings. He was worried in particular by the fact that so many of his key men had been dispersed or were away. A week later he told the committee he was afraid that the coup might fail. Perhaps a wave of assassination might be better.

They were still in this hesitant mood when the phone rang on 20 July with a long distance call from Alexandria. 'It was my brother-in-law, Ahmed Aboul Fath (the editor of Al-Misri)' Sarwat Okasha goes on to relate, 'He told me that Hussein Sirry was resigning as Prime Minister, that the King was going to impose General Sirry Amer on the cabinet as Minister of War, and that fourteen of us were booked to be arrested.'

There was no alternative now. They had to act immediately. (Curiously enough, the government was still not fully aware of what was afoot, even at this late stage. On 20 July, in fact, Hussein Sirry remarked to his military ADC in half bantering terms: 'I hear that there's some trouble in the army. Is this so?' The aide was genuinely surprised. 'I haven't noticed anything myself, Your Excellency' he replied, and has never stopped wondering ever since how he could have been so mistaken.)

The revolt was planned in two stages. The first objective was to seize control of the army itself by occupying the general headquarters with the 13th battalion of the infantry, while tank and armored car units took over such nerve centers as the airport, the radio station, the Telephone exchange, and other key points. Once this had been achieved, the King would be dealt with. Sa'et el-Sefr' (zero hour) was set for 1 am on 23 July, when the streets of the capital would be clear, and senior army officers safely asleep in their beds.

As so often happens to the best laid plans, a number of last moment hitches cropped up. The events of 22 July 1952 run like the script for a thriller.

The heat that afternoon was torrid; the temperature rose to 117°F and the whole of Cairo felt like a turkish bath. Mohammed Naguib, who, because he was so obviously under surveillance by the secret police, was not due to take any part in the actual *coup*, spent the afternoon at the Rowing Club on the Nile. As the sun began to sink behind the pyramids and a breath of cool air floated down the river, a newspaperman brought him alarming news. He had just heard from Alexandria that Hilali Pasha was forming a new cabinet, and that it was intended to arrest what was described as 'a group of conspirators of which Naguib was the chief.'

In another part of the city a young officer was knocking at the door of Abdel Nasser's flat, just as Gamal had slipped back to change into uniform. Captain Saad Tewfik was one of the Free Officers, but not one of the seventy actually involved in the coup. He explained that he was on duty at the Ministry of Interior and he thought he had better slip over and warn him. News had just come through from Alexandria. The King had learned that a *coup d'état* was being planned and had been on the phone to his chief of staff. All divisional and brigade commanders had been ordered at once to GHQ at Koubbeh.

'It was a nasty moment' Nasser admitted later, 'The only thing to do was to act immediately. With a bit of luck, though, it might be possible to round up the whole high command together at headquarters.' Taking Captain Tewfik with him, he jumped into his little black Austin Ten and drove to Abdel Hakim Amer's house. 'Sa'et el-Sefr (zero hour) had to be brought forward from 1 am to midnight—earlier, if possible. But how to alert everyone? With Amer and Tewfik, he rushed off again in the Austin to find Anwar Sadat. But the ebullient Sadat, the man who had been breathing revolution for years, had made himself scarce by taking his wife and daughter to the cinema. All they could do was leave a message to call Amer at once.

Their next destination was the house of the Free Officer who was storing their weapons. He, too, was out. Nasser swore under his breath. Were all his efforts, the ten years of careful planning, to be upset at the last moment? In front of Kasr el Nil barracks he could see the white uniformed police forming up. This was not part of his plan. The little black car raced on to its next port of call.

Suddenly a couple of motorized policemen loomed up and ordered them to pull over to the side of the road. Then one of them asked gruffly for the occupants' papers. 'What's the trouble?' asked Nasser. 'You are driving without lights' snapped the policeman. 'Don't you know that's forbidden?'

Nasser said nothing. It was quite true. He had forgotten to turn on his sidelights. The other police officer peered suspiciously into the car and asked why it was that he was driving without lights. Had they been up to something wrong? Were they running away from something?

For a few lunatic instants the fate of the revolution was in the balance. It would have been the height of absurdity at this particular moment for the two leaders to be hauled off to the police station for a trivial traffic offence. The policeman continued to stare at their papers. At last, after a long-winded reprimand, the police got back on their motorcycles, and the revolutionaries, exchanging a nervous smile, drove off towards Heliopolis to meet up with their fellow conspirators.

Minutes later, they saw a column of headlights coming down the broad, tree-lined boulevard from the direction of the barracks. At a distance, it was impossible to know who they were—their own troops, or units suddenly mobilized by the King. Nasser parked the car off the road to make sure. The first khaki vehicles passed; then a staff car stopped. A platoon of machine-gunners surrounded the Austin. A young lieutenant pointed his revolver at Colonel Nasser. 'You can go' he said, motioning to Major Amer and Captain Tewfik. 'But you, you're a Colonel. All senior officers are being taken in tonight. I'm sorry, but you must consider yourself under military arrest! '

They remonstrated, but it was no use. This was the penalty of being so secret a leader. 'Take him into custody' snapped the young lieutenant.

But at this moment a jeep bounced up, and the commander of the machine-gun battalion got out. It was Colonel Youssef Sadik, one of Nasser's closest friends.

'What on earth's going on?' he shouted.

'I've been arrested by your men' replied Nasser with a grin. Quickly he sketched out the position and the meeting that was going on at GHQ. 'Let's go right in and catch the whole bunch of them' he said.

The column moved off towards Army headquarters at Koubbeh. Outside GHQ, Abdel Hakim Amer took charge of the operation. The low squat building was swiftly surrounded. For a few minutes, the guards put up a token resistance. Then the shooting ceased. Amer, Sadik and Nasser ran up the stairs, revolvers in hand, and burst into the chief of staff's office. Only one of the generals inside made any attempt at resistance, firing three shots from behind a screen in the corner. The others put up their hands without a word.

Meanwhile, Hussein el Shafei's tanks were occupying the broadcasting station and the airport, while Khaled Mohieddin's squadrons took possession of the huge military depot at Abbassiah. They were now ready to strike. Apart from the brief skirmish at GHQ, in which two guards were killed—the only casualties in the coup—Cairo and the nerve centers of the army itself fell into the Free Officers' hands without a shot being fired. Despite all the last moment hitches, the operation went through like clockwork. By one-thirty in the morning of 23 July, the thirty four year-old Nasser, who had plotted revolution for over ten years and taken barely an hour to carry it through, sat at the chief of staff's desk with a handful of colleagues and faced up to the looming, unexplored problem of running a nation. Outside the window, there was a sudden commotion. Someone was bellowing his head off. A counter attack? But it was only Anwar el Sadat, back from the cinema, who in his turn was being stopped by the guards.

Raymond Flower

The success, achieved with such incredible ease in the very nick of time, had now to be consolidated. Two officers were sent off in an armored car to fetch Mohammed Naguib. At three o'clock the general strode in with a broad smile on his face. 'Mabrouk, mabrouk! Congratulations!' he kept on repeating as he shook hands all round, until someone passed over the telephone. It was Hilali Pasha, the Prime Minister, calling from Alexandria. For half an hour he argued with Naguib, offering every sort of inducement if he would call off the coup. Hilali had thought he was dealing with a simple mutiny of malcontents whose grievances could be solved by a few concessions. By the time he hung up he realized that it was much more than this.

Other calls were also coming through, with news of successes outside the capital. But Nasser knew quite well that the hazards were still tremendous. A number of things could happen to turn the coup into a fiasco. The British troops in the Canal Zone were the greatest danger; which is why, even before zero hour, Aly Sabri had been dispatched to the American Embassy to reassure the Ambassador and enlist his support. It is unlikely that the coup came as much of a surprise to the Americans. Jefferson Caffery's staff had been covertly in touch with the Free Officers' movement for some considerable time, moreover, a veiled hint had been passed at a cocktail party two nights previously to the US naval attaché. But it is certain that Caffery's influence did much to quieten fears at the British Embassy, who had already alerted GHQ in Fayed. They accepted that it was an internal matter, which did not justify intervention.

On the upper floor of the Army headquarters building, the lights blazed throughout the night, and in the excited atmosphere of bustle and congratulation, the first decisions were taken. Naguib, it was agreed, should be styled 'Commander in Chief of the Armed Forces of Egypt'. The revolution should be announced in his name. Amer scribbled out the text of a proclamation on some loose pages of an exercise book. Copies were rushed to the newspapers, and at six o'clock in the morning Anwar el Sadat read it over the air from the captured studios of Egyptian State Broadcasting. So much for the first phase. Next came the question of civil government. Ali Maher Pasha, who had so often held office in times of emergency, seemed the ideal man to handle affairs smoothly and deal with the king. Also, he was acceptably anti-British. Anwar el Sadat was off again, this time with Kamal el Din Hussein. They found the ex-premier in his bath, and inclined to be prickly. Nevertheless, an agreement was reached, and Naguib, at his first press conference, was able to announce that Ali Maher would head the Council of Ministers.

The following day word came through from Alexandria that Farouk was planning a counter-coup, and an appeal of his to British GHQ at Fayid for intervention and protection was intercepted. The elimination of Farouk was becoming an urgent necessity. Nasser was very insistent about this. 'Farouk must leave the country within twenty four hours', he told Naguib, 'Within forty eight hours at the most.' Some of the other officers were by no means convinced. They were after Farouk's blood. During the small hours of the night, a dramatic discussion took place. It was the trial of Farouk. Gamal Salem echoed the words of old Aziz el Masri, whom he had consulted on the best way to deal with the King. 'A head like Farouk's only interests me after it has fallen,' the old fire-eater had snorted, 'You must kill, and go on killing, if you want to purge the country.' But Nasser himself argued for exile. Once blood started to flow, there might be no way of stopping it. Moderation would improve the image of the revolution, and the sight of the gross monarch in the nightclubs of Europe would, if anything, tend to justify it. In the end, a vote was taken. Six of the revolutionary council voted that Farouk should hang, seven that he should be exiled.

Mohammed Naguib and Anwar el Sadat flew down to Alexandria, and handed the army's ultimatum to Ali Maher. There was no beating about the bush in it. 'In view of your misrule, your violations of the constitution, your contempt of the will of the nation...' ran the text,'...the Army, which represents the strength of the people, has ordered that Your Majesty abdicate in favor of the heir to the throne, His Highness Prince Ahmed Fouad, on this day, 26 July, and that you quit the country on the same day before six o'clock.'

'The Prime Minister went as pale as death as he read it' recalls Sadat, 'He murmured, almost under his breath, "Farouk never listened to what I told him. He is only getting what he deserves."'

Ali Maher never disclosed what went on during his lengthy interview with Farouk that morning, but the sight of tanks surrounding the palace and the sound of firing seemed to have convinced the king that resistance was useless. Soliman Hafez, the lawyer who prepared the actual act of abdication, remembers that Farouk did his best to appear calm, though his nervous coughs and shuffles betrayed the panic that had gripped him. The first time he signed the document his hand trembled so much that the signature was illegible. He apologized and signed it again.

A few minutes before six o'clock, dressed in the full uniform of Admiral of the Fleet, Farouk came slowly down the steps of Ras el Tin palace, followed by Queen Narriman, and the infant king in her arms. All afternoon had been spent packing whatever he could lay hands on: 204 suitcases and trunks had already been loaded on to the royal yacht. At his request, the American ambassador accompanied him into the safety of the vessel. Then four officers joined the ex-monarch on the bridge. They were Mohammed Naguib, Gamal Salem, Hussein Shafei and Ahmed Shawky. Whatever emotions Farouk felt were hidden behind the dark lenses of his glasses. But his voice was husky. 'What you have done to me, I was on the point of doing to you' he said to Naguib, as they shook hands, 'You will find out in due course that it is not an easy thing to govern Egypt.'

A few minutes later, the majestic shape of the Mahroussa edged out of the harbor, and to the booming of a 21-gun salute, disappeared slowly into the vivid hues of the summer sunset.

It was not just the end of a reign, of the dynasty that Mohammed Ali had founded: it rang down the curtain on a whole epoch in Egypt.

Chapter 18

From Colonel to President

The first intimation that any Egyptians had of the revolution being made in their name was Anwar el Sadat's voice over the radio early in the morning on Wednesday 23 July. 'Egypt has just passed through the darkest period in her history' they heard the ex-terrorist declaring, 'Degraded by corruption and on the point of collapse owing to instability. These destructive factors affected even the army...that is why it has been purged...Egypt will welcome our movement wholeheartedly...'

Soon bewilderment gave way to wild enthusiasm as the benign, pipe-smoking figure of Mohammed Naguib, surrounded by an anonymous bunch of young officers in shirt-sleeves, was seen driving through the streets in an open car and frequently stopping for an orgy of hand-shaking and kissing of babies. It all seemed so pleasantly friendly and informal compared with the disdainful caperings of the King. Only among some of the foreign communities was there a feeling of uncertainty and apprehension, as if the cozily corrupt world that they knew might be coming apart at the seams, and anxious secretaries in the Embassies scratched their heads wondering what to reply to the cables which were flooding in from abroad. The specialists in Arab affairs and the British military mission in particular were the most put out. They just did not know what to make of the coup. Was it simply an army matter, something to do with the officers' club elections? General Naguib was known to have fallen foul of the King, and to be possibly connected with the Moslem Brotherhood. They had been saying for years that a benevolent army dictatorship was just what the country needed—yet Naguib was not one of the officers which the Mission had groomed for such an eventuality. He was thought, if anything, to be rather anti-British in his views. And the others, Naguib's 'boys'? Anwar Sadat had been imprisoned during the war for his Nazi activities, and again for his part in the murder of Sir Amin Osman. Khaled Mohieddin was supposed to be a communist. Shawki and Youssef Sadik were known to be hotheads. It all sounded ominous, particularly in the middle of an extremely hot summer. Yet the Americans were reassuring. They seemed to know more than anyone else about it all.

Nahas and Fouad Serag el Din flew back from their summer holiday cures at Aix-les-Bains to make a great show of solidarity with the revolutionaries, and forecasted a return to power for the Wafd. There were newspaper reports each morning that the military junta had been in continuous session through the night. Farouk, at Capri, denounced the 'communist' takeover of his country. Radio Bucharest praised 'the people's movement which has just struck down Egyptian feudalism'. A decree was passed abolishing the titles of Pasha and Bey. But at the same time, there was the arrest and summary hanging of two ringleaders when workers rioted at a spinning mill at Kafr el Dawar.

Authoritarian, perhaps, but communist, surely not. So ran the reports from the British Embassy back to London, though precisely how the junta could be described was still anyone's guess. However, the cables added hopefully, it looked as though the officers would put an end to the nonsense of Egyptian sovereignty over the Sudan, and would be more realistic about the question of the Canal Zone base.

Indeed, if the revolution at this stage had any predominant color at all, it was surely just khaki. Uniforms were suddenly to be seen every where: in the streets, in the cafes, in the clubs. Mohammed Naguib made a triumphant tour of the provinces, to be met at every stop with rapturous applause and cries of 'Yaish Naguib!' The world's Press blandly assumed that it was he who had masterminded the whole coup. It concentrated on the rugged, homely features of the general, and paid scant attention to the young officers around him. Sefton Delmer of the London *Daily Express* dismissed them as his 'incompetent colonels'. No one could guess that the general, as limited in his powers as a Venetian Doge, reported each morning to a crowded upstairs room in the headquarters building to receive his daily instructions from the 'boys' whose debates had gone on endlessly through the night. Few people, indeed, knew that a whole philosophy of statecraft was being laboriously hammered out from scratch in these marathon nightly sessions, which would eventually bring fundamental changes to every strata of the country's life, and have a pervasive influence throughout Africa and the Middle East.

Nasser and his friends had spent a whole decade planning their coup against heavy odds. They knew exactly what they were out to destroy: the corrupt monarchy, the feudal power of the great landowners, the stranglehold that foreigners had everywhere, the British occupation of the Canal Zone; but they had no precise idea of what to substitute for these long established institutions. They had vague visions of the kind of society they would like to see substituted, but next to no knowledge of the techniques of government which were needed to bring it about. Most of them had read little apart from military manuals, adventure stories, and the nationalist propaganda in the daily papers. But Egyptian nationalism, right from its early days, had always seen everything in terms of black and white, of cops and robbers, and had been more concerned with getting rid of things rather than building things up.

Now, manifestly, for the first time since the Pharaohs, Egyptians from the soil of the Delta were running the country. A whole fresh political philosophy had to be charted from the ground roots up. And so to the upstairs landing of the military headquarters building came an entirely new stream of visitors: university professors, engineers, lawyers, journalists, agriculturists, eggheads and Marxists, who through interminable debates slowly began to blueprint the answers to the problems confronting the military leaders.

Thus seven hot summer weeks of suspended animation slipped by. The man in the street began to shrug off the coup simply as an army revolt against Farouk, and the ex-Pashas in the Mohammed Ali Club speculated how best to persuade the officers to go back to their barracks and put a new king (Prince Abdel Moneim, perhaps?) on the throne. Then suddenly, with the first breezes of September, Nasser struck. Some forty of the *ancien régime* politicians were arrested. Ali Maher was dismissed and Naguib became Prime Minister in his place. All royal property was confiscated, and a new law prohibited any person from owning more than 200 acres of agricultural land—the balance being taken over by the state on terms which amounted virtually to confiscation. This was followed up by a wholesale reduction in rents, and new labor regulations which made it difficult (or at any rate expensive) for workmen and employees to be fired from their jobs. Equally surprising, for Egyptians so long brought up on the 'Unity of the Nile Valley' theme, was a policy declaration offering the Sudanese the choice between total independence and unity with Egypt.

At the beginning of 1953, the regime made a further show of strength. Political parties were suppressed, and it was announced that for the next three years the country would be run by 'The leader of the revolution and members of the military committee'. The image was reiterated: a junta was involved, not just a general. But still Nasser himself kept in the shadows, virtually an anonymous figure, until on the afternoon of 18 June 1953, nearly a year after the coup, he stood out for the first time in front of an open-mouthed crowd outside Abdin Place to tell the world that the monarchy had been abolished, and that henceforth Egypt would be a republic with Naguib as president and himself as his deputy. The secret was out at last. Observers who had long suspected the presence of an *éminence grise* behind the genial, pipe-smoking general no longer needed a sensitive political nose to scent where the power really lay, and indeed who it was who had been the real author of the revolution all along.

But the public did not warm to the tall, rather saturnine figure of the colonel in the same way as it did to the good natured 'man with the pipe'. Naguib had done a tremendous public relations job. If the revolution had been so widely and smoothly accepted, not only in Egypt, but where it mattered abroad, it was more than anything due to his personal popularity and his reassuring charm of manner. Selwyn Lloyd might sniff about 'this nondescript regime', but barely a month after the coup a London newspaper was suggesting that Naguib should be made C-in-C of the Allied forces in the Middle East, and Jefferson Caffery, the American Ambassador in Cairo, was equally starry-eyed. 'My boys' as he liked to call Naguib and the junta, 'can save Egypt from the red tide that Farouk's and the Pasha's abuses could not have failed to let loose over the country' he declared. 'They are going to carry out reforms and raise the people's standard of living. We shall encourage them'—which indeed the Americans did. Washington backed his words with economic aid under Point iv and cultural agreements forming part of the Fulbright program, and John Foster Dulles, after visiting Cairo in the spring of 1953, described Naguib as 'one of the outstanding Free World leaders of the post-war period', and added, at a press conference, 'Egypt is now on the threshold of a great future'.

On a less cozy level was the fact that, perpetually alert against counter-revolutionary moves, Nasser had right from the start been building up the apparatus of power from behind the scenes as painstakingly as he had engineered the revolutionary coup itself. Before very long, his secret police were probing into every corner, and were kept under surveillance themselves by other sleuths. The techniques of totalitarianism were adopted without any apparent misgivings, and items such as lie detectors' could be noticed by the most casual visitor to the Ministry of Interior. Censorship of the press and even private mail became almost total. To those who objected to such creeping authoritarianism the unmistakable presence of senior ex-Nazis who had escaped the Nuremburg net was no less ominous. Yet on the other hand there was always the genial shape of Naguib to dispel any serious feeling of alarm. It was unconceivable that he should be trying to turn himself into an Egyptian copy of Hitler. He was obviously far too nice and straightforward a person for that.

But that was one of the troubles, and perhaps the clash between the benevolent general and his revolutionary 'boys' was inevitable from the start. Nasser had never intended him to be more than a figurehead. Yet as time wore on, Naguib steadily grew into more than just a symbol. In people's minds he became the true 'father' of the revolution. Having been brought in by a telephone call at the last moment, he was now stealing all the thunder. This was bad enough, but worse still, from Nasser's point of view, was the blunting effect the moderate-minded general was beginning to have on the sharp edge of revolutionary progress. Naguib made no secret of his distaste for quite a number of things that were being done in his name, often without his knowledge, and in the end he made it clear that he would no longer tolerate being just a rubber stamp. He began to insist that, as President of the Republic, his voice should be heard. The truth, of course, was that at the bottom of his heart Naguib was still one of the old régime himself. He was far too easy-going to be able to stomach the sort of total upheaval that Nasser's revolution implied, and as such he unconsciously represented the best hope for all those, right-winged and left-winged alike, who hoped for release from the autocratic system that Nasser was erecting.

When it finally came to a trial of strength between the two of them, Naguib was no match for the wily colonel. His enormous popularity carried him through the first clash when Nasser, who had ordered him to be put under arrest, was forced to stand by his side while the President told a wildly cheering crowd that their differences had passed like a summer cloud'. But Nasser went on to deploy his tactics with the skill of a master chess-player (he was often portrayed, perhaps symbolically, in front of a chessboard). He pretended to accept Naguib's policy that the revolutionary junta should be disbanded and retire to its barracks in preparation for a return to normal, old-style democratic life. Press censorship was lifted, and political freedom was promised. For three feverish days it seemed as though the revolutionaries had committed hara-kiri and that Nasser's whole dictatorial world had crumbled. But some careful work had been done back-stage. Opponents had been purged and friends alerted.

Naguib suddenly found himself caught in a trap. He had been brought to power by an army revolt against a discredited political system, and was now apparently engaged in reversing the coup in favor of the electoral party bosses and the big land-owners—or, alternatively the Moslem Brotherhood and even the communists. A general strike, organized by the unions, but which was really just window dressing, brought the whole population out into the streets, and the army, led by the Free Officers, surged to Nasser's support. It was a dangerous, diabolical piece of double play, the tactic of taking one step back and two steps forward (borrowed, no doubt, from Lenin), and for these frantic hours the whole future of the country seemed to be cooking in a vast, bubbling cauldron. Then Naguib gave in, and the dye was cast. It was not to be freedom, with its democratic uncertainties, but 'big stick' authoritarianism of the revolutionary council and police-state rule. Nasser had won. He was now on the threshold of his staggering career as master of Egypt, and a reign as dramatic as any in its lengthy history.

Chapter 19

Positive Neutrality

In what political and economic direction would this thirty-six-year old dictator, the first real Egyptian to rule Egypt for two and a half thousand years, seek to steer his country which had been mismanaged for so long by foreign sovereigns and exploited by an energetic and industrialized Europe? By religion, Egypt is Moslem, linked with Asian, Indian, African and even Chinese Islam; and since Islam itself sprang from Arabia, it is only natural that Egypt, as the biggest and potentially the most powerful state in the middle East, should feel destined to be the leader of the Arabs, especially since the great mosque-university of Al-Azhar makes Cairo a vital power-point in the Islamic world. Yet a glance at the map shows that Egypt is in fact in Africa, its very existence depending on the Nile waters which spring from deep down in that hot, perplexed continent, and the physiognomy of the fellah, as well as his passive character with its furious undertones, is more African than levantine. At the same time, Egypt is a Mediterranean nation, linked to age-old trading traditions, and for over a century its economy had been geared to Western free-enterprise routines. Few countries, it must be admitted, have a personality so agonizingly split. In his own writings—or at any rate in the thoughts he expressed to Mohammed Heikel, who ghosted them into a slim volume called *The Philosophy of the Revolution*—Gamal Abdel Nasser voiced the dilemma, and his own aspirations.

'As I sit in my study I often ask myself, "What is our positive role in this troubled world, and in what scene do we play that role?"' he wrote. 'We are in a group of circles which should be the theatre of our activity, and in which we try to move as much as possible. We cannot look at a map of the world without realizing our place therein, and the role assigned to us by that position. We cannot ignore that there is an Arab circle surrounding us and that this circle is as much part of us as we are part of it; that our history has been merged with it and that its interests are linked with ours...We cannot ignore that there is a continent of Africa in which fate has placed us and which is destined today to witness a terrible struggle for its future. This struggle will affect us whether we want it or not.

'Nor can we ignore that there is a Moslem world to which we are tied by bonds forged not only by religious faith but also by the facts of history...

'All these are fundamental facts, the roots of which lie deep in our life.

'History is full of glorious achievements of heroes who carved great and heroic roles which they played at decisive moments on its stage' he continued. 'History is also full of roles of glorious heroism for which no actors were available at decisive moments on its stage. 'I do not know why I always imagine that in this region there is a role wandering aimlessly about in search of an actor to play it. And I do not know why this role, tired of roaming about in this vast region, should at last settle down, exhausted and weary, on our frontiers beckoning us to assume it as nobody else can do so.

'Let me hasten to say that this is not a role of leadership. It is a role of interaction and experimentation with all these factors, a role for us to harness the powerful energy latent in every part of this vast region and carry out experiments with that tremendous force to enable it to play a decisive part in ameliorating the future of humanity.'

These pipe-dreams—the germs, indeed, of his whole ambition—which he expressed with such disarming candor, pointed the way the revolutionary leader's mind was working and were received with considerable misgivings by political analysts in the West, where the memory of *Mein Kampf* had not been wiped out. Such ambitions sounded inconvenient, to say the least; and undoubtedly the tragedy of the situation was that Nasser was as little disposed to understand and have any regard for the vital interests of the West as statesmen in Whitehall and the Elysee were prepared to put themselves in the shoes of non-Europeans who had been humiliated to their very core by Western occupation. In the 1950's the winds of change were still blowing softly, and these statesmen could not, or would not, appreciate that after centuries of subjugation to one foreign Power after another the basic, burning desire of every Egyptian was to run his affairs in his own way without exterior interference—to be master of his own destiny, no more, and no less.

Nasser ends his little book by saying, 'When I analyze the elements of our strength, I cannot help being struck by three sources standing in bold relief, which should be taken into account before everything else. The first of these sources lies in the fact that we are a group of neighboring nations welded into a homogeneous whole by every possible material and moral tie that would unite any group of nations. The second is our land itself, and the position it occupies on the map of the world—that important strategic position which makes it the crossroads of the world—the main route of its trade and the highway of its armies.

'There remains the third source. This is oil...a vital element of strength.'

Whatever else it may do, this slender volume reveals Gamal Abdel Nasser as a patriotic idealist animated by an overwhelming desire to promote the welfare and expansion of Egypt and the Arab cause, with an almost naive disregard for existing international interests. His destiny, as it soon became evident, was to lash the winds of change up to hurricane force and to become a vital factor in the cold war. Few Egyptians at this period felt personally involved in the great struggle between East and West, most of them having little reason for feeling that the capitalist system is superior to the communist one, or that communism is better than capitalism; but the Egyptians had their own chip on their shoulders. By tactful and sympathetic handling it would not have been impossible to keep Egypt in the western camp. As it was, the unimaginative and extraordinarily ham-fisted policies adopted by London, Paris and Washington alike only hastened the appearance of the Soviet Union on Egyptian soil, and the barely disguised antagonism of the West was a poor alternative in Arab hearts to the warm glow which soon began to radiate from the north-east. On the home front, meanwhile, Nasser's immediate aim was abundantly clear. The dissolute monarchy had been destroyed; the corrupt old political parties had been disbanded; a start had been made on social and agrarian reforms, and what Nasser now wanted more than anything else was to eliminate the last bastion of colonialism which kept Egypt firmly in the tutelage of England—the presence of some 70,000 British troops in the Canal Zone. This was what the press called the 'national problem'.

The Canal Zone base, which had grown like Topsy during and after the war, was currently the largest military installation that Britain had anywhere in the world, and services such as the RAOC quite openly admitted that their inventories were so completely out of date that no one knew for sure what stocks lay buried in the desert. (A rough estimate, at the time of Suez, put a price tag of £250 million on the stores there.) To a certain extent, the Canal Zone base replaced the lost Indian Army in Imperial strategy, and constituted a vital bastion in the Cold War. Fundamentally, therefore, the British never expected or intended to quit—particularly in view of the lever it gave over the oil regions of the Middle East. The 1936 Treaty by which the base had been legitimized did not run out until 1956 and specifically envisaged a period of prolongation. General Erskine, the GOC, made no bones about the matter. 'You can take it from me' he privately confided in 1952, 'we shall never leave the Canal Zone.' If the decision to evacuate was taken only a couple of years later, it was because experience had shown during the riots of 1951 that the base could not exist against a hostile hinterland. Previously, there had been an element of play-acting about the negotiations for evacuation. The British had wanted to retain the base, and Farouk had needed the British presence as an insurance policy against his own people. So the base had remained, despite periodic outbursts from the Wafd, because it was to the interest of at least two sides of the old triangle of power in Egypt that it should remain.

But once the Free Officers came to the negotiating table, the position had fundamentally changed. Nasser needed the British to go so badly that he was prepared to accept a good deal less than the nationalists' cry of 'unconditional evacuation', and to negotiate a new agreement with professional realism. On the other hand the British Government, realizing that Nasser meant business and that in any case so large a concentration was no longer compatible with the requirements of nuclear strategy, were less adverse to phasing out what Churchill called 'this costly base'. And so a curious compromise was worked out whereby the army was evacuated leaving the skeleton base to be run by British civilian contractors.

The evacuation agreement was initialed on 27 July 1954 and came into force on 19 October 1954. If it smelt a little too strongly of 'mutual defense' and disappointed extremist opinion sufficiently for the Moslem Brotherhood to make an assassination attempt on Nasser, it brought him a sudden and soaring prestige through the Middle East as a man would could get results with the 'Imperialists'. From this moment onwards Gamal Abdel Nasser became a hero in the eyes of most Arab nationalists, his picture appearing in shops and coffee-houses from Aden to Aleppo. The agreement had four other crucial and perhaps predictable results.

The power void which had been created in the Western defense system in the Middle East was replaced by the American-inspired Baghdad Pact—the 'Northern tier' which seemed such a splendid idea to John Foster Dulles (who had not been entirely a spectator in levering the British out of military primacy in the oil area) but which was worse than anathema to Nasser and indeed all other progressive nationalists in the Middle East, who were utterly opposed to Nuri-es-Said's power shift to Baghdad, or indeed to any alliance between the Arabs and the West. By the same token, it cleared the ground for Russia—against whom the Baghdad pact was principally directed—to jump the cordon and begin flirting with Egypt for her own account. And it brought apprehension to Israel, whose Prime Minister described the evacuation as an 'abandonment of Israel to her fate'. Finally, the eight shots fired at Nasser by a Moslem Brotherhood terrorist as he was explaining the evacuation agreement to a rally in Alexandria exposed a spectacular plot by the Brotherhood to assassinate Nasser and 116 of the Free Officers and replace Naguib in power. This gave an excuse for a wholesale and bloody purge of the Brotherhood which shocked public opinion, but which completed the *coup d'etat* of 1952 by removing every potential challenge to Nasser's power. 'Lift up your heads, oh citizen, for the days of oppression are over!' was the slogan displayed on posters throughout all the streets of Cairo to celebrate the evacuation agreement. But, as in the days of Ancient Egypt, there was now one man before whom all heads must be bowed. The Colonel had become not only a President, but a Pharaoh.

An impressive stream of VIP's now began to flock to Cairo to pay their respects to the new Pharaoh of Egypt. Tito of Yugoslavia came and gave some interesting advice on the benefits of centralization and the evils of private enterprise. Ten days later, Nehru of India gave some useful tips on how to play off the East against the West. He was followed by Sukarno of Indonesia, who, having mildly scandalized his host by bringing to the presidential dinner table a couple of Pan-American air-hostesses he had picked up in the hotel lounge, then delighted him with the remark that, 'the nations of Africa and Asia are no longer the tools and playthings of forces they cannot influence'. Another brief visitor was Anthony Eden, whose attitude towards the President was (in Nasser's words) 'that he was talking to a junior official who could not be expected to understand international politics'.

A few days later, in April 1955, Gamal Abdel Nasser stepped into an Air India plane at Cairo International airport and took off on his first trip outside the Arab world. Twenty-nine nations were represented at the Bandung Conference—monarchies, feudal states, republics, communists and anti-communists—of every political persuasion, but all with certain things in common. None of the delegates had white skins, almost all of them had been under colonial domination, all were fired with the intoxicant of nationalism, and most of them were neutralists (which in those days meant, practically by definition, anti-West). For Nasser, the youngest of the delegates and the only one to appear in uniform, Bandung was an experience of immense significance. He was loudly cheered and made much of by a number of envoys, and in particular by Chou En-Lai who went out of his way to win Egypt's friendship, all of which brought home to him that Egypt was a power in the resurgent East—the 'Third Block', neither capitalist nor communist, which nevertheless represented five-eighths of the world's population. He returned to Cairo with much more of a global outlook, having established for himself a position as one of the Big Four in the Afro-Asian world, a fact that did not go unnoticed either in Peking or Moscow.

Yet in a different direction a whole sequence of misunderstandings, mistrusts, and disagreements was developing, which was rapidly to turn the Middle East into a ferment and culminate in a catastrophe of historic proportions.

Already in 1953 John Foster Dulles had unsuccessfully tried to persuade Egypt to join in a Middle East alliance sponsored by the USA, the object of which was to keep Russia in check, to contain any spread of communism in the area, and to protect American oil interests. The subsequent Baghdad pact was essentially a marriage between Western commercial interests and the old Pasha class of statesmen intent on maintaining the status quo. It could have no appeal for people of Nasser's generation and persuasion who were working for an Arab renaissance. From the moment the pact was signed, it inevitably set the West on a collision course with the forces of Arab nationalism who might otherwise, with careful handling, have come to terms with the USA, whom they admired, and even their old masters, the British and French. The Arab view was that defense of the region must come from within, through social reform, progress and their own nationalism: by means of an independent, non-aligned pan-Arab pact, and not through an unpopular alliance forced on them from outside. Nasser himself was quite clear about this. He said publicly and privately that Egypt would sign no external defense alliances.

Yet if Nasser was not prepared to go in for cold war alliances with the West, Egypt was still pro-West in the sense that it was non-communist and aware of the dangers of communism. Until 1954, indeed, the regime enjoyed what Dean Acheson termed 'the active friendship of the United States'. Forty million dollars of development credits had been granted and American experts of every kind were to be seen in Cairo. Basically, American policy had sought to integrate Egypt into a Middle East defense pact in exchange for the sale of arms to the Egyptian army, and to control Egyptian economy by means of a loan to finance the High Dam at Assouan. The announcement of the Baghdad pact despite Egyptian opposition, and a sudden renewal of activity by Israel put an end to the honeymoon.

On 28 February 1955 Nasser was woken up in the middle of the night by a phone call to tell him that Israeli troops had smashed across the armistice line at Gaza in a carefully planned raid that seized a supposedly invincible strong-point and inflicted sixty-nine Egyptian casualties. The Israeli prime minister declared the next day that if Egypt insisted on maintaining a technical state of war with Israel, she must put up with the consequences. But to Nasser it was a moment of truth. 'The Gaza disaster was the alarm bell' he admitted later. 'We at once started to examine the significance of peace and the balance of power in this area.' Which meant that he redoubled his search for modern weapons.

Quite apart from the Israeli situation, Nasser relied more than anything on the army for his personal power, and ever since the revolutionary coup he had done all he could to keep the officers in the armed services loyal to him. He had put young captains and majors and squadron leaders into high government jobs to maintain their support. He had given the officers' corps innumerable privileges and turned them into a new élite. The armed forces he had taken over in 1952 had been poorly equipped and suffered from a sense of humiliation over its far from glorious achievements. To the new breed of young officers it was intolerable that the Egyptian forces should remain forever in a position of inferiority. What they wanted in 1955 was tanks and jets—the most modern to be had.

Nasser's military missions were actively seeking armaments in the West. But Britain, France and the United States were trying to keep peace in the Middle East by rationing the sale of military hardware. And Congress had passed a law banning the shipment of American weapons to any country that would not agree to American control over their use. All of which meant frustration to the Egyptian purchasers.

The first hint of an alternative source of supply came at Bandung, when Chou En-Lai offered Nasser arms. Then at a diplomatic reception in May 1955 the Russian Ambassador took him into a corner and asked him point-blank whether his government would be interested in the purchase of arms from the Soviet Union. Two months later Mr. Shepilov landed in Cairo as a 'special envoy' from *Pravda,* apparently on a journalistic jaunt, but in fact to lay the foundations for a deal. Even so, Nasser was in two minds about taking so decisive a plunge to the left. But in September, even as Israeli forces invaded and occupied El Auja, a demilitarized zone under the 1949 armistice, Egyptian intelligence discovered that France was secretly arming Israel. Nasser hesitated no longer. The contract between Egypt and Russia was signed on September 24.

Anticipating the furore which would be caused when the news broke, he planned to keep the deal secret for as long as possible. However, on 27 September Sir Humphrey Trevelyan, the newly appointed British Ambassador, got wind of what was afoot and sought an immediate interview. Miles Copeland, a Madison Avenue man who had been retained by Nasser as public relations advisor, recounts in "The Game of Nations" how he and Kermit Roosevelt of the CIA happened to be in his office when the Ambassador was announced.

'What do you think I ought to tell him?' asked Nasser, rolling his snaky eyes in a lost-little-boy way.

'Well, Mr. President' replied Roosevelt with a sudden flash of inspiration, 'Why don't you soften the thing up a bit by calling it a Czech arms deal rather than a Russian one? Sounds better, you know.'

And so the Czech arms myth was born, invented off the cuff by an American. But it suited the Russian book too, and the following evening, as he opened an 'Army Fair' on Gezira island, Nasser made the announcement. 'The West refuses us the means of defending our existence' he told a cheering crowd. 'We have received an offer from Czechoslovakia to supply us with the weapons we need, on a purely commercial basis, against payment in cotton, and the agreement has just been concluded.'

Even so, within hours the headlines around the world carried the news: 'Communists to arm Egypt', and Nasser was more than ever the darling not only of Egypt but of much of the Arab world. He had touched a deep chord in the masses of the Middle East: their hunger for what they called 'dignity', which was no more than the freedom of acting off their own bat, rather than being at the beck and call of the West. But by a single act the balance of power in the Middle East, so dear to Whitehall and the Pentagon, was completely upset. The gates had been flung open for Russian penetration, and the downhill path to Suez and its aftermath had begun.

Chapter 20

Slap, Counter-slap

Gamal Abdel Nasser had still not quite achieved his role of the West's chief bogeyman. In the weeks following the Czech arms sensation neither London nor Washington really believed that Egypt was heading for war, and in an effort to counteract Russia's diplomatic victory, the Western powers sought to preempt their position by an equally dramatic move—the financing of the Assouan High Dam.

Of all the problems the revolutionary government had to face, the poverty of the fellah and the basic standard of living of over twenty five million Egyptians crammed into the narrow valley of the Nile was the most overwhelmingly urgent. A bare two per cent of the country—six million acres squeezed between the vast rainless deserts—was capable of sustaining life, and the population was increasing by half a million human beings every year. Anagraphically and ecologically, the prospects were appalling. A dam had been built by the British at Assouan at the turn of the century, but its validity had long since been superseded, and the idea of building a second, far bigger dam had been studied for decades. In 1947 the hydrologist Adrian Daninos, realizing that south of Assouan the Nile flowed through a huge natural basin, evolved a scheme for a dam nearly twenty times the size of the existing one. Egypt's problem, in its essential, was that of trapping and storing the life-giving waters of the river which otherwise flowed uselessly out into the Mediterranean when the Nile flooded every September. The experts argued that enough water could be stored to put at least another two million acres under cultivation, together with an impressive potential of hydroelectric power for industrial expansion. Clearly the building of this mammoth dam was a matter of life or death for Egypt; the only realistic measure to counter the population explosion, to bring big new areas of desert land into cultivation, and to give a fresh impetus to industry. One of the Revolutionary Council's first actions had been to set up a study group for the project, and two years later Nasser officially announced the decision to go ahead with the Saad el Ali—one of the most ambitious engineering ventures ever contemplated. 'Seventeen times larger than the Great Pyramid' he had described it—a slogan that filled Egyptians with pride, but which his enemies scoffed at being a 'demagogic pyramid'.

Without doubt the cost of such a gigantic project was way beyond Egypt's financial possibilities. Indeed, only two countries in the world had the resources to build it: the USA and Russia. Some of Nasser's advisors had warned that acceptance of Russian arms would so antagonize the Western Powers that further aid from them would be jeopardized, but his own assessment of the situation (based on the tactics of Tito and Nehru) was different. At heart a gambler, he set himself out to play the East against the West for all he was worth. The formula was deliciously simple. Adroitly handled, he did not see that it could fail.

Indeed, during the winter of 1955 and the early days of 1956 it seemed to work like a charm. Having secured his deal with Russia, he started flirting again with the West. By now the British were moving out of the Canal Zone in accordance with the 1954 agreement, and to make any political capital out of the withdrawal it was obvious that a rapprochement with Cairo was desirable. Sir Anthony Eden's speech at the Guildhall indicated the hope that what was termed 'the febrile plant of Ango-Egyptian friendship' was growing stronger. He hinted that a solution to the Arab-Israeli conflict might be found, and Nasser, despite the fact that it was political dynamite for any Arab leader even to consider a compromise which might meet Israel half way on her territorial claims, stated that Eden's proposals offered 'a very good basis for negotiation'. At the same time, the British Government quietly gave their assurance that the Baghdad pact—which Nasser considered to be directed above all against Egypt—would not be extended.

In this more hopeful climate, it was confirmed at the beginning of 1956 that the World Bank would advance 200 million dollars, the USA 55 million dollars, and Britain 15 million dollars to finance the first stage of the construction of the High Dam. But the money men were taking no chances: their terms were that Egypt's budget would be strictly controlled by the international bank, that all accounts would be scrutinized, and that Egypt would not have the right to raise any other loans'-All of which implied a return to economic (and consequently political) control from outside, which was precisely what the revolution, with its memories of the nineteenth century loans and their outcome, was out to stop. So, inevitably, as negotiations proceeded in New York, the Russian envoy in Cairo was also having talks with Nasser, and he likewise announced that his government was ready to give Egypt technical and economic aid to build the Dam. Although the terms of the Russian offer were vague, it looked as though the Powers were prepared to outbid each other. And then, almost overnight, everything went ridiculously wrong.

General Templar, the CIGS, turned up unexpectedly in Amman to discuss bringing Jordan and the legendary Arab Legion, still commanded by Glubb Pasha, into the Baghdad pact, and Nasser, infuriated by what he considered a blatant breach of faith, began a virulent propaganda campaign on Cairo radio against Britain and Jordan. Shortly afterwards, Mr. Selwyn Lloyd passed through Cairo, and at the very moment that he was in the Egyptian President's office (and from all accounts laying down the law about Cairo's attitude to Jordan) a message came in that Glubb Pasha had been dismissed by King Hussein and given just two hours to leave the country. No doubt Nasser must have smiled as he passed on the news; but the British Foreign Secretary jumped immediately to the conclusion that the incident had been timed with the express purpose of humiliating him. (It later transpired that Nasser had nothing to do with the ousting, which was probably the result of King Hussein, who had long resented the general's special position, having read in the *Observer* that Glubb Pasha was the 'uncrowned king' of Jordan.) The following day, in Bahrein, supposedly a friendly British protectorate, Mr. Lloyd was roughed up by a hostile crowd, and this again was attributed to the blandishments of Cairo Radio. In one way or other Selwyn Lloyd, by no means the least pompous of men, seemed fated to fall foul of an evil Djinn so far as Egypt was concerned; he became obsessed with the notion that all Britain's problems in the Middle East were due to the activities of a fanatical colonel who seemed able, by remote control, to stir up trouble wherever he pleased.

In the spring of 1956 a parallel obsession over Nasser began to germinate—this time in France. With the loss of Indo-China still fresh in their minds, the French had now to stomach the defection, through independence, of both Tunis and Morocco, and were determined that Algeria should not take a similar path. In March, Monsieur Pinaud went to Cairo to persuade President Nasser to stop supporting the Algerian nationalists. Nasser reminded him that the Algerians were 'our brothers...we cannot deny our Arabism', and countered with the request that France should stop arming Israel. It was another example of how not to make friends and influence people. Monsieur Pinaud returned to France discomforted.

Finally, the tangle of antagonisms was completed in Washington, where the Jewish lobby was hard at work. Fighting had flared up again on the Israeli-Egyptian as well as the Israeli-Syrian borders. Along with the French, the Canadians (by arrangement with the Pentagon) had agreed to sell jets to Israel. Yet, as a result of Mr. Hammarskjold's tireless efforts towards a Palestine settlement, there were hints that the Soviet Union might support a Great Power embargo on arms shipments to the Middle East, while belligerent noises from Israel advocating a 'preventive war' against the Arabs led Egypt to realize that if she were not careful she might easily find herself engaged in a war with her armaments supplies in jeopardy. At this moment Abdel Nasser remembered his talks with Chou En-Lai. Cairo newspapers began to argue that 'Russia is not the only alternative for obtaining arms apart from the West'. An Egyptian military mission left for Peking (which would obviously not be affected by the UN arms embargo) and in May Egypt suddenly recognized Red China. Coincidentally, at one of the many heads of States' junkets in Cairo, Nasser joined Pandit Nehru and President Sukarno in reaffirming their joint adherence to a policy of neutralism. Neither of these developments were to Washington's taste. 'The principle of neutrality...is an immoral and short-sighted conception' snorted John Foster Dulles. Congress began to show signs of impatience, and Zionist spokesmen gleefully pressed home the point that any financial help to Egypt, and particularly the Assouan Dam project, would serve only to bolster the prestige of a 'megalomaniac crypto-communist' dictator.

Realizing that the tide of public opinion was turning against the loan offer, the Egyptian Ambassador in Washington, Ahmed Hussein, flew back to Cairo and warned Nasser that he must act quickly if he wanted to conclude the agreement with the World Bank. Although reluctant to put his head into such an economic noose, Nasser finally agreed. The dam was, after all, absolutely vital to Egypt, and he judged that his prestige—particularly now that the last British troops were just leaving the Canal—was sufficient to ride any hostile opposition in the country. On 9 July, Mr. Eugene Black, President of the World Bank, confirmed the loan offer in a letter to the Egyptian finance minister. On 17 July Ahmed Hussein returned to New York and made a statement on landing that Egypt had accepted the terms of the loan.

It was a moment of extraordinary international significance. Apart from the purely idealistic conception that enlightened capital should be used to raise the standard of living in developing and poverty-stricken countries in Africa and Asia, this breath-taking project with all its financial connotations was obviously going to bind Egypt with more than just gratitude towards the donor-nations. It was the culmination of a great deal of patient diplomacy by the American and British Embassies in Cairo, and indeed the historic point at which revolutionary Egypt had at last been conclusively won back to the West.

The expected reaction in Washington was joy at such a hard-won diplomatic success. Instead Mr. John Foster Dulles, who—however unpredictable as a person—had nevertheless been trained as a lawyer as well as a diplomat, did the precise opposite to what was expected. Perhaps he had been listening too much to the Jewish lobby or to the anxiety of his friends in the oil world; but whatever the motives may have been that prompted him, the American Secretary of State decided that now that the Egyptian Government had finally presented itself as a supplicant for aid, the moment was right to diminish Nasser's stature by a slap-down of global dimensions. Unilaterally, without consulting his allies or advising the Egyptian Government, he abruptly withdrew the US offer in a terse statement issued to the press which was chiefly a castigation of the Egyptian economy and its government. No doubt he reasoned that such an unparalleled diplomatic rebuff would be enough to topple the Cairo regime, and demonstrate to the world at large and developing nations in particular that it did not pay to play Moscow off against Washington.

Conceivably, the American action did not come entirely as a surprise either to Christian Pinaud, who only a few days previously had declared publicly that he had 'enlightened' Mr. Dulles about Nasser, or to Anthony Eden who, smarting already from editorial censure on the scuttling from the Canal Zone base, was all the more chagrined by the jubilation of the Egyptians when the Union Jack was finally hauled down as the last British soldiers embarked from Port Said after seventy two years of occupation. But the timing was unexpected. Just the day before (18 July) Sir Toby Lowe of the Foreign Office had reaffirmed at a cocktail party in honor of the Egyptian Minister of Commerce that Britain welcomed and was prepared to go ahead with the loans. Forty eight hours later, the British Government followed the American lead, issuing a statement to the press that the loan offer had been withdrawn, and only subsequently notifying the Egyptian Ambassador to the Court of St. James.

On the critical day of 20 July, Gamal Abdel Nasser left Belgrade, where he, Tito and Nehru had been holding a Big Three meeting, a summit, as it were, of the Neutralists. There was a good deal of argument about the wording of the final communiqué, which reaffirmed their policy of 'positive co-existence', but Nasser had every reason for feeling satisfied as his plane took off for Cairo with Nehru aboard. The Indian leader was to be the guest of honor at the celebrations on 23 July marking the fourth anniversary of the revolution; this in itself emphasized Egypt's increasing stature in the uncommitted world. On 23 July there was to be a grand parade of Egypt's new weapons, and the highlight of Nasser's speech would be the announcement of the building of the High Dam at Assouan. The plane landed at three in the morning and was met by glum-faced members of the Cabinet who gave Gamal the news of the American withdrawal. Sending Nehru off to Koubbeh Palace, Nasser immediately closeted himself with his advisors while Cairo, with the temperature at 117°F in the shade, seethed in a stew of rumors, and people openly placed bets on the identity of Nasser's successor. To many Arabs, it was a repeat of Lord Killearn's brutal ultimatum to Farouk in 1942. Even at this stage of development in the Middle East, it seemed inconceivable that any regime could survive such a calculated blow from the Great Powers.

But both Egyptians and Western statesmen were discounting the character and the almost predictable reactions of a man who more than once declared: If someone spits in my face, I spit back at him ten times.' To a man like Nasser, with the blood of the Saidis in his veins, hatred of enforced subservience to the West was part and parcel of his make-up, ever since he had been a schoolboy agitator. Moreover the Assouan High Dam project was not just a diplomatic ploy, it was absolutely vital to the welfare of the country. Behind locked doors, chain-smoking members of the regime worked round the clock planning their reprisal. Word was given that the President would make a major speech at Alexandria on 26 July.

By seven o'clock that evening—exactly four years to the hour that Farouk had steamed out of the harbor into exile—a huge crowd had converged into Mohammed Ali Square. On the balcony of the Bourse, the same balcony where in 1954 an assassin's bullets had narrowly missed him, Nasser appeared before a battery of microphones. He seemed quite relaxed, and began speaking in an informal, baladi way ('baladi', which means literally 'of the village', is the Egyptian's way of describing his typical, down to earth way of life). For the first time the crowd heard their hitherto austere President talking to them like one of themselves. He began by making fun of the American diplomats and their problems in dealing with Mr. Dulles, and then he switched to a description of Mr. Black of the World Bank. 'When he came into my office he reminded me of Ferdinand de Lesseps' he declared, pronouncing the name in a hissing tone, 'the Frenchman who had charge of building the Suez canal for the Khedive. Yes, Mr. de Lesseps' he added, launching into a diatribe against what he called 'mortgage colonialism'. So far, it sounded like the mixture as before. But suddenly his tone changed and the vast audience was galvanized as if by an electric shock.

'Egyptians!' he cried in a deep, angry voice which rasped through the balmy evening air, 'for too long we have been robbed by that imperialistic company, that state within a state, the *Companie Universelle du Canal Maritime de Suez*. But we shall be robbed no more; for I can tell you now that at this very moment the company is being nationalized, and its premises taken over. From tonight, the Suez canal belongs to us. Do you hear me?'

The whole square erupted in a frenzy of excitement. Complete strangers embraced and thumped each other's backs. Nasser, now seized with a fit of laughter (perhaps only at this moment did he realize what an emotional chord he had touched) went on: 'the Canal will pay for the Dam. The Canal was built by Egyptians. It was built on the skulls of our countrymen. 120,000 Egyptians died digging it. The United States and Britain were going to offer us 70 million dollars to build the dam. But the income from the Canal is 100 million dollars a year. In five years that means half a billion dollars. Let the Americans choke in their fury! We do not need them. We will rely on our own strength. Our Egyptian canal will be run by Egyptians. The dam will be built by Egyptians. To hell with America! Do you hear me?'

In the red dusk all Alexandria was dancing for joy. The sheer audacity of what Nasser had done brought tears to the eyes. Instinctively the mass of humanity in the streets seemed to sense that this was one of the most dramatic moments in their long history. The greatest powers on earth had been challenged and the detested foreigner outwitted; at last they could lift their heads, at last they were really on their own. Whatever the outcome might be, this was a moment of pure rapture, and for anyone who was in Alexandria that evening, an extraordinarily moving experience.

For indeed, as Nasser hissed the word 'de Lesseps' into the microphones, the army, acting on this pre-arranged code-word, had taken over the headquarters of the Suez Canal Company as well as all the strategic points from Port Said to Suez. In London, Sir Anthony Eden, who was host at a dinner party in honor of King Feisal of Iraq, was handed a message and grimly left the table. The following day he denounced Nasser in Parliament as a 'new Hitler'. In the

Chambre Monsieur Mollet warned the 'insolent thief that he would be forced to retract what he had done. Both governments lodged strong formal complaints. Dulles on his side called the nationalization a 'grievous blow to international confidence'. But the Soviet Union supported Nasser's action, and cables of congratulations poured into Cairo from all parts of the Afro-Asian world.

Whatever the legality of the seizure of the Canal Company may have been—and there can be little doubt that it was basically an Egyptian company and therefore in strictly legal terms could be nationalized by the Egyptian Government against compensation, just as many concerns in England and elsewhere had been—it was Nasser's speech, with its demagogic reiteration that Egyptians were in the vanguard of a struggle against Western imperialism that ripped aside diplomatic pretences and laid bare the mutual hatred and distrust of both sides. The spontaneous joy of the Egyptians, which was echoed throughout the Middle East, turning Nasser overnight into a hero of bewitching proportions, was matched by an almost demoniac fury in the West. Eden, Lloyd, Mollet and Pinaud were now not really interested in the legalities of the matter; they were out for Nasser's blood. As the Lacoutures remarked: 'Perhaps the Islamic law is not the only one which cuts off a thief's hands...' Eden declared in a broadcast that the quarrel was with Nasser, not with the Egyptian people. Lloyd, addressing a meeting of Conservatives, spoke of 'knocking Nasser off his perch'. On 31 July, the British Prime Minister announced 'precautionary measures', which included the dispatch of troops to Cyprus, and France was given permission to station troops on the island too. The general attitude in Whitehall was summed up by an official of the Treasury to his colleagues over lunch. 'What we need now' he said, sipping a pink gin, 'is a nice, quick, tidy little war'. In fact, the decision for this very thing had already been taken in secret by Eden and Mollet, and undoubtedly from the end of July onwards the French and British actions were aimed solely at the humiliation and overthrow of the Egyptian leader. 'There was an ultimatum-like quality in almost every word or action by the British and French Governments' wrote Tom Little, 'in the build-up of troops in the Mediterranean area, in the take-it-or-leave-it message of the Menzies Mission, in the repetition—as in the case of the Suez Canal User's Association—that Egypt must accept or take the consequences.'

Dulles, who had triggered off the whole crisis, now became apprehensive lest the Suez affair should develop into a shooting war which might involve the whole Middle East and jeopardize, amongst other things, the US oil interests there. His scheme for a Suez Canal User's association, although predestined to be a failure, was advanced principally to allow a respite for tempers to cool. User nations met at a conference in London, which was fruitless not only because delegates had really been invited to approve the British and French proposals rather than to discuss them, but chiefly because Nasser had refused to attend on the grounds that the very agenda in itself was a demand that Egypt should renounce operating the Canal. In the end it was decided to send a mission to Cairo to put the claim for an international authority to Nasser. The choice of Mr. Menzies to lead this mission was in itself significant. No more obvious example of the old-fashioned imperialist could have been found than 'Pig-iron Bob', or anyone less likely to achieve positive results with a touchy revolutionary leader. Mr. Menzies lectured Nasser like a naughty schoolboy until, his patience at an end, Nasser called an end to the meeting. 'Menzies did not speak as an Australian Prime Minister, but as an Australian mule...he trampled on all the principles by which the twentieth century lives' shrilled Cairo radio. Years later, the head of an Egyptian industrial delegation said to another old campaigner, Billy Rootes, at a luncheon in Devonshire House: If you, Lord Rootes, had headed that mission, there would never have been a Suez war.' The implication is obvious.

For the fact is that, from the moment he had announced the nationalization of the Canal, Nasser leant over backwards to be reasonable. He was prepared to compromise over the canal issue, although he was not prepared to give up Egypt's basic sovereignty over the waterway; it was, after all, too much to expect that in this day and age an independent Egypt would put up with conditions imposed on her when a colony of the Ottoman Empire. He could see that the Suez Canal issue touched the West to the core, and was willing to make a great many concessions to satisfy the Powers that their vital interests in the canal would not materially be affected; yet for all the belligerent noises that were going on in London and Paris he did not, as he told Desmond Stewart in an interview, expect the British and French to take military action. 'Eden proved me wrong' he said wryly to Stewart, 'I had prepared an appreciation of the situation from his angle...I argued that from their point of view they would lose so much, so much'.*

The stage was thus set for the cataclysm of Suez. On the one side, Gamal Abdel Nasser, thirty eight-year-old President and leader of Egypt's revolutionary regime, supported by the mass of his countrymen and with almost the entire weight of opinion of the Middle East, Africa, Asia and Russia behind him. On the other side, Sir Anthony Eden, Prime Minister of England; Mr. Selwyn Lloyd, Foreign Secretary; Monsieur Guy Mollet, Premier of France; M. Pinaud, Foreign Minister; the armed might of these two countries, along with Mr. David Ben Gurion, Prime Minister of Israel and the military forces of Israel; and in the background the apprehensive veto of President Eisenhower, already involved in the US elections.

Dwight Eisenhower was of the school of thought which said that what could not be put on one side of a foolscap sheet of paper was not worth saying. Somewhere in the State Department is a memorandum which was placed before him in the middle of September 1956. It was three paragraphs in length. By all accounts the President of the United States, after reading this pungent document, took up his fountain pen and wrote one word in the left hand margin: 'No'. It was the Anglo-French proposal for the invasion of Egypt.

From this moment onwards, a curious chill developed in Anglo-American relations. There was little or no diplomatic exchange above routine level. The State Department, aware yet uninformed, watched the activities of its British allies with barely concealed suspicion. Anthony Eden was playing his cards very close to his chest. For the curious aspect of the Suez affair is that while everything was put on a crisis footing, while British regiments were openly on their way to Cyprus and the French fleet was readied and the French staff was in London, it was all considered to be simply a matter of diplomatic maneuvers, of power politics. Despite all the publicity which was being given to troop embarkations and military preparations, no one really believed that these were more than just stage management. In the whole of England, only half a dozen people knew that the decision for war had actually been taken. This strange state of affairs was emphasized by the story of the cabinet meeting when Anthony Nutting, the Minister of State at the Foreign Office, ventured to raise some objections to the policy which was being laid down. Eden brushed aside his protest with an impatient gesture. 'It is obvious' he snapped, 'that you have never served in a war cabinet'. 'Since when, Mr. Prime Minister' replied the startled minister, 'have we been at war?'

By the end of September, a working agreement had been reached at the United Nations on six principles to govern the operation of the Canal, and Egypt, to the surprise of most people, had demonstrated her ability to keep the traffic through the waterway moving even with the roster of new pilots which had once more reached normal levels. Moreover with America opposed to an Anglo-French display of force and more and more canal users drifting into tariff agreements with the successfully operating Egyptian management there seemed every reason for supposing that the summer crisis was nearing its end.

But although it is fashionable in today's egalitarian world to play down the role of the individual in history with the argument that the man of the moment acts simply in accordance with the tendencies and the pressures of the moment and is personally anonymous, in the case of the Suez tragedy the personalities and the prejudices of the key figures cannot be discounted, since the decisions and consequently the responsibility were theirs alone. On 15 October a plane touched down at a secret rendezvous in the south west of France, and the following day, after this clandestine meeting with David Ben Gurion, the decision for the invasion of Egypt was confirmed in private between Eden and Mollet. The French plan had been for a direct attack on Port Said and Alexandria simultaneously. It was jettisoned in favour of a joint landing at Port Said and an advance on Ismailia and Suez. It is just as well to keep in mind what was being done. Without consulting Parliament or Chambre, allies or United Nations, these men were embarking their governments on an adventure which hardly had the least chance of success, for even if the Canal Zone had been occupied it would have been untenable against a hostile hinterland, and even if Nasser had fallen (which was unlikely) no Western-orientated statesman could have formed a government. The only elements who could possibly have benefited were what remained of the Moslem Brotherhood or the Communists, and in all probability, as Dulles feared, Egypt and the entire Arab world would have erupted in a paroxysm of violence against everything concerned with Britain, France and the West as a whole. This was the risk which was being taken, and the kindest verdict of future generations may be that an ailing and neurotic Englishman was led up the garden path by a wily Frenchman and an even wilier Jew.

Note:

"Least of all" as he later told Nutting, "did it enter Nasser's head at any stage in the Suez crisis that France and Britain would risk destroying every vestige of their influence and good name in the Arab world by using Israel as their stalking-horse for an attempt to seize the Canal by force" (Anthony Nutting "Nasser" p. 148).

Chapter 21

Tripartite Response

On Monday, 29 October 1956, Gamal Abdel Nasser took his family into the country for a picnic. It was his son Abdel Hamid's fifth birthday, and after the stresses of the past few weeks he felt justified in taking a few hours off. The previous day had been full of urgent dispatches: in Hungary the Russians had entered Budapest; in Damascus there had been riots; in Jerusalem the French consulate had been sacked by a furious Jordanian crowd in protest against developments in Algeria; Israel had announced mobilization because of the situation in Jordan—all crisis news, but not, he thought, immediately affecting Egypt. They lunched under the banyan trees at the Barrage like any ordinary Egyptian family (though no other people were allowed near the Barrage that day, of course) and returned home in the evening for a birthday party. Nasser was playing games on the floor with the children when his secretary suddenly broke in with a message. The Israeli army was attacking. He rushed into his office on the other side of the house and called up Abdel Hakim Amer, who confirmed the news. Two Israeli brigades had crossed into Egyptian territory, heading for the Gulf of Akaba. Other armored columns were advancing into Sinai. There were reports of parachute landings at the Mitia Pass. The Egyptian High Command, Amer admitted, who had been expecting an attack on Jordan, were taken completely by surprise. Nasser studied the map and gave orders for a stand to be made at Abou Aweigila. The following afternoon he received a top-priority coded message from his Ambassador in London. It made so little sense that he sent it back to be decoded again. The Ambassador reported that Mollet and Pinaud had arrived that morning in London, and that he and the Israeli Ambassador had been handed a joint Anglo-French ultimatum. This demanded that the belligerents should order an immediate cease-fire and each withdraw to ten miles from the Canal within a period of twelve hours, in default of which British and French forces would 'intervene in whatever strength may be necessary to secure compliance' and would also move into the Canal Zone to guarantee freedom of transit through the Canal.

Abdel Nasser could hardly believe his eyes. Egypt had been invaded, yet she was being asked to withdraw her troops from Sinai, from the Canal, from Egyptian territory. It didn't make sense.

In London too, the ultimatum sounded puzzling. A lot of people thought they had heard the news wrong. In Fleet Street Stephen Barber, assistant editor of the *News Chronicle* and one of the astutest minds on Middle Eastern affairs, snorted as he reset the front page of the paper. 'Eden's gone mad' he said tersely, 'stark, staring mad. We're about to make the biggest cock-up in history.'

The Israeli Government—whose troops were nowhere near the Suez Canal—immediately agreed to the ultimatum. President Nasser, in a towering rage, sent for the British and French ambassadors. 'Your ultimatum is categorically rejected' he told them. 'Egypt will defend her dignity'. The ultimatum had come as a tremendous shock, but—as he admitted later—he did not believe, until the bombs actually began falling, that the British and French would attack Egypt. He was sure it was a piece of bluff. He knew that, apart from the paratroopers at Mitia, no other Israelis were within 200 kilometers of the Canal.

The time limit expired at dawn on 31 October. Nothing happened. And then, at seven-thirty in the evening, the bombing began. Only then did Nasser realize that Britain and France were indeed intending war. Only then did he send the order to the Egyptian army to withdraw from Sinai and to concentrate on a single front between Ismailia and Bilbeis. Fighting a savage rear-guard action, the Egyptian forces withdrew as best they could, but many, caught up and surrounded, continued the battle until they were obliged to surrender. There was no pell-mell flight towards the Delta, no general picture of a rout as the Israeli propaganda was claiming. Nor was there an Israeli defeat, as Cairo radio shouted. Nasser took the only course he could. Realizing that an Anglo-French invasion of the Canal Zone was now almost certain, he concentrated his strength in the heart of Egypt. Moreover, as the first wave of RAF and French bombers zeroed in and destroyed the Egyptian aircraft on the runways of Almaza and Heliopolis—only a mile or so from Nasser's own house—and reports came in that much of the air force had been annihilated in the initial attacks, he took another drastic decision: against the angry pleas of the air force staff, he ordered all remaining serviceable aircraft to be flown to safety in Upper Egypt. He could not spare them for action in Sinai against the superior French and Israeli jets, especially as they would have to run the gauntlet of the RAF on the way. He needed them for a more important occasion—the time when fighting began in the Delta itself.

From the start, he took personal command over the armed forces as well as all aspects of strategy, propaganda, and diplomacy. As the RAF raids continued surely one of the strangest bombardments ever known, since Brigadier Fergusson, who was in charge of 'Allied psychological warfare against Egypt' broadcast ahead of time which targets would be attacked and warned everyone to keep clear—Gamal Abdel Nasser began an offensive of his own. Always a gambler, he now staked up the biggest gamble of his career: that his friends would pull the chestnuts out of the fire for him. He gambled on a diplomatic victory to overcome a probable military defeat. He knew that the entire Afro-Asian world and many of the countries of the West were appalled at the aggression on Egypt. He knew that in England itself public opinion was violently split over the action. He knew, likewise, that he could count on the support, at this moment, of both Russia and the United States. And so round the clock long-distance calls went out from his office to his ambassadors and Heads of State all over the world, lobbying for help.

There was another thing he knew, which Eden and Mollet and the mandarins at the Foreign Office and the Quai d'Orsay could never understand, although their embassies in Cairo had repeatedly stressed it, which was that in a national crisis such as this, when the soil of Egypt was being threatened by Britain and France, and above all by the arch enemy Israel, the ordinary people of Egypt, perplexed and frightened though they may have been, would stand behind him. While the RAF was dropping millions of pamphlets over Cairo urging the population to rise up against 'The tyrant Nasser', he himself was driving to Al Azhar for Friday prayers where, addressing the multitude squatting on their mats as 'my brothers', he told them that each of them was a soldier in the national liberation army. 'We shall fight a bitter battle' he said, in words not so different from another leader on another occasion, 'we shall fight from village to village, from house to house, and never surrender'. He was literally mobbed by the crowd as he left the mosque and was hardly able to reach his car. There could be no doubt about it. The people—even those who had previously loathed his policies—were now firmly on his side.

There was a chimeric through-the-looking-glass feel to that first week in November; perhaps more so, indeed, in England than in Egypt. No one who was in London at the time will forget the strange hysteria which affected almost everybody. The country was split into two clear-cut sides on the issue. The Hawks, as they would now be called, were delighted that strong action was being taken at last. They had watched with increasing dismay as the victorious Great Britain of 1945 abdicated her imperial position and became the hapless Little England of the fifties, at the mercy of any small nation or colony. The fiasco of Abadan and the retreat from the great base in the Canal Zone only exasperated the frustration they felt at the loss of India. It was high time, they believed, that the rot was stopped and that Britain (the defender of freedom) reasserted herself. The Doves, on the other hand, were appalled at the return of such ponderously Victorian gunboat diplomacy. They could not stomach the idea that Britain (the defender of law and order) should cold-bloodedly lead a quite naked aggression against a smaller nation over a matter which should be dealt with by the United Nations, and thereby run the risk of setting the whole Middle East on fire and triggering a nuclear war. Although on the whole Conservatives were hawks and the Labor party and the Liberals were doves, the split was by no means along party lines. As many staunch Tories were dead against the action as the numerous cloth-capped trade unionists who applauded it. Passionate arguments went on in the pubs and the common rooms of colleges and the smoking rooms of clubs all over the country. For once the traditional phlegm of the English was forgotten. Families thumped the dinner table and people quarreled in the streets. In the hallowed precincts of the Athenaeum two bishops were reported (perhaps quite inaccurately) to have come to blows with one another. The cabinet itself was split. Anthony Nutting resigned from the Government together with several of Eden's top aides, and the Mother of Parliaments was the scene of unparliamentary scuffles in which members denounced Eden in terms practically as savage as Cairo radio itself.

After the initial attack and the start of the RAF bombing, a curious hiatus occurred, lasting four days, during which time communiqués from Cyprus and London charted the snail-like progress of an assault convoy sailing eastwards from Malta. It was difficult to understand whether an invasion was in progress, or not.

Meanwhile, as time wore on, the diplomatic battle for world support was increasingly moving in favor of Egypt. On November 2 an American resolution at the UN General Assembly called on Israel to withdraw behind the armistice line and for other member states not to put 'military goods' into the area. Britain and France vetoed the resolution, but after a nine-hour debate it was subsequently carried by 64 votes to 5. Only Australia and New Zealand (and Israel of course) supported the Anglo-French position, but on the eve of the actual landings in Egypt Robert Menzies sent an urgent cable to Eden. 'Don't do it!' was the laconic message from Canberra.

The initial British and French airborne assault on Port Said, which finally took place at dawn on 5 November was therefore launched in defiance of the United Nations and world opinion. The paratroops met with light but determined resistance; by the afternoon they had encircled the town and the local Egyptian commander had indicated his willingness to discuss surrender terms.

Within the hour, Sir Anthony Eden interrupted a noisy debate in the House of Commons to read the text of a signal which had just come in from operational headquarters in Cyprus: 'Military commander Port Said now discussing terms. Ceasefire ordered.' Instantly it was assumed that Nasser had capitulated, and Eden was given a standing ovation.

At that precise moment, Nasser had just put down the telephone after curtly ordering the firing to go on, if necessary until all Port Said lay in ruins. His next call was to Bulganin in Moscow, who responded with notes to Britain and France and Israel announcing that Russia was prepared to use force to 'crush the aggressors and restore peace'.

At dusk the fighting was resumed and the following morning at 4.40am the main Anglo-French force landed at Port Said. By afternoon the town was completely in their hands and British armour, under Brigadier M. A. H. Butler, was heading down the narrow causeway between the Canal and Lake Menzaleh towards Ismailia and Suez.

In the meantime Sir Anthony Eden, no longer the flushed and triumphant figure waving the cease-fire signal in the Commons the previous evening, was being subjected to such diplomatic pressure that he was almost at the end of his tether. Apart from world-wide condemnation of the invasion, the Russian note had contained a broad hint that unless Britain and France halted their attack at once, London and Paris might be bombed and the world's first atomic war touched off. This rattling of rockets by the Kremlin could probably be discounted, but the run on sterling which had started at the end of October had accelerated on 5 November to such an extent (£100-million was needed for the day's rescue operation alone) that the Treasury reported that if immediate support of something like £1,000-million from the USA was not forthcoming, sterling would have to be devalued within twenty four hours.

On 31 October, James Reston had written in the *New York Times:* 'When Eisenhower first heard of the ultimatum the White House crackled with barrack-room language the like of which had not been heard since the days of General Grant.' In the afternoon of 6 November Eisenhower spoke to Eden on the telephone. He did not mince his words. If Eden did not order a ceasefire by midnight, he pronounced with the subtlety of a drill sergeant, he would break the pound. At this the harassed Prime Minister completely collapsed.

The order to cease fire was greeted with incredulity by headquarters in Cyprus and no less so by Brigadier Butler as he raced towards Ismailia. At first he ignored the signal. It was only when the radio operator of his tank handed up a further direct order; 'Prime Minister to Brigadier Butler. You will stop at once' that he finally halted the advance. But he did not hide his disappointment. Back in Cyprus he told newsmen: 'I couldn't have felt more frustrated by the midnight ceasefire, because I know we could have taken Ismailia at the latest by lunchtime.' But no academic argument could hide the fact that the whole operation had been a monstrous fiasco and that Nasser, although he won no battle, had won the war. As Stephen Barber had predicted, it had been the 'biggest cock-up'—a nadir, indeed, in British imperial history. In one week of unexampled madness, England had incurred the censure of practically every nation in the world and had forfeited, perhaps forever, her pre-eminent position in the Arab world. Moreover the actual mechanics of the whole operation had been badly bungled.

It is now generally accepted, even in the most hawkish circles, that the military intervention was a ghastly error, and moreover that it had been carefully planned in concert between the three aggressor nations: Israel, France and Britain. To discount such collusion would now be unpardonably naive, despite the impassioned but unconvincing denials at the time from just about everyone in Whitehall, including the Prime Minister himself. The difficulty is to understand why it was that the operation went so completely off the rails; to explain away the ridiculous ultimatum to Egypt which bore no relation whatsoever to the situation at the time it was issued, as well as the embarrassment of the military command in Cyprus who were so plainly caught on the wrong foot during these vital days between the ultimatum and the actual landings at Port Said. Nor is it easy to comprehend the unwisdom of launching the action on the very eve of the US elections.

When in due course the secret documents of the Suez campaign come to light, it will be possible to establish the truth of what actually happened. In the absence of these, the most plausible explanation is that for some reason the whole operation was triggered off several days before the planned timetable. This would make sense of what is otherwise nonsense.

In all probability the plan, already drafted in detail by 16 October, was for the Israelis to launch a sudden attack in Sinai during the first week of November, with the idea that after three or four days of fighting their advanced troops would be nearing the Canal, so that on 5 November, the eve of the US elections day (when Eisenhower would have been temporarily powerless) the British and French Governments, their hands raised in horror at the threat to shipping in the Canal, would issue their joint ultimatum, with foreseeable results. While the Americans were still at the polls the bombing of Egypt would begin, and within twenty-four hours the amphibious invasion would be under way. Before Washington or the United Nations could take any action, the Canal Zone would be occupied and a strike force would probably be converging on Cairo to make an end of Nasser.

But it seems likely that Israel, mistrusting her allies or afraid that Eisenhower would somehow manage to dissuade Britain and France at the last moment, took advantage of the sudden uprising in Hungary—a most fortuitous smoke screen from their point of view—to jump the gun and go it alone. Quite possibly the French were forewarned and did not oppose this change of plan. Almost certainly Eden was taken by surprise. He was a sick man, already beset by misgivings, and his conspirators in Paris and Tel Aviv had no intention of allowing him an opportunity of opting out at the last moment. Faced with a *fait accompli,* Eden panicked and collapsed. The ultimatum was issued without any alteration which under the changed circumstances turned it into a highly irresponsible document, and willy-nilly the operation began. But the change of dates took the planners by surprise and upset the logistics; hence the elephantine slowness of the convoys converging on Cyprus, and a whole traumatic week of delay before the landings could begin, by which time world opinion ensured its termination thirty six hours later.

Suez has become a sort of skeleton in the cupboard so far as England is concerned. It is still a subject that tends to be dismissed with a shrug, or at any rate minimized. Three years after the event, a general election was held and won by the Tories with barely a mention being made of the Suez debacle, which is one of the least palatable watersheds of British imperial history. Only recently has the euphoria begun to lift, and a new generation of Englishmen, less concerned with (and maybe fundamentally opposed to) the values of 1956, has realized, accepted, and denounced the basic attitudes and concepts of the men who were responsible for such a disastrous and indeed criminal episode. 'Guilty Men' was the headline in a major newspaper at the time. However, the world, mercifully, had progressed in some aspects since Nuremberg. Sir Anthony Eden disappeared, in a civilized manner, to the obscurity of a peerage, and perhaps it was Gamal Abdel Nasser, of all people, who closed the Suez incident with the most dignity when he said: 'We will forgive—but we will not forget.'

The price of this forgiveness was admittedly high. On 5 November, Nasser had broken off diplomatic relations with Britain and France and ordered the seizure of all British and French property. Once the Suez invasion had been halted and the danger had passed, he worked off his spleen on the nearest and most convenient victims—the defenseless Jewish, French and British residents in Egypt. Before long he had ordered the mass arrest, internment or expulsion of a great many of the fifty thousand Jews in the country. The deportees, most of whom had lived all their lives in Egypt and knew no other country, were allowed to take £5 and a single suitcase of personal belongings with them. The same fate awaited holders of British and French passports, including a large number of Maltese and Cypriots, and the British public was treated to the unaccustomed sight of Anglo-Saxon refugees by the hundred at Dover and Heathrow (where, until regulations were relaxed, they were made to pay customs dues on the few possessions they had been able to bring!)

The knock on the door came always in the middle of the night, and in many cases those being deported were required to sign declarations in Arabic confirming that they were leaving of their own free will and renouncing any claim on their property. This was called 'Egyptianization', and Nasser personally scanned the lists of commercial concerns and properties which were being seized. 'We have a heaven-sent opportunity to purge the country of foreign influence' he told his Minister of Finance, 'make sure you do the job properly'. Within a matter of days, British property worth £100 million had been expropriated, including hospitals, schools, and even the prestigious Shell Company of Egypt along with its subsidiary, Anglo-Egyptian Oilfields. British and French professional men were barred from practicing and British and French concerns were prohibited to sue in the Egyptian courts. Even British and French films and books were banned. The Ministry of Education was ordered to sever all cultural ties with England and France. Textbooks were to be rewritten to exclude, as far as possible, any mention of the two countries which had dominated Egypt for a century and a half. Among the reasons given by Eden for the Suez intervention was the protection of British property. A rasher statement has rarely been made in the House of Commons. British assets in Egypt which were in no danger prior to the invasion were totally forfeited as a result of it. Apart from this cost in human misery (tardily compensated as a result of public outcry by a commission which was still splitting legal hairs with some of the claimants twelve years after the event) the bill which had to be footed by the British taxpayer was staggering: £100 million for the expense of the operation, plus about £250 million of stores and equipment in the canal zone base which were quietly surrendered to Egypt (who had seized them all anyway) as a quid pro quo for the damage by the bombing of Port Said. 'As a matter of fact, the damage to Port Said wasn't really serious' a top Egyptian official confided some years later, 'and actually it helped us a lot by destroying slum areas which might otherwise have taken years to clear.'

Undoubtedly, although Egypt lost such military battles as there were, she won the war, which ironically provided a tremendous boost for the very man it was intended to destroy. Nasser's position, which up to this point had still been uncertain despite his previous successes, was now immensely strengthened in Egypt and throughout the Middle East. Moreover, as this latter-day Saladin himself said, casting his mind back no doubt over the whole period of European primacy since Napoleon's invasion; 'We were able after Suez to nationalize all the foreign assets in our country, and by that Suez has gained back the wealth of the Egyptian people.'

Chapter 22

United Arab Republic

Swept up by an extraordinary wave of popular worship throughout the Middle East, Nasser now began to capitalize his success in wresting control of the Canal from the foreigners in the hope of becoming Pharaoh not only of Egypt, but of all the Arab world—the first of the circles of influence he had dreamt of in his *Philosophy of the Revolution*. He accelerated his international maneuvering and support for radical and progressive movements from Morocco to Baghdad. To him, the fundamental struggle was to eliminate the last vestiges of colonialism—which to all intents and purposes meant Western influence and commitments in any shape or form.

But the very success that Nasserism seemed to be having in the aftermath of Suez caused a nervous reaction among those who preferred the status-quo to the fundamental changes so loudly championed by Cairo Radio. Nasser's bid for leadership of the Arabs led to increasing hostility from the other Arab governments, most of whom were still conservative—and also from Washington, who now began to wish it had not opposed the Suez action so decisively.

Early in 1957 the United States set up what was known as the 'Eisenhower Doctrine'. This proclaimed that international communism was a threat to the Middle East, and promised that financial aid would be given to any government who opposed it. At the same time the USA joined in the economic blockade of Egypt which Britain and France had started after Suez. Dulles, who had triggered off the Suez Canal crisis by alienating Nasser in the first place, and then had baled him out, became intent on building up a pro-Western, anti-Communist, anti-Nasser block in the Middle East—which inevitably had the effect of making Nasser more than ever the darling of the Kremlin.

There were many crosscurrents in Arab politics at this period, and many shifts and changes in the wind, but in its essentials the struggle could be defined. Ideologically, it was between the Arab nationalists and the conservatives. Materially, it was between Russia and the United States, with oil as the prize.

Lebanon, Iraq, Jordan and Saudi Arabia, with their conservative governments, accepted the Eisenhower doctrine. Syria, which had the same pan-Arab neutralist outlook as Egypt, refused it. Instead, fearful of becoming the victim of a coup from either the left or the right (Communist influence and Soviet prestige were strong and an Iraqi take-over plot had been discovered) the Syrians took a bold if desperate initiative. They asked President Nasser to form an immediate and comprehensive union of Syria and Egypt.

Although Nasser realized the dangers of such a marriage, he could hardly fail to be attracted by the chance to extend his frontiers as far as Mesopotamia. It was an opportunity which might not recur. And so at five o'clock in the afternoon of 1 February 1958 Gamal Abdel Nasser and Shukri el Kuwatly of Syria stood side by side on the balcony of Abdin Palace in Cairo and announced that Egypt and Syria would from then on be 'a single state, a single army, a single party'. The curious phenomenon, to be known as the United Arab Republic, had come into being.

When, early in 1959, a 'financial agreement' patched up relations between London and Cairo sufficiently for former English residents, who had been outlawed since Suez, to go back to their homes, they found that officially speaking they were not returning to Egypt at all, because Egypt no longer existed. It had become the 'Southern Region of the United Arab Republic'.

This inelegant nomenclature was symbolic, in a way, of the changes that had occurred during their twenty-nine months absence. Even if on the surface things seemed so comfortably the same, in fact everything was fundamentally different. The old Egyptian warmth remained: indeed many English people who had braced themselves for a frosty reception were overcome by the kindness of their welcome back. Casual acquaintances embraced them in the street; club servants clasped their hands; dhobis, ferrashes, taxi-drivers and all the little folk they had ever known seemed spontaneously glad to see them again. The easy enchantment of Oriental life was unaltered: tric-trac in the side-walk cafes, the fruit and *lamoun* vendors in the street, the *foul* and *tamia* stalls, the tennis professionals knocking up at the club, the long cooling drinks at the open air cinemas, the little shops which produced such marvelous hand-sewn shoes and shirts—all these and such like things were much the same as ever. And yet the ambience was now quite different. It was not just the visual impact of Cairo which had changed with its huge new vertical blocks whose concrete shapes shimmered in the Nile, and its astonishing new television tower rising like a rocket out of Gezira, all of which emphasized Egypt's organic desire to leap forward into a new era. It was that the leap had in fact been taken.

European Cairo was no longer a smart and privileged village set delectably apart from the great teeming capital. It was now only a memory clinging to familiar buildings. The old spacious patrician past, built up by three generations of British colonial administrators, French bankers and Italian merchants had been replaced by the indigenous present, spilling over from the mediaeval heart of the city with all its noise and dust and overcrowded bustle. It was the same in Alexandria. The European skin, or veneer, had gone forever. The Egyptians had taken over. It was as simple as that.

Since Suez, Egyptians had been steadily moving into the private houses and flats which had been seized from the British and French and Jews, and had quickly bought up the property of other foreigners who had seen the writing on the wall and had left of their own accord. Many of the newcomers were young officers who now formed the new elite. To ensure the army's loyalty Nasser had put them in charge of the banks and insurance companies and firms which had been 'Egyptianized', and most of these officer-businessmen, bathed in unexpected affluence, were now living very much the same sort of life as the Europeans they had replaced.

The Suez War had fundamentally changed the direction of Egypt's development. But for it, European influence would probably have continued to come to terms with Egyptian militarism. As it was, the bombs which destroyed Port Said had caused a powerful sense of injustice, breaking the traditional links with the past, and generating a new feeling of national awareness. Ordinary people felt welded into a nation for the first time, and were determined, more than ever before, that the land and resources of the country must be for Egyptians alone.

The sanctions which Britain and France, and subsequently the USA, sought to impose after Suez in the hope of cracking the Egyptian economy had a contrary, stimulating effect. As Egypt entered the sixties, there was a suspicion of greatness in the land—a greatness of promise, at any rate. Far from bringing Nasser to heel, the Western measures gave a sharp impetus to his aim of industrializing the country and freeing it from foreign financial ties. Faced with an economic blockade from its traditional trading partners, the UAR turned to West Germany and the Eastern bloc to sell her cotton and help her set up a crash program to create new industries.

For while the traditional trading links had been discarded, the UAR, although totalitarian, was still far from being a Socialist state. In 1959 the public sector only contributed eighteen per cent of the gross national product, and businessmen were encouraged to go in for manufacturing. The idea of turning themselves into industrialists appealed to many of the merchants who were suffering from import restrictions and could remember the fat profits that local factories had made during the 1939-45 War. Whereas a decade previously the search had been made for franchises and agencies, the rush was now for licenses to manufacture. Anyone who fancied himself as an entrepreneur was now studying a project of one sort or another to make anything from toothpaste to tractors, and there was a heady, almost pioneering atmosphere in private offices as well as in the newly opened premises of the Five Year Plan, the government authority established to blueprint this industrial revolution.

Some of the manufacturing projects were undoubtedly valid, but others were sheer skywriting. Above all, they failed to take into account the almost total lack of managerial talent capable of dealing with the complexities of modern industrial processes and of pushing through an over-ambitious program in too short a space of time.

In the old days, experience had not been lacking. Some of the cleverest business brains in the world had operated in Cairo and Alexandria, but they had mostly been Greeks, Armenians and Jews, and if they held Egyptian passports, it was for convenience, not from birth. Most of these folk had seen the writing on the wall in 1952, and by the end of the fifties they had quietly left to make newer and bigger fortunes for themselves in Geneva, Milan or San Paolo. The Egyptians who had stepped into their places had neither the knowledge nor the flair, and even at the highest levels of government it was surprisingly difficult to draw a line between viable prospects and sheer self-delusion.

Typical of the atmosphere in this heady period was the Ramses car factory. Trucks and cars had already been assembled from knocked-down (CKD) parts for some years, but thanks to a British initiative the first steps to actual manufacture of an Egyptian car were taken in the pre-Suez epoch, and the Phoenix 2SR6 sports racing car made an appearance at Le Mans and Rheims in 1956. The development of the Phoenix project (named after the fabulous firebird of ancient Egyptian mythology) was taken over by a well-known Midlands firm, Meadows of Wolverhampton, who produced a sort of meccano set car which could be built virtually anywhere in the world.. After the signature of the Anglo-Egyptian financial agreement, a couple of prototypes of this mini-car were sent out to their original point of inspiration and within hours of their arrival a group of Egyptians began negotiating for the manufacturing rights. They enlisted the help of Abdel Hakim Amer, C-in-C of the UAR armed forces, who promised to speak to Nasser about the idea. The following afternoon, they were invited to show the cars to the President.

Hurriedly removing the English nameplates, they drove the prototypes to Nasser's private house at Manshiet el Bakhry, where they found him playing tennis with Amer. With perfectly straight faces they said that they had been working for several years to produce an all-Egyptian people's car, and that given government support they could have a factory in production within three months—in time for the Revolution Day celebrations on 23 July.

With an equally straight face, Nasser spent over an hour testing the cars and examining them from every angle. At one point he wriggled underneath and then poked out a Presidential head, to remark with a large grin; 'Did you know that I was once an instructor in engineering at the military academy?' Finally, patting the short Michelotti-designed fiberglass body, he agreed to back the project provided that certain changes in the specification were made.

'Tell Aziz Sidky (the Minister of Industry) to push this matter through' he said to Hakim Amer. 'Make sure he gives it top priority. 'And then he added, rather significantly, 'We've been getting too many promises and too few results from our industries in the public sector. Let's see what the private sector can do.'

Shaking hands with the promoters before turning away, he added, with the ghost of a wink: It will be the first deal with England since the agreement...Let's see what co-operation we get from the English.'

When the jubilant partners got back to their office, there was a message awaiting them; 'The President suggests that "Ramses" would be a good name for the car.'

Bureaucratic procedure was swept aside, and the components for twenty-five cars were hastily shipped from England, reaching Alexandria with about a week to spare. The cars were assembled, painted in eye-catching colors (one in red, white and black of the UAR's flag) and were on display in Liberation square in Cairo for the 23 July celebrations. They were hailed by press and television as a symbol of the industrial sophistication of the UAR. 'The All-Arab People's Car' ran the slogans' 'Built by Arab hands for the Arab people!' A much-publicized cartoon showed discomfited western statesmen seated on camels eyeing a Ramses with Nasser inside it. The caption read: 'They thought we only had camels whereas we are now making our own cars! '

Along the desert road, not far from the Pyramids, a hundred acre site was allocated to the Ramses firm, and soon huge factory buildings were emerging from the sand where five millenniums previously the minor Pharaohs of the 5th Dynasty had built their tombs. The Ramses was given a monopoly in the mini-car field, which meant that no competitive small machines could be imported or produced in the UAR.

A delegation from Cairo traveled to England to order the components for the first 10,000 cars and negotiate credit terms. They were welcomed politely but soon discovered that the British Government was by no means enamoured with the idea of helping to boost the UAR's industrial image—at any rate so long as Cairo delayed the desequestration of British property and kept Colin Crowe (the British Charge d'affaires) and his team kicking their heels in ministerial anterooms—indeed pressure was brought on the unfortunate manufacturers in the midlands—who naturally had been overjoyed at securing such an important order—and a bland President of the Board of Trade made it clear that no components for the all-Arab car would reach the factory by the pyramids where it was '99 per cent manufactured'. The luckless delegation took an afternoon plane from London to Stuttgart, where they were rather more sympathetically received, and a few weeks later the first shipment of parts for a substantially modified 'Arab People's car' left the NSU factory at Neckarsulm for Cairo. For twelve years or more, the consignment of parts has continued in much the same way to the factory by the Pyramids—which has now been nationalized and makes furniture when periodic shortages of hard currency holds up the supplies of components for Ramses cars, over two-fifths of which are now effectively manufactured in the UAR.

The Ramses incident illustrates the cynicism of both the Oriental and Occidental attitudes, while underlining the hostility which continued to bedevil relations between London and Cairo. As it was, the West Germans made the most of this particular prize, along with a great many other industrial projects in the UAR, including later on the production of military hardware and even some tentative manufacture of rockets.

The advantages of industrial collaboration with the UAR was frequently stressed, and the line taken was a reiteration of Nasser's own 'circles of influence' theme. 'Strategically, we are in a vitally important position' as the Minister of Industry once bluntly put it. 'We are potentially the leaders of the Arab world. We are likewise the gateway to Africa. We need your help in getting our industrialization going. In return we will be your springboard into the vital markets of the Middle East and Africa. We have one of the most powerful radio stations in the world, broadcasting in seventy-eight languages. We will use it to boost our jointly produced products. We also have political and barter agreements with a number of countries with whom you cannot deal because of their currency shortages and import policies. But by manufacturing your products in UAR factories, using our cheap labor, it will be possible to penetrate these markets.'

West German industry was quick to see the strength of this argument, and later the same principle, applied instead to political penetration, became one of the major reasons for the Russian involvement in the UAR.

But in the twilight days of 1960, the UAR was still Western orientated, and apart from Russian military equipment and the promise of the Assouan High Dam, only a few Russian bookshops, a cinema showing Russian films, and Russian participation in sports events were the tangible evidence of Soviet infiltration. If the UAR was moving eastwards, it was still a very tentative shift. Geographically speaking, and in accordance with her neutralist platform, she was still west of central. Of the ubiquitous newcomers on the Cairo scene in the early sixties, the great majority were Germans.

On the last day of September 1961, one of the Badrawi Ashours held a reception for the marriage of his daughter. Like the Free Officers themselves, the Badrawi family sprang from fellah stock, and as befitted the feudal lords of Mansourah, it was a lavish spree. The tennis court at the ex-Pasha's villa in Dokki was covered over to form a huge buffet and one whole side of it was piled high with crates of French champagne. The atmosphere was rather less formal than in similar binges in the past, and towards the end of the evening a few hilarious guests in dinner jackets were seen, somewhat unsteadily, to be clinking glasses—but not to the bride. The Badrawi's themselves pretended not to notice, although they were possibly aware what the toast was about. Two days previously, a group of Syrian officers in Damascus had made a coup, and Syria had seceded from the United Arab Republic. Nasserism had proved too much for the Syrians, who resented being treated as junior partners in the union, and disliked the single-party system which was being imposed on them. Above all, the Egyptian officials who had been steadily taking over their country seemed to the Syrians to be arrogant, overbearing and disruptive.

Right from the start, the merger had worked badly. The Syrian army objected to being under Egyptian command; the civil servants felt upset that most of the executive and legislative power was being switched to Cairo; and the free trading Syrian businessmen did not take kindly to the controls which were imposed on them. The mass of the people might still revere Nasser, but the middle classes had become heartily sick of the union with Egypt.

Nasser's instinctive reaction was to send in troops, and he even alerted his paratroops, but on second thoughts, when it became obvious that this would simply lead to civil war, he gave up the idea. Perhaps he too was disenchanted with the whole affair. 'For three and a half years, we have nothing but trouble in Syria', he told the Egyptians in a televised speech. 'Almost three-quarters of my time was spent trying to solve Syrian problems.' But he did not disguise the fact that it was a serious blow, and his enemies in the Arab world did not hide their pleasure. In Egypt, a great many people were secretly delighted too. They hoped it might lead to his downfall.

Discussing the setback with Tito shortly afterwards, Nasser (who by now was developing a dogmatic sense of mission) blamed himself for having underestimated the reactionary elements in Syria, and complained that the wealthy classes were always opposed to him. 'We made a dangerous mistake', he explained. 'We have never been prepared to come to terms with imperialism, but we came to terms with reaction...and now in Syria, capitalism and feudalism joined forces with imperialism to wipe out the gains of the masses and strike at the socialist revolution.'

Tito is reported to have given him some down-to-earth advice. In Yugoslavia, there were no such problems, for the very good reason that there were no rich people, and no such things as capitalism and feudalism. The solution was simple: stop the rich being rich—eliminate the bourgeoisie.

These were precisely the lines along which Nasser was thinking. He suspected that if he did not act against them immediately, there was a serious danger that the Egyptian middle classes would follow the example of the Syrians and stage a revolt of their own. Before they had time to act, he determined to destroy the roots of their power.

In November 1961, 1,200 of the wealthiest families in Egypt were placed under sequestration, which meant that their property was seized from them, as well as their businesses. About the same time all banks, insurance companies and export houses, as well as several hundred industrial and trading companies were nationalized. This drastic confiscation of all major sources of wealth meant that almost overnight nearly ninety per cent of the industry and commerce of the country had been taken over by the government, or 'Egyptianized' as Nasser called it.

Shortly afterwards all foreign-owned land—amounting to about 150,000 acres—was expropriated, and the assets of the Greeks, the only foreign community so far untouched, estimated at 120 million pounds, were also seized. Nasser described the 1961 nationalizations as: 'The biggest triumph of the revolutionary drive in the economic field.' The country's economy had been changed more fundamentally than at any time since Mohammed Ali. Socialism had hit Egypt with a vengeance. It had become, in the words of the economist Charles Issawi: 'a totalitarian socialist state'.

Chapter 23

To Orchestrate the Arab World

Since the early days of his power, he had always been known as El-Rais, 'the Boss', and sometimes half-affectionately as 'Jimmy', but now to everyone in Egypt he had become just 'He'. He was at once the most hated, the most admired, and the most feared man in the Middle East. He sat alone and remote in his study in the two story villa he had built at Manchiet el Bakhry, between Abbassia Barracks and the suburb of Heliopolis, and nobody in the land dared to guess where he would strike next. His hands held all the reins of government, and his snake-like gaze seemed to take in everything that was going on, down to the most trivial detail.

If a person drew out more than a thousand pounds from the bank, he knew about it. If someone applied for an exit permit to leave the country, his approval had to be sought. If an import permit was given, Gamal Abdel Nasser had vetted it first. All promotions and appointments were decided by him. He alone knew the ramifications of the three separate secret intelligence systems dealing with espionage and counter-espionage inside the country and abroad, each of which had orders to keep a close check on each other's activities.

For more than five millennia, the ancient land of Egypt had known absolute rulers of every description; yet El-Rais had a style quite different from any of his predecessors. Austere and Cromwellian in his private life, he lived unostentatiously in a suburban house no larger than that of any successful professional man in Europe or America. He never set foot in the high spots of Cairo, and cleaned the city's nightlife up to the point that belly dancers had to cover up their navels. Yet while stressing a low-keyed good-family-man image, he was by no means indifferent to the trappings of power, and the swift rush of his motorcade through the streets of Cairo—the huge black Cadillac flanked by outriders and tailed by a dozen black Chevrolet saloons—or the fleet of silver Ilyushins in which he traveled abroad, were as impressive in their jet-age splendor as the ornate cavalcades of any Pharaoh. He was never prepared to wear a white tie or even a dinner-jacket, yet the banquets he gave at Koubbeh Palace were as lavish as in the days of Farouk, and were cooked and served by the same staff.

His daily routine varied little. He would get up at seven o'clock in the morning and read the main Cairo newspapers over breakfast, checking that the editors were following the orders given to them. About nine o'clock he would walk across the hall to his office and spend the morning initialing dossiers, reading reports from his ministers and his ambassadors, and issuing instructions.

He never had any meetings in the morning. If he spoke to a minister, it was always on the telephone.

After lunch, which he usually had with his family, he would take a siesta and sometimes, very occasionally, he might play tennis with Abdel Hakim Amer or Zacharia Mohieddin on the private court in his garden. Then, at five o'clock in the afternoon, the real action would begin with a series of conferences, meetings and interviews lasting far into the night.

In Cairo, especially in the summer, business and professional men tend to work in the evening when the heat of the day is over. Nasser followed this habit. The later the hour, the more relaxed he felt. Some of his most important meetings would be held after midnight. It was about then that he had supper—highly salted white cheese, tomatoes and onions, with a glass of orange juice, served on a tray in his office. When he finally went to bed, he would take an armful of magazines with him and read for a couple of hours.

Magazines were his favorite hobby, and he often spent hours glancing through *Time, Life, Newsweek, L'Express* as well as the many Arab-language publications. He was also fond of movie films and had a private projection room set up in his house. His choice was usually for westerns and musicals, and sometimes he would put on two or three full-length feature films one after the other. A favorite film of his was 'Lawrence of Arabia', and when he heard that his censors, for political reasons, had banned it, he countermanded the order and gave instructions that it should be shown throughout the country. It was good propaganda for the Arabs, he said.

Huge posters of Nasser with a toothpaste grin were plastered all over every city and village, and in every shop-window and in every office, but he himself rarely appeared in public, save for prayers at the mosque on Friday mornings, and at meetings of the National Union. Even to his ministers and to foreign diplomats he was an inaccessible figure, and he tended to give priority to the representatives of the smaller neutralist nations rather than to those of the western powers, whom he enjoyed keeping waiting. Even so, a constant stream of visitors from all over the world came to the house at Manshiet el Bakhry, walked through the banks of potted flowers at the entrance, and were inevitably photographed shaking hands with Nasser in front of a black marble fire-place and a rather indifferent Spanish painting of two peasant children.

In contrast to the complicated protocol for seeking an interview, the actual meeting with Nasser tended to be relaxed. As often as not during the summer months he would come slip-slopping across the hall in his slippers, dressed in an open-necked shirt worn outside his trousers—although on more formal occasions he would wear a neatly-pressed business suit, correctly but not too elegantly cut, and a striped tie. He would escort his visitors into the drawing room, which with its reproduction Louis XVI gilt furniture, glass chandelier, and aggressively new Persian carpets, was a replica of any suburban Egyptian home, and no sooner were the guests seated than the inevitable 'ahwa masbout'—small cups of highly spiced Turkish coffee—would be served.

The conversation usually flowed quite easily. Just as in the old days of the Free Officers, he had the knack of making his visitors feel that the barriers were down, and that it was 'themselves and Nasser'. He would put over his arguments with such ingenuous frankness that even his most equivocal pronouncements sounded eminently reasonable. He spoke good English and many foreign diplomats and journalists who disliked his politics nevertheless confessed after meeting him that they had been won over by the apparent sincerity of Nasser himself.

Much of his charisma and his appeal to the masses was due to this 'man to man' approach, which came over impressively on the television. Even people who hated him would shake their heads after watching him on television, and would murmur, despite themselves; 'He is a good man!'

Undoubtedly, under his guidance, a great deal of good was being achieved. In the 'sixties, schools were being opened at the astonishing rate of one a day. Medical services were being improved and the Ministry of Health's budget in 1962 was four times that of 1952. Clean drinking water was being piped to every village in the Delta and Upper Egypt. Eye diseases, once endemic, had been almost entirely eliminated, and good progress had been made in combating bilharzia and malaria. The difficult question of birth control, so vital in a land where the population increases by half a million a year, was being seriously tackled. The standard of living of the industrial labor force had improved, as well as its working conditions. Huge blocks of popular flats were being built to house slum-dwellers. The road transport system was being bettered. Electricity was more widespread. Women's position in the structure of society had been liberalized, and indeed a woman was Minister of Social Affairs.

Anyone returning to Cairo after a few years' absence had to admit in all honesty that a great deal had been done. But more important than the superficial and outward signs of social emancipation—that tarbouches (considered as a symbol of the old Turkish domination) were no longer worn, that shirts and pants were replacing galabiyas, and that the streets and shops were full of girls in pert western-style dresses—was the pervasive and almost tangible feeling of pride which people had acquired, of being able at long last to hold their heads high, which was strangely moving to any sympathetic observer. 'Dignity' was what the Egyptians themselves called it. For all its authoritarian muddling, the regime had managed to weld men and women into a community, and made them proud to be Egyptians.

On the other hand, there was a seamy side to the revolutionary movement. A high percentage of the population was non-productively lounging in mushrooming government offices; the secret police was full of wasters and bully-boys who threw their weight unpleasantly around; and the increase in centralization could only lead to more bureaucracy than ever before. Ministers were little more than rubber stamps for presidential diktats, and corruption was as rife as in the days of Farouk. The much-vaunted Liberation Province, set up to reclaim a huge tract of desert between Cairo and Alexandria had become an open scandal, and its produce, by any normal accounting, cost double the market value to grow. The same cost factor applied to the steel forged in the huge new factory at Helouan. Industrialization was barely denting the country's formidable economic problems, and the government factories were inefficient even with relatively cheap labor, so that the heavy debts contracted to finance their development were obviously going to be a serious mortgage on the future.

As far back as 1956 Nasser had sought to put his powers on a constitutional basis, and a single party National Union had been formed to replace all the previous political parties. Candidates had all been carefully screened and few of them were prepared to get out of step with the President, who himself once described the National Union as 'a mere organizational facade, unstirred by the forces of the masses and their genuine demands'. During the period of the merger with Syria, the National Union was extended to both regions of the UAR, but continuous changes and amendments made the set-up so complicated that in the end it was virtually self-defeating. Nasser began to feel the need to revitalize the system and give a measure of initiative to the masses who since the dawn of history had been politically apathetic and left everything to the government. At the same time he wanted to guarantee the future of the revolution against his enemies who were still covertly waiting for an opportunity to strike.

Six months after his humiliating rebuff in Syria, he introduced the National Charter. Written entirely by himself, it represented an attempt by the architect and sole chief executive of the revolution to codify his political theories and to devise a system which, while protecting himself from deviationists, would give the mass of the people a chance of being associated in the process of government. The 30,000-word document also revealed that the President of the UAR still nourished some ancient grudges.

The National Charter dwelt at length, for instance, on how England had robbed India and Egypt of their wealth to develop the industries of Lancashire, and declared that countries with an imperial past should be 'compelled to offer the nations aspiring to development part of the national wealth they sapped when that wealth was a booty for all looters'. It added that political democracy should not be separated from social democracy and 'cannot exist under the domination of any one class: democracy means the domination and sovereignty of the people—the entire people.' The National Union, henceforth to be called the Arab Socialist Union, would be the authority representing the people and the guardian of their rights. The fellahin and the workers would have half the seats in it 'since they form the majority of the people'.

An important chapter dealt with the right to criticize, which was described as 'an important guarantee to freedom' and this was followed up by the equivocal statement that 'the decisive guarantee for the freedom of the press lies in its belonging to the people'. In a pronouncement 'on the inevitability of the socialist system', the Charter stated that the working day had been reduced to seven hours; and that labor was entitled to participate in management and profits. Every citizen should have the right to education, medical care, to a job suited to his ability and to a guaranteed pension. Women, moreover, 'must be regarded as equal to men', and they must work together to produce more food.

'Of course God provides sustenance,' Nasser declared to his audience as he introduced the Charter to them; 'We know this and the Prophet Mohammed said we were to rely on God, but he did not tell his followers to rely only on God and do nothing else.' The National Charter, the Arab Socialist Union, and the National Assembly did in fact represent a genuine attempt by Nasser to spread authority downwards and outwards, although it was difficult to see how it could succeed in a totalitarian state. For all the talk of freedom of the press, only a very foolhardy journalist would have attempted any real criticism of the government's policies, and even Nasser's closest colleagues such as Zacharia Mohieddin, found themselves elbowed out into the cold if they suggested policies at variance with El-Rais. 'We do not allow any deviationists to remain among us,' he proclaimed in a subsequent speech. 'Should a person deviate...the Arab Socialist Union must speak up and seek to expel him.' The periodic witch-hunts did not encourage initiative or independence of thought. Whether he realized it or not, Nasser's brand of idealism went hand in hand with a cynical ruthlessness.

In fact, as he sat behind his seven-foot mahogany desk at Manshiet el Bakhry, with its ten hot-line telephones, Gamal Abdel Nasser seemed ever-increasingly engaged in a round-the-clock struggle against all and sundry at home and abroad: on the one hand to beat the social, economic and anagraphic problems in Egypt itself while stamping out any signs of dissension within the country; and on the other to out-maneuver his international enemies and take control of the whole Arab world. To achieve this ambition, his agents were busily fomenting trouble where-ever they could. In particular his sights were aimed at the conservative regimes which by their nature were opposed to everything he stood for—the Syrian 'Reactionary separatists' as Cairo Radio called them; King Faisal of Saudi Arabia; King Hussein of Jordan; and the most reactionary ruler of all, the Iman Ahmed of Yemen. There was also Israel, of course—although the Zionist state had less priority in his thoughts than might be supposed at this stage.

In Iraq, a pro-Nasser coup eradicated the Royal Family and brought Brigadier Kassern to power,' and in the Lebanon a revolutionary group all but brought their country into the Egyptian camp. But this was nipped in the bud by President Eisenhower, who sent the US Marines into Lebanon and Jordan to safeguard their identities. From then onwards, Nasser's campaign to unite the

Arabs under his aegis suffered a bewildering number of ups and downs. Kassern developed into a bitter rival who railed against Cairo increasingly until he was overthrown in his turn, and another pro-Nasser faction under Colonel Araf took over. At which, caught as she was between the militantly Arab nationalist regimes of Baghdad and Cairo, Syria was subjected to another coup and this time the Ba'athists seized power.

Syria, Iraq and the UAR all now considered themselves to be progressive states dedicated to 'unity, freedom and socialism', and for a moment it seemed possible that a tripartite state might come into being under Nasser's leadership. Such a federation was, in fact, proclaimed on 17 April 1963, but that was all. The Syrian Ba'athists were not prepared, to give Nasser the control he demanded; and only three months later relations between the prospective partners had deteriorated to the point where Nasser declared angrily that the UAR was not prepared to enter a union with 'a fascist, nazi, prison government'. So much for Arab unity.

A year later, Nasser made a further attempt to regroup the Arab leaders when Israel announced in 1964 her intention to divert the Jordan river from Lake Tiberias into the Negev desert. Using this as a pretext (anything to do with Israel was political dynamite, and no one could refuse to come) he called an Arab summit conference in Cairo, But although some bridges were mended during it, and the UAR at least got back on speaking terms with nearly everyone but the Syrians, the conference showed that as far as unity was concerned 'its echo was larger than its voice', as the old Arab proverb says.

Even as the national rivalries and political dissensions in the Arab world grew, the UAR's relations with the west continued to deteriorate. With President Kennedy, there had been a brief flowering of mutual comprehension and even friendship which could have led to a rapprochement, but the Johnson administration had soon become openly hostile to Nasser. The British Labor Government shared this dislike, which was hardly surprising, even among fellow socialists. Nasser's policy of non-alignment, which meant unremitting opposition to western bases in Africa and the Middle East, along with his constant support for radical revolutionaries against pro-Western regimes (as in the Congo) let alone his socialist policies which had obliterated the vast western commercial interests in Egypt without proper compensation, could only lead to mounting hostility in Britain and the United States. Inevitably both London and Washington, in their efforts to counterbalance his disruptive influence, found themselves supporting the enemies of Nasserism wherever it was necessary.

El-Rais himself seemed to relish this trend, and in 1965 he even broke off diplomatic relations with West Germany—despite the close links between the two countries and the massive aid to the UAR's industrial development—in anger at Bonn's reparations agreement with Israel. Steadily, as he veered away from the West, Nasser moved the UAR into the Soviet orbit.

Raymond Flower

The Russians had been playing their game gently and astutely. The 'Czech' arms deal of 1955 had opened the door, and this initial breakthrough had been consolidated by technical and economic aid after Suez, along with massive purchases of cotton, which cushioned Egypt considerably from the effects of the western boycott. The next step in the Russian involvement had been to underwrite the Assouan High Dam, and this firmly established the UAR as a client state.

Soviet imperialism did not seem to worry Nasser; he considered that he could harness Russian cold-war maneuvers to his own expansionist plans, and was confident that he could disengage himself from the bear's hug at any moment that he chose. Moscow, quietly intent on using the UAR as a springboard for penetration not only into the Middle East but into the depths of Africa as well, could well afford to keep the hug at handshake pressure. On many subjects—not least of which the need to eliminate western influence and all foreign bases in the area—Krushchev and Nasser saw eye to eye. El-Rais fitted so perfectly in Moscow's plans that Krushchev, visiting Assouan for the inaugural ceremony of the first stage of the High Dam, expansively created Nasser a hero of the Soviet Union—the most prestigious honor that the USSR can award.

To this cozy partnership the Yemen War can be attributed.

In the summer of 1962 the aged Imam Ahmed of Yemen died, and was succeeded by his son Badr. Days later, on 28 September, a group of Yemeni officers led by Brigadier Abdullah el Sallal revolted against the new Imam and proclaimed a republic. Badr escaped and with Saudi help rallied support among the Yemeni tribesmen. Nasser swiftly answered Sallal's call for assistance, and soon the Egyptian army was heavily involved in the hills of Yemen. But the Royalists dug themselves in, and what had initially looked like being a walkover for the superior Egyptian forces turned progressively into an Arab Vietnam.

The war dragged on for five years, and at its height was costing half a million pounds a day, which was clearly beyond the UAR's means. Yet if Egypt was supplying the manpower (of which she had no shortage) she was not entirely burdened with the financing of the campaign. In exchange for Soviet military hardware and the High Dam at Assouan, Nasser was prepared to throw all his weight into the effort of subverting the Yemen. There were political as well as geographical considerations behind his gamble. Politically, of course, it was part of his unsleeping struggle for leadership of the Arab world, and by definition a confrontation between the forces of progress and reaction; geographically this feudal corner at the southern entrance to the Red Sea represented a strategic point, as the Kremlin was well aware, from which to strike at the oilfields of the Persian Gulf.

As the war dragged on its weary and murderous course in the hills of Yemen, it became apparent that the UAR's expeditionary force of over 60,000 men was not getting the better of the tough, primitive Yemeni tribesmen, despite daily bombardments by Nasser's new Russian jets and even (it is asserted) the use of poison gas. Backed by arms and money from Saudi Arabia, the Yemeni royalists continued to fight back, and what should have been a quick victory for the Egyptians grew into a prolonged and fruitless campaign which eventually dropped out of the world headlines to become a forgotten war in a remote land which added no luster to Nasser's image. The idealistic major who had re-returned from Faluja vowing that he would 'think a thousand times before committing his countrymen to war' had changed a good deal in fifteen years. He was now well on his way to having caused more Arab deaths than any other man in history.

At a Cairo cocktail party around about this period, an American lady journalist rebuked a diplomat who was voicing this unpalatable fact. 'Do you realize', she declared almost angrily, 'that you are talking about the most significant figure in the Middle East since the Prophet Mohammed?'

The correspondent of a London newspaper, standing near by, shrugged his shoulders. Asked what he believed Nasser himself thought of the situation in the Yemen and in Egypt itself, he suggested that in his heart of hearts Nasser must be saying to himself: 'How very tired I am...and what a dreadful mess I've made...'

Chapter 24

Seventy Hours in June

Even as he finally began to disengage his troops from the Yemen in the spring of 1967, Gamal Abdel Nasser must at last have realized that his grandiose plans to orchestrate the Arab world had failed. But if the Yemen expedition had proved to be a disaster, it was nothing compared to what was to follow. Not even in his worst dreams and nightmares can Nasser have envisaged the catastrophe which was to strike Egypt in the summer.

On 10 May four top-secret intelligence reports reached his desk at Manchiet el Bakhry. One was from his own espionage network, the others from the intelligence services of Russia, Syria and Lebanon. Each spelt out the same ominous news: The Israeli army was massing on the Syrian border, and an attack on Damascus was imminent.

For months the tension between Israel and the UAR had been as low as it could be, given that the two countries were technically still at war. Nasser had been far too preoccupied with other problems—the war in Yemen, the reactionaries in Arabia, and his efforts to dislodge the British from Aden—to bother a great deal about Israel. He was more concerned with fighting reaction and propagating socialism than in starting a war with the Jews.

By the same token Israel was not expecting any immediate trouble from the UAR. Their ships were still denied the use of the Suez Canal, but this was an old story; the Gulf of Tiran was open to them and a UN contingent was guarding the Sinai frontier. It was a different matter, however, with Syria, whose Ba'athist leaders had taken a sharp turn to the left. The continuous raids by El Fatah guerrillas from Syria, some of them quite deep into Israeli territory, were becoming intolerable. To put up with such constant harassment was an admission of defeat in itself, and although Israeli jets had shot down six Syrian jets over Damascus on 7 April in reprisal, the Knesset was under pressure from its more militant members to launch an invasion into Syria and put an end to the Ba'athist regime.

On 8 May, a Syrian delegation had flown to Cairo to enlist Nasser's help. The Egyptian President was evasive, and told them he would first have to be convinced that Israel was effectively planning an attack as they suggested. Two days later the intelligence reports on his desk confirmed their fears.

For Abdel Nasser, it was an extremely awkward development. The last thing he wanted was a war with Israel. Much of his army was still bogged down in the Yemen, where it had lost a great deal of men and equipment, and what was left was needed in Egypt itself for internal security. Although Abdel Hakim Amer (as

C-in-C) insisted that the army was ready 'to push Israel into the sea', Nasser was perfectly aware that his armed forces were in no shape for a conflict just then. On the other hand, if the Israelis invaded Syria and the UAR failed to retaliate, his prestige in the Arab world would be lost forever. As it was, whenever he had urged moderation in the past—as he frequently had—his enemies had accused him of being in league with Israel. To maintain his position as spiritual leader of the Arabs, he could not afford to stand idly by.

Caught in this embarrassing dilemma, Nasser decided to bluff it out. He began to put on a great show of force. He paraded his infantry and tanks through the streets, making sure that they passed through Garden City under the windows of the American Embassy. At the same time he made belligerent noises. All of which was intended to convey the message that he would come to the rescue of Syria.

As part of his bluff, he ostentatiously sent reinforcements into Sinai, and arranged for the local commander to ask General Rikhye, the UN delegate, to remove the United Nations armistice force from the border area. General Rikhye replied that this was outside his competence. Under the terms of the UN agreement with the UAR it was a legitimate request, but must be negotiated directly between President Nasser and the Secretary General, U Thant.

Upon which Nasser felt obliged to make an official demand to U Thant to withdraw the UN troops from Egyptian territory. He calculated that the situation was getting tense enough for the Powers to intervene and bring pressure on both Israel and the Arabs to resolve the crisis. Had this happened, his tactics would have succeeded.

Instead, U Thant did the opposite to what was expected. He agreed on the spot to Nasser's request. The UN forces who had kept the peace on the frontier between Israel and the UAR for eleven years were suddenly withdrawn, and Nasser's hand was called.

Always a gambler, he now upped the stakes. On 22 May he occupied Sharm el-Sheikh and denied the Gulf of Akaba to Israeli shipping, thus sealing off the vital port of Eilat. Such a bold and reckless move was characteristic of Nasser: he was only happy when holding the initiative, and certainly at the time it looked as though he had scored a heavy blow at Israel's expense and was winning the game of international poker.

A worried U Thant flew off to Cairo with proposals for a peaceful settlement of the crisis, which Nasser—operating masterfully from a basically weak position—was only too eager to accept. President Johnson spoke on the hot line to Mr. Kosygin and the leaders of the superpowers agreed to put pressure on their 'clients' to avoid a shooting war. On 28 May at a press conference, Nasser made some particularly pugnacious remarks to coincide with the arrival of Charles Yost as a special representative from President Johnson, but an agreement was nevertheless drawn up between them. The crisis was to be resolved through diplomatic channels; the question of the Straits of Tiran was to be submitted to the International Court at The Hague for arbitration, and Zacharia Mohieddin would leave for New York to negotiate a settlement between the contestants. Charles Yost left Cairo on 3 June, two days before the war started, having reportedly assured Nasser that Israel would take no offensive action so long as the negotiations were on. That weekend Nasser relaxed for the first time for nearly a month. His tactics seemed to have succeeded, and he was emerging from an awkward situation with his reputation enhanced.

Twenty-four hours later, the world came crashing down about his ears. Savagely and mercilessly, the Israelis had called his bluff.

Until the middle of May, Israel had adopted a wary, but relaxed attitude towards the UAR. As the largest and most influential of her Arab neighbors, the UAR was automatically enemy number one. But for years Nasser had proved the most moderate of the Arab leaders, at least so far as his policy towards Israel was concerned, and in recent months the danger had shifted towards the north where the Syrian Ba'athist regime was training and equipping the El Fatah guerrillas. Finally the decision had been taken to put an end to these activities by overthrowing the Damascus regime. Israeli intelligence reports had indicated that the Arabs, and in particular the UAR, were in no fit state of preparation to come to Syria's aid.

Nasser's actions from 10 May onwards entirely changed the situation from Tel Aviv's point of view. The highly publicized mobilization of troops, the demand for the withdrawal of the UN peace-keeping force, the threats from Cairo Radio, and finally the closing of the Straits of Tiran showed that Nasser, the number one enemy, had belligerent intentions after all. Or had he? Was it only bluff? Israeli intelligence had full information, down to the smallest detail, about the UAR army's capabilities. The men in Tel Aviv were aware, probably better than Nasser himself, that the Egyptian army could not stand a war at the present time. The State of Israel, by its very nature and geography, was an aggressive incursion into the Arab world. To subsist at all, moreover, it had to expand. The conviction grew in Tel Aviv that the opportune moment had come to fracture the pinched borders imposed in 1948 and 1956 and achieve security against Israel's hostile neighbors by pushing out to frontiers which were easier to defend. Such an opportunity might not reoccur. Throughout the country, the same hawkish attitude prevailed. 'Munich!' growled people from Safad to Beersheba, 'If we let the Arabs get away with it this time, when we can really knock them for six, we shall have lost a heaven-sent chance...Don't let's have another Munich!'

Premier Levi Eshkol, by nature a moderate, might personally still have been inclined to compromise, but on 20 May, when news came through of the blockade of the Straits of Tiran, his colleagues in the Defense Committee forced his hand. They argued the necessity of attacking immediately: the people of Israel had waited long enough over the years for the international negotiators to relieve them of the peril on the frontiers. Time was no longer on Israel's side. The Arabs had a growing build-up of military hardware, thanks to Soviet shipments. But the UAR was not yet ready. Everything pointed to the advantages of a lightning campaign—immediately.

On 21 May, secret orders went out for total mobilization. Nothing that subsequently occurred—U Thant's efforts at mediation, the warnings from the Soviet Union, the diplomatic pressure from the United States—altered the situation. In fact Nasser's intransigence, and King Hussein's sudden flight to Cairo on 30 May, piloting his own Comet, to sign a mutual defense pact with the UAR placing the Jordanian army under Nasser's overall command in the event of war, only served to stiffen the Israeli determination. When Moshe Dayan became Defense Minister the following day, his first action was to scrap a plan with the limited objective of seizing Gaza, and to give orders to concentrate instead on taking the whole of the Sinai peninsular and reaching the Suez Canal.

Five days later, the Israelis attacked. At 0845 (Cairo time) in the morning of Monday 5 June, the first wave of Mirage and Mystere fighters went in. The day and the hour were carefully chosen. Attacks are usually expected at dawn, at which moment the Egyptian defenses would have been at maximum alert—but four hours later their concentration would be relaxed. And since the Egyptian brass reach their offices at nine o'clock, a quarter of an hour earlier they would all be on their way to work and caught up in the Cairo traffic. But most important of all, Israeli intelligence knew that a top-level staff meeting was scheduled that morning in Sinai, and that consequently most of the combat units would be temporarily without their commanders.

The first wave of the air strike was directed against ten airfields and was meticulously scheduled so that all the aircraft should reach their targets at precisely the same moment and achieve maximum surprise. By far the greater part of the Egyptian airforce was caught on the ground—in fact, the only airborne aircraft were four unarmed planes flown by an instructor and three trainees. At the Abu Suweir air base near Ismailia, the Egyptian pilots were drinking coffee when the Israeli jets streaked in and destroyed their MIGS lined up on the runway. Eight other formations of MIO 21s were simultaneously blasted to bits as they taxied to the end of the runways at the other airfields.

Barely had the first wave struck their targets than a second wave was behind them and a third wave on the way. The Israelis were operating an incredibly fast turn-round time. Less than ten minutes after they had returned to base they were off again. Within an hour of their first attack they were over the targets a second time. Instead of coming in directly from the north-east, they swept in from the west across the desert to attack the airfields round Cairo, flying not more than ten or fifteen metres above ground level to dodge the radar. Their objective was to annihilate as many of the Egyptian MIG fighters and long-range bombers as possible and to render the runways unusable.

Raymond Flower

Cairo, showing the modern blocks along the Nile with the Citadel and the Mokattam Hills in the background; (below) Nasser, the universal provider. Huge placards such as this were often to be seen in Egypt.

J. Allan Cash and Bruno Barbey/Magnum

Napoleon To Nasser

Raymond Flower

The grief of a nation at the loss of its leader is caught in this striking icture.

Rene Burri/Magnum

LEFT
The scenes at President Nasser's funeral
in September 1970 were a final affirmation of his extraordinary grip on the
emotions of the Egyptians.
Bruno Barbey/Magnum

A courtyard inside the Mosque-University of Al Azhar, Cairo.

Egyptian Tourist Centre

For 170 minutes, the Israelis pounded the Egyptian airfields without let-up. During this time they destroyed 300 out of the 350 Egyptian combat aircraft, including all thirty of the long-range TU 16 bombers. The dimension of the disaster was stupefying. In less than three hours, Nasser's airforce was almost totally destroyed. The sheer magnitude of the Israeli attack—and the fact that their aircraft were coming in from the direction of Libya, where Britain and the USA had air bases—led the Egyptians to suppose that British and American planes had taken part in the raids. It seemed inconceivable that the Israelis alone could have pulverized the UAR'S much-vaunted Russian jets in so short a space of time.

This attack took not only the Egyptian airforce, but everybody else in Cairo completely by surprise. Some anti-aircraft firing was heard at nine o'clock in the morning, but people took little notice and went about their business as usual. The idea of a war was far from their minds. An hour later, the sirens started wailing. Presently Cairo Radio came out with the announcement that the UAR had been subject to a 'treacherous aggression'—one of the truest statements it had ever made. But soon the propaganda machine was at work and communiqués were broadcasting a stream of Egyptian successes: 40, then 50, and then 70 enemy aircraft shot down. By the end of the day, Cairo was claiming 130 Israeli aircraft destroyed. Despite the air-raid sirens and often intensive anti-aircraft fire, the streets crowded up and each announcement of a higher score had people shouting with joy and bugging each other. No one had the slightest idea of what had actually happened. Not even Nasser.

It was only quite late in the afternoon that he learnt that his airforce had gone. Nobody had dared to tell him immediately. Afterwards he related ruefully how he had spent the first vital hours of the war pouring over maps to decide where to order a defensive stand in Sinai, and it was only at about four o'clock that somebody finally plucked up the courage to say: 'We've no more planes...'

At 0915 (Cairo time), just half an hour after the jets had started annihilating the Egyptian air force, Israel's armour crossed the border and began punching through the Egyptian defenses at Khan Yunis and Rafa, not far from Gaza. The Israeli tanks plunged forward in waves, ahead of mechanized infantry riding open half-tracks. The speed and momentum, and above all the surprise of the Israeli thrust carried it through. Once the defenses were breached, the armour fanned out: one column made a right-flanking movement to capture Gaza, while others headed for El Arish on the coast and El Kantara on the Suez Canal. During the seventy-two hours that it took the Israeli army to reach the canal, Israeli jets pounded the Egyptian armour, transport and infantry as relentlessly as they had done to the Egyptian air force.

To all intents and purposes, the Six Day War was won in the first three hours, for whoever won the air won the desert, however good the ground troops. The

UAR lost 700 of its brand new Russian T55 tanks, and over 100 pieces of artillery, pulverized by the Israeli jets. The Sinai desert was littered with blackened metal, some of it blasted by gunfire, some of it charred by napalm. On the winding Mitia Pass, hundreds of trucks and jeeps lay tangled on top of each other in a grotesque and gruesome traffic jam.

The whole operation was brilliantly planned and ruthlessly executed. Pressmen who managed to get up to the front were unanimous in their praise of the tough, commando-trained Sabras who fought with their turrets open under the heaviest fire. Equally astonishing was the virtuosity of the Israeli intelligence service, which apparently knew the radio frequencies and codewords of each Egyptian divisional unit, and even the names and nicknames of its officers, and continuously sent them false orders, with the result that many tanks were trapped, and others were sent on wild goose chases until they ran out of fuel.

By late on Thursday night, when the UAR Government agreed to an unconditional cease-fire, little remained of Nasser's army save thousands of stragglers, abandoned by their officers, struggling hopelessly towards home. Many of them never made it, and were left to perish in the fierce desert heat from thirst and exhaustion.

In Egypt itself, the press and radio continued its incessant barrage of propaganda, with constant repetition of the wholly fictitious statement that American aircraft from Wheelus Base in Libya and British Canberras were operating with the Israeli air force. On Friday 9 June Cairo Press carried in banner headlines; Israelis suffer more reverses on all fronts—UAR smashes back.' But in small print underneath was the factual admission: 'Ceasefire accepted.' The great mass of Egyptians was kept wholly in the dark about what had happened at the front, and had no idea of the catastrophe the country had suffered.

But behind closed doors at Manchiet el Bakhry, the cruel facts could not be ignored. Overcome by the appalling sequence of events, Nasser himself was in a state of collapse. His air force had been destroyed, his army had been routed in one of the swiftest and most decisive defeats ever known, and the Israelis were on the banks of the Suez Canal—the same canal that he had so painfully wrested from Great Britain. The Russians had not lifted a finger to hinder the enemy's advance; world opinion was overwhelmingly on the side of Israel; his closest colleagues were at loggerheads with him. Four days ago, he had ridden high on a pinnacle of success. Now everything he had built up was totally destroyed. Israel had won. The reactionaries had triumphed.

Some of his advisors were whispering that he should retire into the background, if only for a while. All of them believed that the only hope now was to back-pedal the revolution, eat humble pie, and crawl under the wing of America. But this was too bitter a pill for Nasser to swallow: rather than this, he would resign. 'Zacharia Mohieddin always wanted to compromise with

America,' he said wearily, 'If it has now come to that, he had better take over from me. He has my blessing.'

At seven o'clock the following evening he appeared on radio and television for the first time since the war had started. Word went round in the mysterious way it does in Egypt that something dramatic was happening, and nearly every adult in the country was waiting to hear what the President would say. When the familiar features appeared on the screen, the face was that of a man at the end of his tether. Slowly, stumbling over the words, the broken Pharaoh read out from a prepared text.

'Brothers,' he said, 'we have been accustomed together in times of victory and in times of stress, in the sweet hours and in the bitter hours, to speak with open hearts and to tell each other the facts...And now we cannot hide from ourselves that we have met with a grave set-back in the past few days...I tell you truthfully that I am willing to assume the whole responsibility. I have taken a decision with which I want you all to help me'—there was a lump in his throat as he uttered the words: 'I have decided to give up completely and finally every official post and every political role and to return to the ranks of the public to do my duty with them like every other citizen.'

He then nominated Zacharia Mohieddin as his successor to the Presidency, and concluded by expressing a hope that the working classes would carry on the Arab socialist revolution.

An extraordinary, unparalleled thing now happened. Like a swarm of bees, from every street, from every house, people began pouring into the center of the city, many of them with tears in their eyes, shouting 'Nasser! Nasser! Nasser! We need you, Nasser! Don't abandon us!' In the warm twilight the wave after wave of tortured faces was an incredible sight to see. Huge crowds gathered outside the National Assembly building chanting Nasser's name. An even larger crowd, thought to be nearly half a million strong, made its way along the five mile boulevard to Manchiet el Bakhry, and spent the night outside Nasser's house waving hastily painted banners imploring him not to resign.

Throughout the length and breadth of the Delta, it was a crazy, hysterical scene. At Port Said the Governor had to plead over the public address system to prevent the whole population from marching to Cairo, arguing that if the town were emptied, the Israelis would occupy it.

When on the strength of such passionate support Nasser withdrew his resignation the following day, it was immediately assumed in Europe and America that the whole affair had been a put-up job to restore his shattered prestige and authority. But those who knew Egypt had no doubt about the sincerity of the crowds, and such an experienced eyewitness as Eric Rouleau of *Le Monde* stated quite categorically: 'I have traveled the world a good deal but I've never seen a whole people plunged into mourning like this and crying in anguish as they did...the answer was given to me by one of them who in the morning wanted Nasser out, and in the evening was shouting for him to stay: "For us Nasser is a sort of father. One can be angry with one's father and criticize him, but one doesn't want him to go. I felt lost without him."'

The scenes at Nasser's funeral three years later amply bore out this assessment.

Chapter 25

Agonizing Re-assessment

What should have been the end to his career had therefore turned into a new beginning. But it was the beginning of the end.

Although the masses had shouted him back to power, Nasser's image was irretrievably tarnished. And he was now faced with a bitter post-mortem within the army itself, as well as a growing conflict between the left and right political wings: between those who sought to accelerate the speed of Arab socialism, forging closer links with the USSR, and the technocrats who believed that the only solution for the country's plight was to patch up relations with the West, and concentrate on solving the tremendous economic problems which could not be shelved.

As the struggle for political leadership unfolded through the hot summer months of 1967, it crystallized into a confrontation between Gamal Abdel Nasser and Abdel Hakim Amer.

Amer, like Nasser, had resigned from his position as C-in-C when the Israelis reached the Canal, but unlike Nasser, he had not been reinstated. In fact, having been head of the armed forces he was in disgrace for the disaster which had occurred, and for which he privately considered that El-Rais was directly responsible. He had never been so fervent an idealist as Nasser. He had concentrated his efforts on building up Egyptian striking power rather than in propagating Arab socialism, and in the bitter aftermath of the Six Days War it was to Amer that many of the malcontents—particularly in the army—began to turn. In the end these two close friends, who as colonel and major had blue-printed and executed the revolution, found themselves at odds with each other.

Like any Mameluke bey in the high middle ages, Amer surreptitiously mustered his followers at his villa in Dokki. The plan was for him and a group of senior officers to retake command of the army by means of a forged presidential decree while Nasser was in Khartoum for an Arab summit conference. They would then depose Nasser, blaming him and the Russians for Egypt's misfortunes, and appeal to the West for help to get the country back on its feet.

On the eve of his departure, Nasser's intelligence services—which had saved him from numerous assassination attempts in the past—got wind of the plot, and Amer was taken to Manshiet el Bakhry where in the office in which they had so often conferred during the past fifteen years a final meeting between the two men took place. Just what passed between them has never been divulged, but subsequently the newspapers reported that 'with sadness and regret' Nasser had found it necessary to arrest Amer and fifty other officers who would be tried by court-martial.

At first Amer threatened that if he were brought to trial he would produce incriminating evidence which would compromise a great many people including Nasser himself. Later, he attempted to commit suicide. The doctors saved him, but the disgrace of a court-martial, on top of the army's debacle, must have been too great an ordeal for him to face, because on 14 September he gave his guards the slip for long enough to swallow a phial of poison concealed on his body. This time he died.

Such at any rate is the official story, even if in the clubs and cafés some other versions were voiced. At all events, whether Nasser had his friend eliminated or not, he remained in control of a truncated UAR, in the same way as the Israelis continued to occupy Sinai and dig themselves in on the eastern bank of the Canal. Time and time again, during the months that followed, Nasser vowed to regain the territory he had lost, if necessary by another war. To give substance to his dream, he was prepared to surrender even more of the *UAR'S* independence to Moscow in return for the Soviet weapons needed to re-equip his army and air force.

The Israeli victory had put the Russians in a considerable quandary. Within a fortnight of the cease-fire Marshal Zakharov was already in Cairo to see what could be salvaged from the wreckage of the Soviet's Middle East platform. He was followed by M. Podgorny himself. The Russians had waded too deeply into the Egyptian quagmire to be able to cut their losses and quit. For the sake of their prestige in the Arab world and elsewhere, they had somehow to shore Nasser up: they did so by sending such massive shipments of aircraft and armaments that within six months the military hardware which had been lost by Israeli action was entirely replaced—at the cost to Egypt of still tighter Soviet control as well as staggering new mortgages on the already over-burdened Egyptian economy.

Once, over a drink at the club, a senior government official was asked whether the country could really afford the many ambitious industrial and social projects which were being planned. He replied that the UAR was in the position of a man who borrows from the bank to build a block of flats: while the work is proceeding, he is short of cash, but as soon as the building is completed the rents begin to roll in and he can start repaying his debts. Counting on his fingers, he enumerated the main sources of foreign exchange to the UAR: cotton, which produced £300 million a year; the Suez Canal, which produced £200 million; oil, which produced £100 million; and tourism, which produced £50 million. £650 million in hard currency was sufficient for the normal needs of the country, he had concluded with a confident smile. That was in 1965. (These figures should of course be treated with reserve.)

As a result of the events of 1967, the cotton crop was mortgaged to Russia for years ahead, the Suez Canal was closed, the oil companies were unable to operate (the Sinai oilfields being in Israeli hands) and no tourists were coming any more. To lose all these sources of revenue in a single go required a special brand of irresponsibility. Yet this was what Nasser had done, and the UAR was forced to suspend many industrial and development projects and literally beg for money from the other Arab states.

Nasser had created a new Egypt, and in the end he had almost destroyed it. He had wrested independence from Britain, and then surrendered it to Russia. He had chased out the British only to bring in the Soviets. He had made Egyptians proud to be Egyptians, and led them into an abortive war in Yemen and two staggering defeats at the hands of the Israelis, whose army was now on the banks of the Canal.

To any thinking Egyptian, Nasser was a tragedy. And yet, for all the immensity of his failures, he remained a revered father-figure to the still adoring masses. 'I would have shot Nasser myself,' said a twenty-five-year-old agricultural student in Cairo recently. 'I would personally have taken a rifle and shot him if I'd have had the chance. And yet, when I heard of his death, I cried.'

'Why?'

'When a person dies, you always think of the good things about him. Nasser was a dynamic figure. He was a symbol of the Arab renaissance. It was he who gave us the slogan and desire to "lift up our heads and be proud to be Egyptian". I admired the symbol even if I hated the man.'

Himself only a generation removed from the peasants of Upper Egypt, Nasser's genius was to have articulated the deep yearnings of the Arab masses—expressed in the poems of Ahmed Shawki, the music of Abdul Wahab, the songs of Om Kalthoum, and the stories of Taha Hussein—and to have translated them into positive and historic action. A key figure in the third world of uncommitted nations, he towered head and shoulders over his contemporaries; but precisely because he was so much out of scale with them, he made concord with his neighbors impossible. He was the only Arab leader with sufficient stature to make peace with Israel, but he never did—although in the last weeks of his life both Washington and Moscow were pinning their hopes in him to achieve a settlement which would bring the endless Arab-Jewish conflict to a conclusion.

His last political act, indeed, was to patch up the feud between Yasser Arafat's guerrillas and King Hussein, and, ironically enough, his death from a heart attack on 29 September 1970 as he was seeing off his guests at Cairo airport caused as much consternation throughout the world as any of the masterful actions of his life-time.

Epilogue

Death of a Pharaoh

On the roofs of trains, in dangerously listing lorries, on camels, mules, donkey carts, and even on foot they converged on Cairo. From every province in the country the ordinary people of Egypt, frenetic with grief, thronged to the capital in their hundreds of thousands for the funeral of the man they knew as 'the Boss'. To each beat of the funerary drum a myriad voices along the twenty-kilometre cortege moaned the name: 'Nasser! Nasser! Nasser!' The eighteen heads of state and hundreds of foreign dignatories who followed the horse-drawn gun carriage were literally swept off their feet by a sea of howling humanity. 'It was like being caught in a maelstrom,' said Jacques Chaban-Delmas of France, who had once been a rugby footballer. Since the death of the last of the Pharaohs 2,300 years ago, Egypt had not experienced so heart-rending a funeral; indeed the unrestrained sorrow of so many millions was the final affirmation of Nasser's extraordinary grip on the emotions of his people.

Every nation needs its quota of great men, but the world has a way of carrying on without its giants. The Nasser epoch was over, and with encouraging smoothness his old friend Anwar el Sadat assumed the presidential mantle. Quietly back-pedalling some of the more extreme aspects of Nasserism, he began the uphill task of mending international fences, retrieving lost ground, and achieving internal stability, while the world held its breath at the unhoped for prospect of better things to come in the Middle East. But even as he and his colleagues set about bringing order to chaos, they must have reflected on the truth of Paul Valery's dictum: 'Great man is he who leaves those who follow him in difficulties.'

For all the magnitude of his early achievements, Nasser's titanic years of rule had been little short of a catastrophe for Egypt. He had left his ancient and suffering land in a staggering mess: in hock to Russia, its foreign earnings gone, its armed forces discredited, its people stifled under an avalanche of diktats, and the enemy at the door.

Nonetheless, to the vast mass of his countrymen, Nasser was still the greatest Egyptian since the days of the Pharaohs.

Raymond Flower

Parting Shots

Parting Shots

In the introduction to the previous editions of this book I wrote:
The 19th century and the first half of the 20th century, which represent the 'European interlude',are as exciting a period as any in Egypt's tremendous history, and lead all too logically to the revolutionary trend of the nineteen-fifties and sixties. My object has been to describe the sequence of epochal events from the moment that Napoleon appeared in 1798 until the death of Nasser in 1970, stressing the basic problems and tensions which have bedevilled this ancient land in modern times, but touching only lightly on the enormous technical,economic and political developments of the last two decades. This,then, is intended to be a panoramic introduction to modern Egypt,and I can at least claim to have been on the scene of action for over a quarter of the historical span covered by the narrative.Indeed most of it was written over a period of years at our house on the Nile at Badrashein where, surrounded by the fel-laheen working their fields against the eternal background of Memphis and Sakkara, I had the sensation of being organically in touch with the soil and spirit of Egypt.

Much of my material was gathered in Cairo and Alexandria,and I would be lacking in courtesy if I failed to record my enormous debt of gratitude to all the friends who not only helped with the research, but progressively shaped my thoughts and attitudes towards the land I have lived in since I was three months old. Thanks to them my love-affair with Egypt has never ceased.

On the vexed question of spelling Arabic words, there are many differences of opinion. T.E.Lawrence considered this unimportant. 'Arabic names won't go into English, exactly,for their consonants are not the same as ours, and their vowels, like ours, vary from district to district 'he wrote,'There are some' scientific systems' of transliteration, helpful to people who know enough arabic not to need helping, but a washout for the world. I spell my names anyhow,to show what rot the systems are.' All I can say is that I have tried to write them in the way that is most likely to be familiar to the general reader,and have included a short glossary of Arabic words used at the end of the book

Raymond Flower

Glossary of Arabic Words in the Text

Hakuma government
Ulema religious leader
Caracol police station (originally Turkish)
Sayce attendant, groom
balad village
baladi of the village, indigenous (in the vernacular sense, occasionally derogative)
ibn 'balad son of the village, local boy (in a complimentary sense)
Wafd a political party founded by Saad Zagloul (literally delegation)
molochia a glutinous, spinach-like soup made from a vegetable called molochia.
Suffragi waiter
Daira estate office
Wakil agent or deputy who acts for
Omdah village mayor
Sheikh el balad village head man, assistant to Orndah
Feddan an area of land, approximately an acre
souk bazaaar or market
Musky the chief shopping street in the Arab quarter of Cairo
Khan-el-Khalili Cairo's famous bazaar, originally Persian meaning Khalili's stores
Al Azhar The Mosque-university, the main centre of Islamic learning
Misr-el-Fatat The Young Egypt Party; an extreme, ultra-nationalistic group now defunct
Ras-el-Tin Royal Palace overloking Alexandria harbour
Ramadan Moslem fasting month
Ya'ish! Long live!
Saad-el-Aali The High Dam at Assouan
Sarat el-Sifr Zero hour
Lamoun lime squash, a favourite Cairo drink
Foul and Tamia stewed and fried Egyptian fava beans
Ahwa mazbout Turkish coffee with sugar, medium
Bashi-bazouk Turkish irregular soldier
Nazir literally the man who supervises, a landowner's agent
Cherif a family name denoting descent from the Prophet
El-Rais The Boss
Dhobey Laundry man (Indian word)
Bilad-as-Sudan the country of the Blacks; Sudan
Galabiya a flowing native day or night shirt (slang). In classical Arabic it would be *Gilbab*

Raymond Flower

Sources

A Short Critical Bibliography

Prologue

There is no lack of books on Napoleon, and new ones appear every season, but the standard work on this particular stage of his career is Wheeler and Broadley's *Napoleon and the Invasion of England* (London 1908). In a lighter vein, Carola Oman's *Britain against Napoleon* (Faber 1947) is full of pleasant little details. Duff Cooper's *Talleyrand* (Gape 1932) is also worth reading. For French accounts, I have relied chiefly on Michelet and La Jonquiere's massive *L'Expedition en Egypte* (Paris 1899) but serious students should consult the *Correspondance inédite, officielle et confidentielle de Napoleon Bonaparte: Egypte* (Paris 1810-20) from which the extract from Napoleon's letter to Talleyrand is taken (Vol III p 235). The remarks to Miot are drawn from Jacques Francois Miot *Memoires pour servir á l'histoire des expeditions en Egypte et en Syrie* (Paris 1814).

Chapters 1-3

The most valuable contemporary account of events of this period in Egypt is certainly Sheikh Abdel Rahman El-Djabarty's monumental *Merveilles biographiques et historiques*, translated into French as *Le Journal d'un habitant du Caire* (9 vols, Cairo 1888-96). Sheikh El-Djabarty was born in Cairo in 1754. Originally from Zeilah on the African coast of the Gulf of Aden, his family had by then been settled in Egypt for seven generations and his great-grandfather, Sheikh Ali, was venerated as a saint, to the point that his tomb at Edfu was a place of pilgrimage. El-Djabarty's father was recognized as the greatest Arabic scholar of the day and kept a free lending library. Abdel Rahman was himself a scholar and one of the foremost Sheikhs of El Azhar. He kept a diary from 1780 until 1820 when he was murdered—on Mohammed Ali's orders, it is said—as he was riding his donkey to Boulac. Having been chosen among the Dewan to serve on the General Divan, or local government, set up by Bonaparte with the help of Moslem notables, he was well placed to know what was going on. Volume vi of his Chronicles gives one a vivid day-to-day account of the French occupation as seen through Egyptian eyes, and significantly enough, a good part of it is taken up with complaints about the French methods of 'peaceful coexistence'. Another useful contemporary source is Nikula Ibn Youssef, known as Nicholas Turk, whose *Chronique d'Egypte 1798-1804* was translated from the Arabic by Gaston Wiet and published in Cairo in 1950. Of recent works, the most definitive is certainly J. Christopher Hérold's racy and well-documented *Bonaparté in Egypt* (Hamish Hamilton 1963). Alan Moorehead's *The Blue Nile* (Hamish Hamilton 1962 and now in paperback) should also not be missed. Stanley Lane-Poole's *History of Egypt in the Middle Ages* (London) gives a great deal of useful information about the Mamelukes, but for a detailed study of the Mameluke system one should consult David Ayalon's *L'Eslavage du Mamelouk*. Napoleon's description of Cairo is taken from his *Memoirs* written at St Helena, Lieut. Morgan Morgan Clifford's impressions are drawn from his *Egypt: Journal of a young officer of the 12th Light Dragoons* (privately printed 1802).

Chapters 4-5

Edward William Lane's *Manners and Customs of the Modern Egyptians* first published in 1836 and now available in Dent's Everyman Library (No 315) was described by his nephew Stanley Lane-Poole as 'The most perfect picture of a people's life that has ever been written and is certainly the classic work on Mohammed Ali's Egypt. Although Lane managed to mix among the ordinary people of Cairo and participate in their lives, he was nonetheless a dispassionate observer, and the patterns of life he describes are still recognizable in rural Egypt even today. I have drawn on him for one or two picturesque anecdotes. Otherwise the most rewarding books about Mohammed Ali are Henry Dodwell's *The Founder of Modern Egypt* (Cambridge University Press 1931) and Shafik Ghorbal's *The beginnings of the Egyptian Question and the rise of Mohammed Ali* (Routledge 1928). William Turner's description of Mohammed Ali comes from his *Tour of the Levant* published in 3 volumes in 1820. The eye-witness account of the massacre of the Mamelukes by Giovanni Finati was published by John Murray in 1830. A description of conditions in Egypt is given by the British MP, Sir John Bowring, in his *Report on Egypt and Candia* (Parliamentary Papers 1840 Vol XXI). Helen A Rivlin's PhD thesis, *The Agricultural policy of Mohammed Ali in Egypt* (OUP 1953) is also worth consulting.

Chapter 6

Few historians have devoted more than a paragraph or two to Abbas, and the best information I have been able to find is in Edwin de Leon's *The Khedives' Egypt* (New York 1877). De Leon was American consul in Cairo for more than three decades, and gives an entertaining description of the social life in palace circles during the time of Abbas, Said, and Ismail. Most of my anecdotes come from him. Under Said, there was a great influx of Europeans, and consequently a spate of publications from this time onwards in English and French, although the Egyptians themselves—apart from some Palace-inspired eulogies and underground tracts of a nationalist character—chose to remain silent. They had little choice, to be fair. Of the English offerings, D. A. Cameron has some good material in his *Egypt in the 19th Century* (London 1898), but the book I found most useful is Sir George Young's *Egypt* (Benn 1927). This eminent lawyer, who compiled an authoritative work on Ottoman law in 1905-6, is sometimes considered partisan (by the *Encyclopedia Britannica*, for instance) but to me his often pungent remarks come as a welcome relief from the cant and jingoism of all too many other writers.

Chapter 7

Francois Charles-Roux, the biographer of de Lesseps and a former director of the Companie Universelle du Canal de Suez, wrote the official history of the Suez Canal but although impressive, it is naturally rather one-sided. I have preferred to rely on Hugh J Schonfield's excellent *The Suez Canal in World affairs* (Constellation Books 1952). My quotations are from de Lesseps' own papers. *(Lettres, journal, et documents pour servir a l'histoire du Canal de Suez* published in 5 volumes, Paris 1875-81, but for public consumption more than anything.)

Chapter 8

Mohammed Bey Rifaat has some good material on Ismail in his *The Awakening of Modern Egypt* (Longmans 1947) although it should be remembered that the ex-director general at the Ministry of Education in Cairo was writing about the reigning monarch's grandfather, and therefore had to mind his step. George Young itemizes the European loans to Ismail. The banking aspects are admirably described in *Bankers and Pashas* (Heinemann 1958) by David S. Landes who gives an enthralling insight into the mechanics of high finance and economic imperialism in Egypt. A. J. Butler's

Court Life in Egypt (Chapman and Hall 1887) and Moberley Bell's *Khedives and Pashas* (published anonymously in London, 1884) are full of local color as seen through the eyes of a Fellow of BNC Oxford and *The Times* correspondent, and Lucie Duff-Gordon's celebrated *Letters from Egypt* published after her death in 1869 give a vivid picture of the plight of the fellahin under Ismail, about whom she does not mince her words. My 'Pasha' in Shepheard's bar is an imaginary person, of course, inspired by a well-known Egyptian figure of the *Ancien Regime* with whom I often had discussions about Ismail.

Chapters 9-10

Cromer's *Modern Egypt* (Macmillan 1908) is the standard work on the run up to the British occupation. Generations of young Englishmen have been nurtured on his polished periods, and he crystallizes the attitudes towards Egypt which finally led to the tragedy of Suez. It is useful as a piece of Victoriana but it is no longer, one hopes, taken as gospel fact. Wilfrid Scawen Blunt was also a great Victorian, but of quite a different sort. Mixing constantly with Egyptians of all levels, he probably knew a great deal more about them than Cromer, closeted in his study in the Residency, can ever have done, and his *Secret History of the British Occupation* (Martin Seeker 1907) from which much of Chapter 9 is taken, gives a side of the story which in perspective seems far more convincing than the nostrums of Cromer, Milner or Auckland Colvin. Blunt was undoubtedly devoted to the cause of Egyptian nationalism, and even paid for a barrister to come out from England to defend Arabi at his trial. In a more recent book, *Founders of Modern Egypt* (Asia Publishing House 1962) Mary Rowlatt gives a lively description of the bombardment of Alexandria, drawing from the experiences of her grandfather who was living there at the time. Another eyewitness was John Ninet, a Swiss, whose *Arabi Pasha* was published in Berne (1884). Ninet seems to have managed to ramble quite freely in all the trouble spots, including Arabi's camp on the eve of the battle of Tel-el-Kebir, and I have quoted some of his observations. Arabi's confrontation with Tewfik is taken from Rifaat and from Arabi's own account which Blunt reproduces.

Chapter 11

From their opposite points of view, Lord Milner's *Britain in Egypt* and Wilfrid Blunt's *My Diaries 1888-1914* (London 1918) deal with the British occupation of Egypt, while George Young strikes a balance between the two. John Marlowe has recently published a well documented and dispassionate study, *Cromer in Egypt* (Eick 1970). In *Orientations* (London 1937) Sir Ronald Storrs gives a sympathetic portrait of Eldon Gorst, his former boss, and Baron de Kusel describes the social scene in *An Englishman's recollections of Egypt* (Bodley Head 1914). Lord Edward Cecil's *The Leisure of an Egyptian Official* delighted readers in the 1920s even if it was not altogether appreciated by the official classes in Cairo. It is said that Lord Edward, bored with London, asked Kitchener to dinner at Wellington Barracks, filled him with champagne, and persuaded him to take him out to Cairo as his *ADC*, where he remained to become Financial Advisor. In contrast, the Egyptian attitude towards the occupation is convincingly and pleasantly expressed in Afaf Latfi al-Sayyid's *Egypt and Cromer* (Murray 1968). As my own grandparents were in the habit of wintering in Cairo soon after the turn of the century, and my father as a very young man started our family business way back in 1906, I have been fortunate in being able to draw on their experiences from this time onwards.

Chapter 12

There is no lack of material about the Great War, and those who are interested in its military aspects in Egypt should consult Sir George Macmunn & Captain Cyril Fall's official history *Military operations Egypt and Palestine* (HMSO 1928). On a slightly less formidable level Colonel P. G. Elgood's *Egypt and the Army* (Oxford University Press 1924) gives the required information. But my favorite book is Priscilla Napier's *A late beginner* (London 1966). In this delightful account of her childhood she describes wartime Cairo as seen through a little girl's eyes. It is pleasant, for instance, to ponder with her who the mysterious person called C in C's house down the road could be. I am grateful to her for several pert comments from a tiny eye-witness. Brian Gardner's *Allenby* (Cassell 1965) gives a good picture of 'the bull', as well as the political scene immediately after the war.

Chapter 13

In my glance back at the Sudan I have drawn inevitably, on Lytton Strachey's famous essay in *Eminent Victorians* (Collins 1959) and naturally also on Winston Churchill's *The River War* (Thornton Butterworth 1930). From Wilfrid Blunt's indefatigable pen there is likewise *Gordon in Khartoum* (London 1911). For conditions in the Sudan, perhaps the best description is in Rudolph Slatin Pasha's *Fire and sword in the Sudan 1879-95* (Edward Arnold 1896), while the standard work on the campaign as a whole is Sir Reginald Wingate's *Mahdiism and the Egyptian Sudan* (Macmillan 1891).

Chapter 14

Tom Little's excellent *Egypt* (Benn 1958) traces the history of the country from the Pharaohs onwards, but is a particularly useful source on the political scene from the Declaration of 1922 onwards. As head of the Arab News Agency, Little was in a good vantage point to review events. (Jan Morris, incidentally, was his deputy in the early 1950s, and one wishes this brilliant writer would give us more on her experiences in Cairo). John Marlow's *Anglo-Egyptian relations 1800-1953* (Cresset Press 1954) rarely sparkles, but he serves up all the facts. Lord Lloyd's *Egypt since Cromer* (Macmillan 1934) is in my view too much of a white-washing operation. Amine Youssef Bey explains the Egyptian position in *Independent Egypt* (London 1936) and in the process conveys the flavor of Court circles during Fouad's reign. There is also some excellent fiction set in Egypt between the wars. John Knittel's *Dr Ibrahim* dwells on the frustration of a young provincial doctor, and Laurence Durrell's *Justines, Cleas and Balthazars* mirror the frothily cosmopolitan atmosphere of pre-war Alexandria, which nevertheless had a special grace of its own, as Cavafy so movingly shows. Nor should one overlook E M Forster's *Alexandria* (Doubleday 1961)—perhaps the best guide-book to any city—and his equally delightful *Pharos and Pharillon* (Hogarth Press 1961) from which I have taken George Valassopoulo's translation of Cavafy's *The God abandons Anthony.*

My own 'mood piece' on Alexandria has no source other than my own experience.

Chapter 15

My old friend Georges Vaucher has painstakingly retraced Nasser's early career in his *Gamal Abdel Nasser et son équipe* (Julliard 1959) interviewing schoolmasters and classmates and even tracking down old library slips with the result that we know that while at military academy Nasser read among other things Robert Graves' *Lawrence*, Churchill's *River War*, Buchan's *Gordon*, Liddell Hart's *Foch*, and Emil Ludwig's *Napoleon*, which seems to suggest an already awakened interest in the heroic figure. Another biography in depth is Robert St John's impressive *The Boss* (McGraw-Hill

1960) which although required reading for all American diplomats posted to Egypt in the sixties, and on the whole sympathetic, was unpredictably banned in Egypt. (Luckily the Ministry of National Guidance lent me a copy!) But perhaps the most valuable source on the origins of the revolution is Anwar el Sadat's own *Revolt on the Nile* (Alan Wingate 1957). My quotation at the beginning of this chapter is from Major C S Jarvis' *Oriental Spotlight* (John Murray 1936).

Chapter 16

I have dined out so often on Farouk's 'boutades' that I can hardly remember their exact source, beyond the fact that all the anecdotes I've recounted—and many more—were in current circulation in Cairo. For those who are interested, Michael Stern's *Farouk* (Bantam 1965) has a rich collection of Faroukiana. Most serious historians tend to dismiss the pervasive corruption and theatrical opulence of the last years of Farouk's reign in a paragraph or two, but it should not be forgotten that this now legendary period was very much part of the Egyptian scene, and is still remembered—who knows if not sometimes with a tinge of regret—by many people. And only a short while ago Hans Jurg Badrutt repeated to me what his half-brother Andrea had said about the summer incursion of the Pasha brigade to St Moritz. 'It's quite true' he said, 'We never had any other clients like them. There used to be thirty or forty Rolls-Royces from Egypt in the garage—Egyptians would never dream of having anything but a Rolls-Royce, unless it was a Bentley...We used to have *Concours d'élègance* for cars, for dogs, for women even—but all this stopped with the revolution'. On a more down-to-earth level, Tom Little's *Egypt*, and Jean and Simonne Lacouture's *L'Egypte en Mouvement* (Seuil 1956) published in English as *Egypt in Transition* (Methuen 1958) deal fully with the years prior to the revolution.

Chapter 17

Anwar el Sadat's *Revolt on the Nile*, Vaucher's *Gamal Abdel Nasser et son equipe* and St John's *Boss* each describe the growth of the Free Officers' movement and the *coup d'etat* of 23 July 1952. But I have tended to follow the very detailed account published by Saroit Okasha in *El Tahrir* as well as the descriptions given by Ahmed Aboul Fath in *El Misri* and Ihsan Abdel Khoulous in *Rose el Youssef*, all of whom were participant witnesses during the first heady hours of the new Revolutionary Council. The direct speech quotes in the story of the putsch itself are mainly from these three sources.

Chapters 18-19

The Lacoutures, Tom Little and St John are all excellent on the early days of the revolution, including the out-maneuvering of Naguib by Nasser. I have quoted from Nasser's *Philosophy of the Revolution* (which was largely ghosted by Mohammed Hassanein Heikal). Miles Copeland describes the 'Czech' arms deal scenario in *The Game of Nations* (McGraw-Hill 1969). Desmond Stewart's *Young Egypt* (Wingate 1958) studies the initial achievements of the new government.

Chapters 20-21

Even if official documents are tightly locked away, we have a number of books on the Suez war, and in addition to the Lacoutures, Little and St John, a significant piece of research has been carried out by Erskine B. Childers in *The Road to Suez* (MacGibbon & Kee 1962). As Peter Calvocoressi wrote in the *Observer:* 'This is a bloodhound of a book...and will probably stand the test of time'. Indeed, a decade later, Erskine Childers is progressively shown to be nearer the mark than almost anyone else. On the other hand, Lord Avon's account of the crisis in his *Memoirs—Full Circle* (Cassell 1960) is, unhappily, now discredited in most people's eyes.

Chapters 22-23

Tourists apart, few English people were to be seen in Egypt during the sixties, but Peter Mansfield, who was the *Sunday Times* correspondent in Cairo, documents this period admirably in *Nasser's Egypt* (Penguin 1967). Gordon Waterfield, a former head of the BBC Arabic service, has some useful material, particularly on the National Charter, in *Egypt* (Thames and Hudson 1967). A good analysis of the economic scene is given by Claude Estier in *L'Egypte en Révolution* (Julliard 1965).

Chapters 24-25

To my mind the best accounts of the Israeli-Arab war of 1967 are given by Randolph and Winston Churchill's team in *The Six Day War* (Heinemann-Penguin 1967) and by Eric Rouleau, Jean-Francois Held and the Lacoutures in *Israel et les Arabes—Le 3me Combat* (Seuil 1967) both of which books appeared within weeks if not days of the conflict. Since Nasser's death, Jean Lacouture has published a sparkling biography: *Nasser* (Seuil 1971) and excerpts from Mohammed Hassanein Heikal's "The Cairo Document" (to be published by Doubleday in 1972) have been serialized in the *Sunday Telegraph*. Since Heikal was Nasser's mouthpiece for many years and latterly was probably nearer to the Egyptian President than almost any other person on the political scene, his 170,000 word tome will probably prove to be the 'definitive biography of Gamal Abdel Nasser Hussein—almost an autobiography, in fact.

Finally, Anthony Nutting's excellent *"Nasser"* (Constable 1972 gives a lucid and honest account of Nasser's reign.

Raymond Flower

About the Author

RAYMOND FLOWER's life-long association and knowledge of the Middle East date back to his childhood days in Alexandria. After war service with the Royal Hampshire Regiment, he ran the family business interests in Egypt, became a Name at Lloyd's, and made his mark as a racing driver on the European circuits. Although his appearance with the Egyptian-built Phoenix 2SR6 at Le Mans, Rheims, and other international races was cut short by the Suez Crisis, once Anglo-Egyptian relations were restored he was largely instrumental in setting up the Ramses popular car factory in Cairo.

A graduate of Magdalen College, Oxford, where he read history under A.J.P. Taylor, Raymond Flower has written some two dozen books on a variety of subjects dear to his heart. In addition to Napoleon to Nasser, his publications range from histories of Italy, Southeast Asia and Western Australia to motor racing, winter sports and Lloyd's of London